# *of* Silk Saris
# *and* Mini-Skirts

## SOUTH ASIAN GIRLS WALK THE TIGHTROPE OF CULTURE

## Amita Handa

Women's Press / Toronto

Of Silk Saris and Mini-Skirts: South Asian Girls Walk the Tightrope of Culture
Amita Handa

First published in 2003 by
Women's Press
180 Bloor Street West, Suite 801
Toronto, Ontario
M5S 2V6

www.womenspress.ca

Women's Press gratefully acknowledges financial assistance for our publishing activities from the Ontario Arts Council, the Canada Council for the Arts, and the Government of Canada through the Book Publishing Industry Development Program (BPIDP).

**National Library of Canada Cataloguing in Publication Data**

Handa, Amita, 1964–
    Of silk saris and mini-skirts : South Asian girls walk the tightrope of culture / Amita Handa.

Includes bibliographical references.
ISBN 978-0-88961-406-2

1. South Asian-Canadian women—Ontario—Toronto—Social conditions. 2. Culture conflict—Ontario—Toronto. I. Title.

FC3097.9.S66H35 2002        305.48'89140713541        C2002-904795-1
F1059.5.T689S66 2002

Cover design by Shannon Olliffe
Cover photo by Vinita Srivastava
Page design and layout by Susan Thomas/Digital Zone

10   11   12      6   5

Printed and bound in Canada by Marquis Book

*For my father*

Looking for my souls/soles… Tracing your footprints from (village/pind) Kundar to Toronto, Canada… Miss your gentle eyes and hands… Your telling of life's little secrets in the stories of Masiji, Baba, and Lal Basha… Your pondering in shadows of white shawls and kurtas from Karl Marx to Buddha and Sri Aurobindo… and your many acts of love. Looking for ways to live without my soulmate.

*And also*

To the generation of communities before me who had the courage to migrate either due to necessity or choice, who attempted to construct a sense of home in the cold winterlands of Canada. It is because of them that I have been able to keep a connection to the past, to memory, to a notion of roots. This work is also a tribute to the generation younger than me who have had the courage to begin to claim a cultural/racial space that is rightfully theirs in Canada. It is to them I owe my finding a little piece of myself.

# Table of Contents

# Acknowledgements

I would like to thank the many people who have been instrumental in the completion of this work. First, to those who were library research buddies along the way: Farah Shroff, Rinaldo Walcott, Melanie Randall, Radha Kohly, Tina Sahay, and Amie Parikh. There are also a number of people who provided me the emotional and community support I needed for this project. The days were lonely until I found a community of people in Brampton, including Baldev Mutta, who believed in my work and is a constant source of inspiration as a community leader — I continue to admire and appreciate him as a pioneer in community development. Also, my appreciation to Jas and Rupinder for their help in the initial stages of this research. A special thank you to the Rashid brothers, Meb and Ian, for being witnesses and emotional and intellectual supporters over the years. I especially want to thank such platforms as South Asian Issues Discussed at York University and Desh Pardesh. Both of these spaces have been invaluable for discussions, dialogue, community building, and pushing boundaries. I cannot forget Hiren Mistry for his intellectual support and discussions of dahl, or my family of friends: Vinita, Zena, Junia, and Nicole, who are living examples of creativity and possibility.

Behind every woman is a good sister. I especially cannot show enough appreciation to my sister Manavi for putting up with me over the years — thank you for the emotional and intellectual support, for the labours of love, and so much more. And to my mom, who has shown me, through example, that women can do anything they want to do.

With respect to practical and intellectual support, I would like to thank Kari Dehli, Sherene Razack, and George Dei for their insightful guidance. I would also like to thank the Social Sciences and Humanities Research Council for research funding for parts of this project. Without their financial support, my research would have been greatly limited. I am also indebted to the team at Canadian Scholars' Press/Women's Press, especially to Althea Prince and Rebecca Conolly for their professionalism, support, and hard work on this publication. And finally, most importantly, I would like to thank all of the young South Asian women who shared their lives with me. I thank them for their courage, strength, and openness in sharing their experiences.

# CHAPTER ONE

# Beginnings:
## The Telling of Secrets

*L*et *me tell you about secrets.*

*My first memory of being part of a community is at age four, in 1968, driving in a car by my mother's side, the gas pedal and brake hidden mysteriously beneath her endless yards of sari material. I wanted to be part of it, too. I had my own set of keys, which I plugged into the glove compartment. They swayed and clattered with every turn and every sudden stop. With one eye on my imaginary wheel and one on my mother, I duplicated her driving movements, turning left and right alongside her.*

*At a stoplight, I saw another South Asian beside us, sharing the passage of time from red to green. "Look, Mom!" I shouted with excitement. There was thrill and anxiety in my belly as I tried to get my mother to find what I had discovered on the road before the colours changed. What followed was the kind of momentary celebration that occurs when two old friends meet unexpectedly. Only in this case, the meeting was among ajnabees (strangers). Even at that age, I understood that part of what made this such an important event was its rarity. On such occasions, there was a ritualistic exchange of glances and nods of mutual acknowledgment. And if the stranger was a woman, the exchange would include a sure invitation for chai.*

*I also remember the arduous task of food shopping in the late 1960s. Every month we made a special trip down to Dupont Street to the only Indian grocery store, from our home in Don Mills, which was then the outskirts of Toronto. The Gills, a husband and wife team, stocked their store with eats all the way from India. There, in a dark warehouse full of cats and the smell of spices, I would watch my mother pick out the dry goods, dahls, and attas.¹ If I was lucky, a jar of mango pickle would go into the shopping cart. If it didn't, I would sneak one into the pile of foodstuff strategically at the bottom of the stack.*

*At a later, adolescent age, within the walls of home, I paraded the most recent in salwar kameez fashion sent through many hands and borders to reach me. In the mirror I reflected the walk and talk of Bollywood, mimicking the images of female beauty on the Indian movie screen.*

*I do not remember when the marvel of being part of something larger, such as the feeling of discovering likeness in the car next to my mother's, began to fade. I do not remember when it began, me getting smaller than my body, the darkness of my steps, the shallowness of my voice, or the fear. The fear of discovery at the neighbourhood mall: my mother and Mataji in saris as I dart and hide amongst the clothes in the nearby shops so nobody could see me with them. Or the fear of sitting beside another South Asian in high school. This made my brown feel darker and inevitable. Mixing in among white made it less conspicuous.*

*Those teenage years that sometimes still hover within me are about not being Canadian enough, not being Indian enough, not being white enough... not being. Not being the right kind of daughter, not the right clothes or hair or skin.*

*My parents did not see our front porch steps as a mark of crossing: my crossing into a world they thought they protected me from, the world where I explored my femininity and sexuality. The world of self-bleached jean jackets, faded in all the wrong places. I don't recall the first time I looked at bleach in a new way that took it beyond clothes, to my arms, face, and legs. Anything to keep the secret.*

*I came across one of the many articles that ponder this so-called condition, which describes me as being caught between cultures, half-breed, halfway. I read that what complicates me is "several features peculiar to [my] culture." That my culture expects me to be "passive" and "obedient," that if only I had "Canadian" parents I would be able to "enjoy the freedoms" that those "other" girls have.*[2]

*I want to run and hide amongst the clothes again. I want to protect the secret. I want to tell you that there are no problems, no tensions, and no conflicts. Talking about these experiences makes me part of something lesser, warped, outdated, in the wrong place. Why is it that every time I begin to speak about the tensions of home, I become part of a backward, repressed, outdated culture? Why is it that every time I turn my attention to the issue of racism, I have to construct home as a mythical and infallible place?*

*This is where I am caught: not between two cultures, but between omissions, between fragments of myself.*

Consistent with one of the generic South Asian[3] migratory routes, I am a twice immigrant, my parents having passed through and lived in England, the Empire's headquarters, on their incidental, now thirty-year visit to Toronto, Canada. The memory of driving with my mother at age four reminds me that the landscape of this community has altered enormously in thirty years. Large South Asian populations now inhabit the regions of Scarborough, Peel, and Metropolitan Toronto. The history of migration has fluctuated according to the labour needs of this country. My parents' opportunity to settle in Canada was not accidental, but took place at a time when the country needed skilled professional labour. A hitherto racially restrictive policy was therefore loosened in order to "tap pools of 'appropriate' overseas labour."[4]

This process of migration — the physical movement of large numbers of people and the consequent changes in the consumer goods and services available and in the international economic and geographical ties — has profoundly affected the landscape of Toronto. Consequently, it has potentially significant implications for a redefinition of what it means to be Canadian. The process of migration equally significantly affects the understanding of what it means to be South Asian. Here, community identity must be constructed outside the boundaries of a nation-state and is in constant negotiation through the relationship between Canada/Canadian and "back home."[5] The changes associated with migration are, for Arjun Appadurai, a process of deterritorialization whereby "we as an ethnic group increasingly operate in ways that transcend specific territorial boundaries and identities."[6]

Thirty years later, I now witness and participate in this deterritorialization: a South Asian community of young people, whose sheer numbers have, in some ways, played a part in the formation and overt celebration of cultural identity. At dances and weddings I voyeuristically watch as their arms-in-the-air movements evoke a mix-and-match of Hindi film, hip-hop, and disco dancing. Wondering why people younger than myself have not "lost" more than I, I observe at these gatherings that their speaking of "back-home" languages comes with an ease I cannot match.

In the mid- to late 1990s, I took part in various debates within the South Asian community. Central to these discussions were the issues of cultural retention, the diasporic experience, hybridization, and cultural authenticity. To put it simply, there has been much angst around what it means to be South Asian in a place far away from "home." This quest, the longing for and reinvention of home, takes place within the context of Canadian racism and assimilationism: immigrant parents anxiously watch the younger generation in an effort to gauge what aspects of anglo Canadian culture will be adopted. As South Asians struggle to form communities in the face of white conformity, the underlying concern is the dilution of the values and traditions associated with South Asian-ness.[7] It is feared that if not guided properly, young people, the inheritors and future transmitters of cultural practices and artifacts, could forfeit their authentic, ethnic identity, or worse still, fall prey to the ills of a modern Western society. Most often, the discourse of South Asian cultural retention is protectionist, suggesting that traditions of "back home" should be retained. From this perspective, any change is viewed as a possible precursor to cultural annihilation.

These debates have not only affected the South Asian community but have unsettled the meaning of what it is to be Canadian.[8] In the postwar era, Canada has increasingly been forced to deal with the diversity of its national population. The changing racial and ethnic composition within its borders has led to a lot of handwringing and controversy over the definition and meaning of *Canadian,* as well as concern over the possible weakening of the nation's boundaries. This discourse of nationalism equates *Canadian* with whiteness, and it, too, is protectionist. If migrant populations alter the fabric of a Canadian identity based on white anglo norms, then they threaten the definition of Canadian national identity. And thus, any change is again viewed as a possible precursor to cultural dilution and extinction. While Canadian and South Asian discourses of cultural protectionism may be similar, the former, unlike the latter, has the (relative) social, economic, and political power and representational resources to enforce itself.

Second-generation[9] South Asian youth in Canada are particularly troubling to these discourses because their presence points to the ruptures and contradictions between "modern" and "traditional." Young South Asians struggle to fashion an identity that speaks to their experience of being South Asian in Canada. In so doing, they often unsettle and resist certain mainstream definitions of both *South Asian* and *Canadian.*

But the experience of diaspora cannot be given all the credit for disturbing the notion of cultural authenticity. I am reminded of another story about culture and tradition. My paternal grandmother (Mataji) lived in Ferozepur, a small town in Indian Punjab near the border with Pakistan. Women in this area wore the veil, especially in front of older male company, and she did so after her marriage. Shortly after marrying my father, my mother arrived at her in-laws' to find that she, too, was to observe this aspect of purdah.[10] After one day she approached Mataji, known to be a powerful and unyielding matriarch, with some trepidation and announced she was not going to be covering her head. To my mother's surprise, my grandmother sighed, "Thank God!" Mataji's relief was palpable. She, too, shed her veil that very day. This story reminds me that, contrary to the belief in an authentic home culture, cultural practices do not remain static, even "back there."

But it also tells me something less obvious. Both my mother and grandmother are Punjabi Hindu women. Although wearing the veil is popularly thought of as an exclusively Islamic practice, the location of Ferozepur has meant that its cultural practices reflect a mix of Islam, Sikhism, and Hinduism. Because Hindu temples are scarce in the region, it has been customary for Hindus to pray at the gurdwara (Sikh temple). It was also tradition for one of the sons within a Hindu household to follow Sikhism, which was the path of my maternal granduncle. I grew up in both Hindu temples and Sikh gurdwaras. Of course, even these kinds of religious fusions are subject to political mobilizations around certain rights, territories, symbols, and identities. For example, in the last two decades the movement for an independent Khalistan spearheaded by members of the Sikh community, and the resulting Hindu reaction and backlash, have made ties between these two communities tenuous. The tension between the Hindu and Muslim communities within India dates well back before partition in 1947, and has particular postcolonial manifestations. In India, its most recent representation has been the right-wing Hindu fundamentalist political platforms intolerant of Islam, which have succeeded in gaining access to the official state apparatus.[11]

Ethnic identities, far from being natural or fixed, can also be seen as political articulations. By seeing ethnicity and race as constructed and imagined, political, and strategic concepts, we can begin to dislodge fixed notions of culture. As the story of my grandmother and mother indicates, culture is not static, but constantly being reconstructed and reimagined in relation to and in combination with other cultural sensibilities, narratives, and practices. It is for this reason that the "culture clash" or "caught between two cultures" model often used by the mainstream media and social analysts to account for the experiences of second-generation South Asians is inadequate. This model treats culture as a fixed category, and because it retains some of the assumptions inherent to assimilationist and acculturalist perspectives, it overlooks the power dynamics between mainstream culture and "other" cultural identities. It treats the clash of cultures as a conflict between equals, obscuring the fact that white Canadian is a more acceptable ethnic/cultural identity in the Canadian context than, in this case, South Asian.

## Culture Clash Theories

In the Western world, popular and commonsense understandings of tension between the white mainstream population and non-white immigrant communities situate the conflict as being between cultures.[12] *Culture* here is defined as values, attitudes, habits, and customs. The challenge confronting modern, culturally diverse societies is therefore understood as arising from value conflicts.[13] South Asian adolescents are said to be "torn" or "caught" between the values of a "traditional" (South Asian) culture and a "modern" (Canadian) one. This discourse is prevalent in both mainstream representations of the South Asian community and in the discussions of South Asian researchers, analysts, service providers, and community members. Given the power dynamics between minority and dominant cultures in Canada, this way of understanding tension between them is a way of managing the threat of modernity and westernism, on the one hand, and the threat to the centrality of white ethnicity on the other. Young women are central in this East-West conflict, both in its representation and in the ways in which accepted ideas of East and West position and imagine their respective identities.

Studies of second-generation South Asian youth in the West focus mainly on the process of acculturation and assimilation. This approach tends to measure the "success" of immigrants by the degree to which they assimilate into mainstream Canadian culture. The focus is on the immigrant's degree of cooperation and the adaptability of her/his culture, rather than on the degree of adaptability of the dominant culture. It does not recognize assimilation as a prerequisite for social, economic, and political opportunity.[14] However, many analysts have shown that assimilation, far from being voluntary, is a coercive process. Racial strife is not just attributable to cultural difference and misunderstanding but is a matter of economic exploitation and power relationships between dominant and minority groups.[15] The "common cultural life" immigrants are expected to assimilate into is based on white anglo conformity, and immigrants who continue to hold on to cultural markers that are visibly distinct from dominant political, economic, and cultural systems are not given the same access to opportunities for success.[16]

The degree to which second-generation immigrant youth adapt to dominant Canadian norms and values is, from this acculturalist perspective, seen to indicate the flexibility of their parents' culture. The conflicts youth face are said to result from being caught between two cultures: that of home and family, and that of the larger mainstream society. Youth whose parents are more open to embracing Canadian economic, political, and cultural norms are portrayed as having less conflict in their adolescent years than those whose parents are more reluctant to let go of the "outdated" traditions of their homeland.

The culture clash model tends to overlook how important race is as a determinant of identity. Early 1990s media curiosity about the South Asian subculture in Canada emerging around bhangra day dances, for example, is illustrative of this omission.[17] The day dance controversy was described by an article in *Toronto Life* magazine: "Daytime dances, which mainly attract teenagers, have become the focus of an ongoing conflict between generations within the city's 120,000-strong South

Asian community. At its core the conflict involves the usual parent-child issues — clothing, choice of friends, dating, parties, curfews — and dances serve as a powerful symbol representing them all ... Complicating matters are several features peculiar to the culture ... Indian children are expected to be passive and obedient." The article goes on to describe the life of a young girl who is "expected to come directly home after school; no hanging around the streets or at the local malls, mixing with boys, getting in trouble ... Is this what it means to be 16? ... It's certainly not what it means to most of the girls and boys her age at school who enjoy so many freedoms that are apparently unquestioned in Canadian culture."[18]

In David Hayes' article, the sixteen-year-old South Asian girl is juxtaposed with an unstated norm of freedom and autonomy. She is measured against the standard of a Canadian girl of the same age (read: a white girl, because the South Asian girl is not described as being part of Canadian culture) and is portrayed as leading a comparatively repressed life. In fact, the idea of freedom itself is characterized as part of the very fabric of Canadian culture. This type of analysis leads one to identify South Asian family and culture as the only source of constraint and conflict for South Asian girls. Such comparisons between "Canadian" and "South Asian" also tend to generalize the experiences of white youth by reducing questions of freedom and equality to matters of female presence in certain public spaces, heterosexual affiliations in the form of dating, and going to dances.[19]

The culture clash/identity crisis models are problematic for several reasons. First, they treat the cultures in question as equal competitors. This, of course, ignores the existence of a dominant culture (which minority cultures are expected to assimilate to) and the presence of systemic racism in Canada. In a nationwide survey over two decades ago, 80.5 percent of respondents of British origin identified themselves as "Canadian."[20] It was found, however, that for the respondents *Canadian* was another word for "British." The Canadian culture they were loyal to was actually structured by (white) British values and sensibilities.[21] In 1992, research findings indicated that Canadian antagonism towards immigrants was at historically high levels.[22] And in 1995, a public opinion poll reported that most Canadians preferred an English-speaking Canada to a multicultural one.[23] The September 11, 2001, attacks on the World Trade Center in New York forged an even greater divide between an "us" and a "them." Despite the Canadian government's commitment to multiculturalism, (anglo) British values and sensibilities continue to form the core of Canadian cultural identity.

Second, the culture clash model tends to view conflict as beneficial to identity formation. For example, Peter Weinreich explains "an individual's conflicts in identification with others as being an important psychological impetus for personal change. In this view 'identity' conflict is regarded as being more frequently a resource than a liability."[24] Weinreich cautions, however, that the generational conflict within minority communities should be kept in "perspective because such tensions tend to exist in all communities, since they are in part the result of changing values accompanying the normal processes of adolescent self-concept development. There is no evidence that they are greater in minority communities, only that they are based in different issues, ethnicity being a salient one ... Perhaps too often these [problems] are perceived as coming from within minority groups rather than from deficiencies in societal institutions."[25]

While I agree that problems and conflicts within minority communities are sensationalized in mainstream institutions and media, presenting them as a universal adolescent experience does not take into account the importance of race in the formation of identities in multiracial and assimilationist contexts and societies.

After reading the day dance article in *Toronto Life* magazine, I became interested in exploring what was being termed "culture conflict" among second-generation South Asian youth. Hayes' reading of conflict within the South Asian community did not, to my mind, capture the complexity of my own experience of growing up second-generation in Toronto. On the other hand, in an effort to dispel some of the mythologies created by the identity crisis approach, many antiracist perspectives I came across in discussions and scholarly writings seemed to cast aside the conflicts, crises, and complexities that young women sometimes do face.[26] I began to reflect on the role that race and racism played in my experiences in a predominantly white high school and analyzed the conflicts in my home during these years. It became clear to me that the article's characterization of conflicts facing young women is not fabricated, but represents in very real ways some of the struggles that many South Asian teenage girls confront. While Hayes' portrayal of young women emits a particular message about South Asian values and family as the source of conflict for young women, I began to realize that the ways in which we as a community of scholars and activists responded to this kind of analysis was protective. At public forums, we steered away from discussing the ways in which women's lives were regulated, yet privately we anguished, obsessed, and even joked over the ways in which our lives as women were restricted.[27]

 Negotiating Identities

In many ways, the tension between limitation and possibility has been a salient thread that has run through much of my life as a South Asian woman growing up in Canada. Understanding and exploring this tension has also been a source of inspiration and motivation. For many years, I have wanted to uncover all of the dynamics that limit, circumscribe, and mute the possibility of the totality of what we articulate, express, and live as second-generation South Asian women.

An example of what I have jokingly and privately called the "uncle or auntie phenomenon" further explains this tension. Recently, I was coming home from a night of dancing with friends at one of Toronto's downtown clubs. It was about three o'clock in the morning and I hailed a cab, sat inside, and began chatting with the cab driver in English. He was a South Asian man. Though we begin chatting in English, by his accent I am immediately able to place him as someone from India or Pakistan, a speaker of Hindi, Urdu, or Punjabi. While at first we both avoid acknowledging and placing each other as part of the same collectivity, inevitably the conversation turns to "Where are you from?" This question does not carry the same weight or sting as the "Where are you from?" I receive so often from white Canadians. In this context, it is more of a ritualistic marking and mutual acknowledgment of something shared, a confirmation of inclusion rather than a disclaimer and verification that "you are not from here." As the cab driver and I establish that our roots go back to a similar region, the style of our interaction changes. We no longer perform and construct ourselves around the rules and regulations of separation between driver and passenger specific to living in the West, and Canada in particular. At this point, I slip into Hindi, as a gesture that I have retained the language, which he may have assumed I had lost. The language here becomes part of a shared text and in some ways allows certain kinds of conversations that usually do not happen in English.

Now the dialogue begins to follow a familiar trajectory that often takes place in Toronto cabs when both the driver and passenger are from "back home." The discussion invariably involves the harshness of living in Canada, the cold weather and people, and a shared consensus that it's not the same as home: "Something is missing." Quite often the driver apologetically explains that he is only driving a cab temporarily or that back home he used to be a teacher, or had a degree in engineering or chemistry. He thought it would be "so different here": "You can make money, but look what happens to the family — everyone is so busy and nobody has any time. It's a lonely life."

As we pull up to the driveway of the house that I share with other female roommates my age, we begin to argue about payment. He does not want to accept the cab fare. "No, we are of the same people," he says. "How can I take money from you?" Sometimes I succeed in full payment, sometimes partial, and sometimes I am unable to persuade the taxi driver at all. Just before I exit the cab, the performative content changes. He wonders whether I am married, and if not, whether I live with my parents and if they approve of me going out so late. "Yes," I say, "I live with them." And yes, they approve, because after all it was only the birthday party of a family friend that I had been attending. While the invention of truth comes so naturally after years of practice, the next day my response always surprises me. There is always a part of me in the moment of lying that thinks about where I really was and feels the shame, the moral weight of knowing the truth. The tension between my performance and the truth always makes me feel uncomfortable.

What strikes me about the uncle phenomenon is that although this man is a complete stranger to me and has no direct connection to my family or relatives, and although I am now at an age where my own mother does not protest about my whereabouts or curfew, he is still a representation, a symbol, if you will, of the kind of moral regulation that I grew up with. This experience is reproduced no matter where I go or what city I am in when I see older South Asians. While they may be strangers, they are symbolic uncles and aunties nonetheless.

The gaze of uncle and auntie always weighs heavily on my shoulders. I am always prepared for the switch, the changing of masks. In talking with other young South Asian women, I learned that my experience of this gaze is not uncommon. The interaction with uncle makes me reflect on my own investment in the self-representation of what I understand to be the script of the good unmarried South Asian girl. I construct a narrative and representation of self in relation to uncle that is congruent with racial and cultural loyalty. To relinquish this investment and expose the truth would automatically align me with whiteness and Western-ness, labelling me a cultural renegade. This seems to be the only other possible racial and cultural position available to me. Because if I admit to transgressing the boundaries that mark the East, I automatically find myself in the other half of the binary — complicit in whiteness and Western-ness. While this book explores quite thoroughly this dichotomy of East and West and the ways in which women have become responsible for upholding and representing Eastern identity, I am also interested here in reflecting on whiteness as a performative category, in relation to the tension between limitation and possibility and in relation to the political risks of exposing truths.

Jasbir Puar uses the notion of the tourist as both a metaphor and a descriptive analytical category for second-generation South Asians, and this can be applied to immigrants in general.[28] The tourist is always in a transient and temporary social space. Second-generation South Asians are always in a state of just visiting, neither here nor there, neither quite in Canada nor back home. As a transplanted community they often occupy the space in-between nations. In this sense they never quite have ownership over the nation-building process, either in Canada or back home. The right to this ownership always appears somewhat arrogated. The space of the tourist, I would argue, is both marginal and "other," and a space of possibility and freedom. It is also potentially subversive. My own process of self-identification illustrates this point well.

Like many of my peers, my experience of growing up South Asian in Canada involved a process of rejection. Part of rejecting the Indian community that I grew up in had to do with a desire to reject certain expected middle-class feminine roles. I did not relate to gatherings of young South Asian women who were concerned about holes in their stockings, wearing the right clothes or shoes, or shaving body hair. The only place I could escape to was the white community. The rules, norms, and regulations did not weigh as heavily on me there. It was as if I was constantly a tourist in this whiteness. I could slip more easily into the grey areas, flaps, and folds of white collectivity. For example, in grade thirteen I felt most closely aligned with one or two other students in the school who, contrary to the dominant script of middle-class teenagehood of fast cars, clothes, and makeup, were opting out for a more hippie sensibility. Here I did not have to worry about shaving hair or wearing makeup and stockings. There was room for me to negotiate and manipulate a femininity outside the norms and rules of both middle-class Indian-ness and whiteness.

But how was this hippie identification received, I now wonder. After all, in the late 1970s and early 1980s, hippie culture occupied a marginal position in relation to other dominant discourses of teenagehood, and I, as a non-white person, may have pushed these fringes even further. (I do not see too many representations of me at Woodstock.) I wonder whether I unsettled the category of "hippieness" at all. And if I did not do it quite properly, if I did not use the appropriate signifiers, was I excused as the tourist, the immigrant that doesn't really know what's "in"? Or was my allegiance to hippie culture missed altogether — was I just a dirty immigrant who did not know how to shave her legs or dress properly? And finally I wonder whether this choice of association to hippie culture was a way (albeit unconscious) of maintaining a tie to my Indian-ness that was acceptable to me — there was space available here to sneak in a nose ring or an anklet if I wanted to, or a skirt made in India. The West has always appropriated, marketed, and distributed certain aspects of the East. So maybe there were moments when I was actually more authentically hippie, as a brown person closer to the spirituality and non-materialism of the East.

In my allegiance to this hippie culture and in some ways to what I understood as a non-materialistic Eastern identity, and in defiance of middle-class femininity, I decided to grow the hair on my legs and under my arms. One of my most confusing moments in terms of East, West, and second-generation identification came during a trip back to India, when one of my aunties was shocked and appalled at the hair growth on my body. This upset my aunt's version of the West, especially because her daughter and all her friends threaded their eyebrows, waxed their legs, and shaved under their arms in a desire for Western, modern productions of the body, an alliance to the good, clean, upwardly mobile, we're-not-backward-anymore life. Why didn't I? "But I'm trying to be more Indian," I protested.

Reflecting on the cab ride with uncle, examining my investment in hiding truths, and thinking about the space of freedom I thought I found for a few years among a handful of leftover hippies, the notion of tourist once again emerges. Somehow my position as tourist, a brown hippie, represents a blunder of appropriation. The hippie subculture did not correspond with brownness. And yet the judgment for breaking the norms of white femininity in marking my body differently did not carry the same moral weight as judgments from within my own community about transgressing the same middle-class feminine norms. While as a tourist I could possibly be forgiven for not performing "it" properly, within my own community judgment had far-reaching implications. It was much worse for an insider, who knew the rules, to transgress them. This kind of transgression seemed unforgivable, made me a traitor.

Through this research I have become interested in exploring the investments we have in performing certain identities over others and upholding certain masks over others, and the emotional and psychological costs of living in a racist society. What does it mean to constantly live in a generational space in which there is constant switching, lying and hiding of truths, experience of shame, and the weight of upholding the image of family and community in a hostile environment?

I have a personal investment in disclosing these secrets and silences, exposing the cracks between the normative boundaries of Canadian-ness and South Asian-ness — and how we perform, disrupt, and subvert these by identifying and inhabiting these cracks. These issues, questions, struggles, and negotiations have been part of the very process of writing this book. I have constantly had to negotiate the political risks of exposing secrets. What erasures do I commit? In a context of racism, where hanging out your "dirty laundry" is even more dangerous because it opens you and your community to more stereotypes, or reinforces stereotypes, is it possible to expose all the truths?

## ✍ Conflicts of Talking Culture

Most studies on South Asian youth have tended to focus on one dimension of their experience to the exclusion of others. Thus, either they produce eurocentric stereotypical portrayals of South Asian culture or they render invisible the contradictions and complexities of the everyday experiences that *are* connected to issues of cultural practice. In the process of this research I began to ponder how I would represent the experiences of women, which include difficulty with parental and community authority, without rendering women as passive victims to a seemingly repressive South Asian culture.

While I could identify the shortcomings in both mainstream representations and academic scholarship on South Asian Canadian youth, I was left with several troubling questions. Is it possible to take up the specificities of South Asian cultural practices without falling into stereotypical representations of South Asian culture and families? Are the experiences of South Asian girls fundamentally different from those of other adolescent girls? When does culture determine their experience, and can experience ever be constructed and conceived of outside of culture? What is culture? Is there a way to acknowledge cultural difference while simultaneously dislodging and subverting stereotypical representations? Once we acknowledge the systems of inequality that shape our experiences, such as race, class, and gender, how do we understand them without overdetermining or underdetermining their importance? These dilemmas have to do with the difficulties of theorizing around culture and difference, and are related to issues of representation and agency.

For my own research, I have found the most useful and relevant insights into the term *culture* in the works of Tony Bennett and Edward Said. Bennett explores the changing meanings of the concept of culture. He traces *culture* in its reference to the perfection of human development to the sixteenth century. In the eighteenth century, human development became coterminous with the Enlightenment notion of civilization. In the context of Enlightenment thinking, Bennett argues, "the development of culture and civilization — a hybrid concept referring to the development of economic, social and political institutions as well as the arts — was regarded as leading towards the creation of more rational, more enlightened patterns of thought and organization."[29] The idea of culture became interconnected with modern Western notions of civilization, advancement, and development. In the nineteenth and twentieth centuries, culture and civilization, once thought to be synonymous, have developed increasingly separate meanings. The former refers to all the practices involving "the arts of description, communication, and representation,"[30] while the latter is more closely tied to and dependent on the process of industrial and technological growth.[31] Culture, in this sense, is seen to be independent and autonomous from social, economic, and political systems. Bennett argues that culture has come to be associated with the sets of values that are in need of preservation and protection from what are seen as the ruthless costs of civilization.

The idea of culture as the perfection and development of human society has also come to have ideological and political meanings. It is enmeshed with notions of nation and belonging. I would argue that there are two commonsense notions of culture: one is tied to ideas about "cultured" art and music; the second is tied to notions of nation and ethnicity. Edward Said explains that this latter definition of culture is equated with "each society's reservoir of the best that has been known or thought. ... In time, culture comes to be associated often aggressively, with the nation or state; this differentiates 'us' from 'them,' almost always with some degree of xenophobia. Culture in this sense is a source of identity and a rather combative one at that, as we see in recent 'returns' to culture and tradition."[32]

I have introduced both Bennett's historicizing of culture and Said's interpretation of culture as an ideological and political category because both these notions are relevant to the arguments in this book. I argue that women and youth have become symbols of the sets of values that are seen to be in need of protection from the process of modern social progress. In addition, certain notions of women and youth are mobilized in order to maintain and assert specific notions of identity and belonging. South Asian cultural identity relies on particular definitions of womanhood in order to assert a distinct Eastern identity vis-à-vis the West.

Because *culture* is associated with the notions of identity and belonging, it has often been used synonymously with *race* and *ethnicity*, words that, while used interchangeably, have themselves been the source of considerable debate.[33] The overlap of the terms *culture, race,* and *ethnicity* can be understood if we examine the shifting notions of difference in the twentieth century. Lila Abu-Lughod argues that culture has come to replace race as a means of explaining and understanding difference. Similarly, Philomena Essed maintains that nineteenth-century arguments about racial inferiority (based on biological and genetic differences) are no longer seen as credible and have been replaced with apparently more tolerant notions of cultural inferiority. Cultural difference has thus become the new marker of socially constructed racial difference.[34] Differences in culture (and not racism) are seen to be responsible for discrepancies in economic and political development, governmental structure, lifestyle, and personal attributes and achievements.

Because the concept of culture has become interwoven and conflated with notions of race, discussions of culture have been opened to eurocentric and racist conclusions. While it is no longer acceptable, for example, to speak about racial differences or incompatibilities as reasons for segregation, exclusion, or intolerance, cultural incompatibility and difference remain a justification for partial treatment of non-white populations in the Western world. In my interviews with young South Asian women, I found that a discourse of cultural difference and conflict obscured the working of race and racism and the idea that white is normal.

Writing about Western Europe, Philomena Essed argues that late-twentieth-century racism operates through a discourse of apparent tolerance. She asserts that tolerance in a culturally pluralistic society presumes that people of colour and other immigrants "accept and internalize the norms and values of the dominant group," while they at the same time are "permitted" to retain their cultural identity (so long as it does not conflict with the dominant social and legal order).[35] Sherene Razack maintains that according to this paradigm people of colour are seen as "not having made it owing to their cultural incompatibility with the dominant culture."[36] Essed argues that the principle of tolerance, which has been adopted in some countries as a way of managing cultural diversity in the postwar era, creates new forms of racism while at the same time rendering race and racism invisible. (The Canadian model of multiculturalism is a paradigmatic case of Essed's sense of tolerance.) Discussing culture and cultural differences therefore becomes perilous in racist contexts, because it may further obscure the racist subtext.[37] Razack maintains that most such discussions are "formulated on the basis of a reductionist notion of culture whereby culture is taken to mean values, beliefs, knowledge and customs, all of which exist in a timeless vacuum outside of patriarchy, racism, imperialism and colonialism."[38] Culture in this context claims "a superautonomy that reduces all facets of social experience to issues of culture."[39] In this kind of climate, any discussion of gender relations within a non-white context raises the danger of reinforcing stereotypical and fixed notions of culture, where gender oppression is seen as an effect of culture.

During the process of my own research I found myself arguing that the difficulties that South Asian teenagers face are no different from the issues that young women from the dominant culture confront — dating, curfew, degree of autonomy. I was reacting to literature that portrayed South Asian culture as backward, repressive, and the source of conflict for women. Yet, on the other hand, I, along with others, have been fighting for the recognition of the need for social services that are specifically geared towards ethno-specific groups. The tension between sameness and difference has been central in most theoretical interrogations of identity. Often referred to as the difference/equality debate, it oscillates between those who believe that efforts should be directed towards addressing the conditions that circumscribe a particular group's social position so that they may enjoy the same rights and privileges as others (the equality position) and those who argue that the focus should be on eradicating the very nature of these differences and conditions (the difference position).[40] An example would be fighting for the right of women to join the military (equality position) or fighting for the dismantling of the patriarchal militaristic system all together (difference position). Linda Alcoff speaks to this postmodern pitfall: "For the liberal, race, class, and gender are ultimately irrelevant to questions of justice and truth because underneath we are all the same. For post-structuralists, race, class, and gender are all constructs, and therefore incapable of decisively validating conceptions of justice and truth because underneath there lies no natural core to build on or liberate or maximize."[41]

The young South Asian women I interviewed provided many examples of this dichotomy. On the one hand they are constantly positioned in relation to race and racial difference, and on the other hand liberal discourses of multiculturalism reinforce the notion of racial equality. The difficulty for them becomes naming experiences of racism within a context that constantly tells them that race and racial difference do not matter. The tension between sameness and difference is connected to discourses of difference and the retention of binary categories that obscure the dynamics of inequality.

Jasbir Puar argues that polarized identities, such as the binaries in culture conflict — East/West, traditional/modern, South Asian/ Canadian, backward/advanced — are perceived as contrasting and oppositional categories. These oppositions are seen to be "mutually exclusive so that the only logical conclusion to anyone struggling with culture conflict is to choose either one side or the other, primarily for the sake of mental emotional well-being."[42] Puar explains that notions of identity that categorize human experience within these dichotomies "consistently reinscribe 'identity' as a fixed, static, and boundaried state. Such an understanding of identity continues to define qualifiable 'difference' in terms of 'sameness' as in 'not the same as.'"

In my own research I found that young South Asian women drew on a discourse of identity that defined "South Asian" in fixed terms. Accordingly, South Asian is seen as rooted in biological markers, such as skin colour, or common ethnic markers, such as language, dress, and religion. This discourse relies on certain fixed notions of culture/race/ethnicity, which are used to construct, define, and circumscribe the parameters of identity. This kind of framework dominates as a means of making sense and interpreting categories of identity. The day-to-day behaviour, experiences, and location of most of these women, however, are often at odds with the parameters of dominant narratives of South Asian-ness. For example, some women defined "Indian" as dependent on language retention and going to religious institutions, yet still considered themselves Indian although they did not observe these aspects of cultural practice. For them the conflict and points of tension emerge from a definition of "Indian" that is dependent on fixed authentic notions of cultural practice, with the simultaneous recognition that this definition of identity excludes them from membership in the group. Most often the definition of "South Asian" depended on a distinction from "Canadian" or "Western." How to be South Asian in Canada, when these two categories of identity appear oppositional and mutually exclusive, was at the forefront of young women's struggles to negotiate and construct a sense of identity.

The debate about culture and belonging, and whether culture is rooted in some original historical source or shared characteristic based on an unchangeable tradition, has implications for South Asian identity. Are we determined by a fixed and unchanging fact of identity — so that to be South Asian means we have to behave and believe in certain fixed ways — or does the way we experience being

South Asian have to do with the way in which the category "South Asian" is defined and constructed?

The debate around whether race, ethnicity, and culture are essential categories or socially constructed ones has deflected attention away from some important questions around how these categories work. Another question became more significant for me: why is there a continued investment in notions of identity that appeal to common, shared, or universal characteristics, experiences, or ideals? I began to understand the questions about cultural difference as part of the problem. Rather than seeking to diminish cultural difference by treating culture as a measurable phenomenon, the question became: how does the notion of cultural difference relate to issues of cultural identity? How do notions of cultural difference operate? How do young South Asian women make sense of them, use them, subvert them? I began to understand discourses of cultural difference as very closely related to how we frame, interpret, and conceptualize notions of cultural identity.

## ⟩⟩ The Sources

From a survey of articles in mainstream media, interviews with young women, and discussions within the South Asian community, I concluded that the notion of culture clash was having real effects, both in the way conflicts and tensions were being named and represented and in the way they were being experienced. It is from here that I became interested in understanding my own (and other women's) investment in upholding certain kinds of representations over others. In my own self-reflection and analyses of interviews with young South Asian women, I was struck by one recurring theme: the continuous negotiation of identities, changing of roles, wearing of masks, and safeguarding of secrets.[43]

This work examines some of the discourses around cultural identity within the South Asian community in the context of early to mid-1990s Metropolitan Toronto.[44] This research has grown out of in-depth qualitative interviews with fourteen young South Asian women of varying religions and primarily from the South Asian subcontinent and parts of Africa. In some cases, the women were interviewed again, a year later. I have used my conversations with the young women as threads to discourses and a source of information about their social world. I also searched mainstream and South Asian periodicals for representations of second-generation immigrant populations, as well as of the South Asian community, and young women in particular. The media sources include *Toronto Life* magazine, the *Globe and Mail, Toronto Star, Winnipeg Free Press, Calgary Herald, Montreal Gazette,* and *Halifax Chronicle Herald*.[45] I use a textual analysis of these representations of the South Asian community and culture conflict to provide a context, juxtaposing how dominant discourses position young South Asian women with how the women position themselves.[46]

As I began to interview the young women, I quickly realized that I was operating according to stereotypical notions of "modern" and "traditional." After being thrown off by the complexities of young women's identities and realizing that they were not easily categorized, I attempted to apply these same categories to my own family. For example, over the years, people have frequently asked whether my parents were traditional or modern. As I begin to describe my mother, however, the cohesive and clear-cut notions of traditional and modern are unable to capture her complexities and contradictions. I have always known my mother to wear a sari. I have always known my mother to be in paid work, cook the meals, drive a car, clean the house, control her own finances, do the household repairs, and garden. In which category should I place her?

Below I provide biographies of five young women who represent a cross-section of those I interviewed. I provide these accounts as a way of demonstrating the broad range of their life experiences and presenting a detailed look at some of their life circumstances. These stories also further illustrate the tension between, and assumptions around, modern and traditional, a theme that I explore throughout this book.

## ALKA

When I first met Alka, a sixteen-year-old Hindu upper-middle-class girl, I assumed that she was traditional and therefore conservative. At the beginning of the interview (conducted in her room) I learned that she was very religious, had two older brothers and a sister with whom she had little connection, avidly consumed the Bombay film industry, and was a classical Kathak dancer. She had pictures of Hindi film stars pinned up above her bed. She described her family relationships as "isolating." She had little or no communication with her mother and brothers and she admitted to feeling suicidal in the recent past.

By the end of the interview, however, I found that I was not able to categorize Alka so easily. Her dancing had caused her some problems in the marriage market and she was unwilling to let go of this aspect of her life to satisfy any potential suitor. This was a source of ongoing tension between her and her parents. She was articulate, outspoken, and involved in many school activities and had aspirations to follow a career as a radio broadcaster. After I interviewed her, she interviewed me on video for a school project. In a follow-up discussion a year later, she told me that she ran away from home one week before her semi-arranged wedding and stayed in a youth hostel in the outskirts of town. She explained that although she had initially met and introduced her fiancé to her parents, his insistence that after marriage she give up dancing, and her parents' pressure to marry, compelled her to run away. At the time of the second interview, she was again living with her parents. She was dating somebody new and kept this relationship hidden from her parents and siblings.

PINKI

I met Pinki, a seventeen-year-old Sikh girl of working-class background, during a crisis. She had recently run away from home for several months to live with her boyfriend. Her parents discovered where she was and took her back home. She was to leave for India for the first time the day after our interview and was afraid that she would be pushed into marriage. She was the youngest in a family of seven. Most of her siblings were married and no longer lived at home. Although Pinki said she loved her boyfriend, she said that their separation was a "good idea." She was concerned about his overindulgence in drinking and his participation in a gang. She seemed to think that their love would endure the separation.

Her mother is not formally educated, and her father is a prominent member of the community. This prominence seemed to affect her position as a daughter. Because of her father's role in the community, her behaviour, she felt, was constantly monitored and regulated. Pinki explained that her conduct was seen not only to reflect on herself, but also on the reputation of the entire family. If she did not follow the family and community codes of femininity, it reflected negatively on her family and consequently her father's standing in the community. While she was very aware of this and the fact that most of her siblings had followed what she saw as the expected "respectable" path, she had still mustered the courage to run away from home.

Part of what surprised me at the end of our interview were my assumptions about her Punjabi accent. As we packed up I casually asked her how old she was when she arrived in Toronto from India. "I was born here," she answered. I commented that of course she must have travelled back and forth to India many times. "I have never been to India," she answered. She explained that she had a Punjabi accent because at home she spoke Punjabi with her parents and at school she spoke Punjabi with her friends, Punjabis being the mainstay of her school population.

SALIMAH

Salimah was an outspoken eighteen-year-old Pakistani girl of lower middle-class background, who attended school in Mississauga and described her group of friends as "culturally diverse." She felt quite restricted by her parents and wished to follow a singing career that she knew she would not be permitted. This was particularly painful for her because she had already been asked to sing by a prominent talent scout. She was in constant battle with her parents about attending social functions at school and dances. She explained that her parents felt it was not proper for a girl to sing or dance, if it was going to be in front of men.

Salimah felt that her parents trusted her and saw her as a proper daughter who did not date, drink, or go out late. While she did her best to maintain her "good girl" image with her parents, she also felt weighed down by the expectations this image placed on her. She was quite outspoken (anonymously of course) on the radio about issues affecting young South Asian women. She felt that publicly talking about the restrictions on young women's lives, if her parents knew, would ruin their perception of her. While she admitted to struggling with depression now and again, she was often in the role of providing support to her peers and younger women who had difficulties coping with the competing expectations of school, peers, and family.

RATNA

For Ratna, an eighteen-year-old Hindu girl of upper-middle-class background, celebrating her South Asian-ness wasn't a "big deal." She explained that she had three older siblings who had been quite involved in the South Asian social scene. She seemed to view the issue of cultural identity and the excitement over the bhangra dances as a bit tedious. She explained that for her, growing up around siblings who celebrated their cultural/racial identity, while perhaps important for a generation who were attempting to claim racial space, was rather limiting. She did not want to be confined to socializing only in the "brown scene" and preferred a mix of friends. The issue most affecting Ratna's life was her Muslim boyfriend. Because of the religious difference and the fact that, according to her parents, she should not be dating in the first place, this relationship was shrouded in secrecy. While she said she really loved him, she was considering ending the relationship. Ratna felt that there was no point in investing in a relationship that she knew her parents would not approve of. Interestingly enough, one of her siblings had married a white Canadian, who despite initial misgivings and resistance was now accepted by her parents as part of the family.

## RUPINDER

Rupinder, an eighteen-year-old Sikh girl of working-class background, described herself as a bit of a loner in relation to her family. She said she preferred it that way. At the beginning of the interview she was very quiet but revealed quite a cynical and sarcastic sense of humour by the end of our meeting. She seemed to feel disenfranchised by both the South Asian community, which she found parochial and judgmental, and by the white community, which she found racist.

Although she had a "soft spot" for her father, she had the most altercations with him of anyone in her family. She was the older of two children. She seemed to be somewhat fearless in her challenge to the authority of her father. Her latest conflict with him had occurred when she had gone out to a club and returned home late. When her father threatened to throw her out of the house, she said, "Fine!" and walked out.

She spoke in great detail about her experience of sexual abuse by a family member. She felt this sexual abuse had profoundly affected her life and yet her efforts to talk to her parents about it had only isolated her further from them, as they now viewed her as sexually promiscuous and "spoiled." She had not spoken about the abuse to any friends or professionals.

With these young women I explored their relationships primarily within the family and at school, and their notions of culture, race, and gender. I observed that regardless of class, ethnic, or religious differences, most of the women had similar concerns. They all named conflict with their parents as the most important issue affecting them, and this tension almost invariably centred on issues of freedom and autonomy.[47] They emphasized the severity of family and community restrictions in relation to dating, choice of partner, vocation, and freedom of movement. I became aware of the significance they placed on what they perceived as a lack of freedom and control over their own lives.

Feeling they had few people to turn to for guidance, many of the women I spoke to were attempting to sort out extremely critical issues on their own. They did not communicate with their parents about most of their experiences in the world of school and peers. They all emphasized the need for secrecy, explaining that community and family approval of their behaviour was extremely consequential and without it they risked social ostracism. In one of the interviews, Salimah reflected on this experience: "I don't think a lot of Indian girls have anybody to talk to. They really don't. I know so many Indian girls who are having so many problems. It is problems with their parents ... They can't handle it. Sometimes they get so frustrated and so upset. I know so many Indian girls who all they used to do is cry. I find they all have the same problems. All they ever say is, 'I have no freedom, I have no life.'"

Some young women were in abusive relationships. Young men seemed to be taking full advantage of the fact that these girls' parents would highly disapprove of their dating in the first place. They used the consequent fear and secrecy as a means to maintain power in the relationship by threatening to disclose the relationship to her parents if the woman wanted to break it off. While most young women feared judgment and exclusion from family and community, they also felt misunderstood by support services offered by school and other social agencies. Rupinder was sexually abused by a family member. When the school and family services found out and decided to intervene on her behalf, against the advice of the girl, her life changed for the worse. Her parents became more reprimanding of her because she had exposed "dirty laundry" outside the family. As a result of the experience she has learned not to reach out for help both within and outside the family and deals with the effects of the abuse on her own.

Another young woman approached her school guidance counsellor in an effort to discuss the conflicts she was facing at home. The counsellor, she felt, was unable to understand her family context and advised that she leave home. As in the case of most of the young women I interviewed, allegiance to home and family was a central component of her identity as an "acceptable" daughter and community member. Rather than solving her problem, advice to leave home made this young woman realize the ineffectiveness of adult systems of support.

The women in my study seemed to be caught between the ineffectiveness of white peer support, mainstream social service agencies, parental guidance, and school assistance. I found that depression, feelings of suicide, and isolation were common to many women that I interviewed. South Asian social and community workers corroborated these findings. They emphasized that the conflict between parents and their daughters was of paramount concern within the community and among the most significant stressors for South Asian parents and youth. Two of the community health nurses, who have frequent contact with young women, disclosed that there was a disturbing increase of depression, eating disorders, alcoholism, and suicide attempts among young South Asian women in Toronto.

## ⟩ꙮ Inside and Outside

The tension between inclusion and exclusion is a theme that runs through much of this book, which at one level is about constructed identities. In order to understand young women's experiences of isolation and depression, and the reasons their lives have become so intensely regulated by parents and community, I explore narratives of South Asian community identity in the West. In these chapters I unravel some of the pressure points in what is being described as a clash of values between South Asian immigrants and their offspring and between South Asian peoples and mainstream Canadians. Rather than reducing the problematic of conflict between immigrant parents and their children to a product of autonomous factors of backward chauvinistic culture or racism, I look at how notions of race and gender position young South Asian women in the diasporic context of Canada. These notions have been central to the construction, imagination, and maintenance of the boundaries around an ethnic identity for both South Asian and white Canadians.

Narratives of identity are produced out of intersecting historical relationships between East and West, and the continuing struggle for political control, with its particular dimensions in the diaspora, positions women in specific ways. While concerns about young South Asian women and the tension between confinement and freedom are seemingly about women, they are equally about an East-West battle that is rooted in a colonial discourse of cultural difference and inequality. An exploration of Indian colonial discourse is thus central to my discussion of South Asian women in Canada. I maintain that the elements of the struggle over tradition and culture that operated in colonial India parallel components of the culture conflict debate in Canada in the 1990s. The notion of tradition as static, and fixed and preserved by women, is a colonial one relied on by both the British administration and Indian nationalists.[48]

In the context of colonial India, historian Jenny Sharpe argues that a nineteenth-century crisis in British colonial authority was managed by the British through mobilizing certain ideas about race and women. She contends that the figure of woman was pivotal in "shifting a colonial system of meaning from self-interest and moral superiority to self sacrifice and racial superiority."[49] I would argue that the moral superiority of white Canadians is restored by a narrative that portrays "other" cultures (in this case, South Asian culture) as backward. Youth, and especially young women, are instrumental to this narrative. Young South Asian women are constructed as in need of rescue from traditional, overbearing, unyielding parents, cultural practices, or families. This message is especially important at a time when Canadian identity, its boundaries and meaning, are uncertain and contested. The uncertainty of the boundaries of white Canadian identity is present in the debates on immigration and reactions to cultural diversity. The narratives of the "backward ethnic" and "immigrant conflict" are best understood in relation to the real or imagined threat that a non-white population presents to the centrality of a white Canadian identity and the maintenance of white power and privilege. South Asians are excluded from the imagination of Canadian national identity. It is partly in response to this oversight that particular narratives about South Asian community, identity, and authenticity have been mobilized.

# CHAPTER TWO

# From Mataji to Myself:
## Formations of East and West

In the early 1990s, I witnessed the birth of Salaam Toronto, spearheaded by Ian Rashid, cultural producer and writer. This small platform for South Asian activists and non-conformists grew into a ten-year-long organization called Desh Pardesh. Gathered in a small room of the 519 Community Centre on Church Street, I watched, for the first time with other like-minded people, aspects of my cultural heritage that I had grown up with. Only, in this instance nonconformity and South Asian-ness came together for me. I watched the same Bharat Natyam–style classical dances that I had gone to see with my parents, and stood in line for the same samosas and chutney I had formed a love-hate relationship with in high school. But it felt different. Dressed in my jeans and T-shirt, as I looked around and saw possibility in wardrobe, I thought, I could have worn my salwar kameez.

## Home as a Site of Crossing

While at my predominantly white high school I spent most of my time trying to hide my brownness (thinking I could), at home my family life involved the celebration of all festivals and the mandatory wearing of the clothes and following of the understood codes of being Indian. My social life consisted of my parents' social life. At home I conformed well to all the expectations of being a proper Indian girl, and at school, I was trying to be anything but Indian. I was leading a double life.

As I entered teenage-hood and attempted to assert my individuality, my parents equated this with the influence of Canadian/Western culture. There seemed to be no other way to read my suddenly strange teenage behaviour. One evening as we all sat around in silence at the dinner table, I asked if I could go to a party that a girl at my high school was having. This question came at a time when we had been having our first series of disagreements around curfew and social activities.

"No," my parents said.

"But, but..."

"But nothing. You can't go. Nothing doing. There is nothing to discuss."

My head drooped down as I fought to keep the tears that gathered from spilling over and becoming part of my aloo gobi vegetables. And something came over me. I had never spoken back to my parents before, but it was too late. Before I was able to catch the words, they had already been propelled from my end of the dinner table to theirs.

"But it's my life!" I exclaimed. This pushed the mounting tension to the edge.

"Your life! Your life! *You* think it's *your* life! Where are you learning such nonsense! This is not your life. That's a Western rubbish, you are Indian!"

Sitting across from Aarti in a crowded coffee shop twelve years after finishing high school, trying to understand this experience, she confided the following — an admission that somewhat comforted my anxieties about duality. "My whole life is based on a lie and my parents probably know that ... The big thing I'd say [is that] conflicts between my parents and me were always about going out, about going out late at night ... It's just the whole thing of the Western culture, that [they say,] 'We're not like them, why do you want to be like them?'"

East and West, traditional and modern, and what they have come to represent, are often the subtext of many of the conflicts within South Asian families. Though the contrast between traditional and modern is most commonly thought to be between first world and third world or industrialized and pre-industrialized nations, this contradiction is not exclusive to my generation living in the West. In my own family, the idea of migrating to the West was the subject of much ambivalence. My paternal grandfather was educated to matriculation (tenth grade), which was considered quite high for his generation. When my father received a scholarship to study at the London School of Economics for a doctorate, there was tremendous excitement and skepticism on the part of cousins, aunties, and parents. My father was the first in his extended family to leave his small town of Ferozepur and go to Delhi. This in itself was considered a big journey in the family, so the news of his sailing away to the foreign lands of the Angrez/English was the grounds for much commotion. There was some doubt how all this burying of nose in books was actually going to help anybody or change anything. In fact, every time he went back home, Mataji pressed his hand to her cheek in a gesture that was both wondering and thanking of god for his return, looking him over as if disbelieving he had survived the big world all this time. And as quickly as she accepted his return home, she would begin scolding the institution of education and the world of books that had taken her only child so far away. His departure from India was associated as much with a sense of pride and accomplishment as with fear: fear about the modern world and its perceived social and moral ills. My father was the only person within the small town of Ferozepur to leave for a scholarship in the "new" world.

As I thought more about the conflict that occurred in my home and that of many other South Asian families, as well as how this conflict has been perceived both within and outside of the South Asian community, several things struck me. I started to understand history as important to the making and perception of this conflict. I also began to unravel the symbolic meanings behind being young, being South Asian in the West, and being female in modern times. The ways in which we understand the concepts of youth and women in relation to East and West are very much a product of the modern era. While the ideas and changes associated with modernity are complex, what is significant to this discussion is that many of the changes associated with modernization have generated a kind of ambivalence — both fear and excitement about the possibility of change.[1]

While the idea of tradition has become associated with the East, fears about modernization and change from traditional pre-industrialized ways of life and customs have also existed in the West. Rapid changes accompanying modernity brought with them an increasing anxiety about the success of the modern era in the Western world from the point of view of the white middle classes. Would modernity really bring about progress and prosperity, or would the freedoms accompanying it lead to social and moral decay and disintegration?[2] Historical research made me realize that youth was conceived of as a period of storm and stress in North America both before and during the influx of immigrants from the non-European world at the beginning of the twentieth century. White, middle-class families and professionals worried about their children in the 1950s and discussed the youth problem at great length. The use of youth to register both anxiety and ambivalence among white middle-class families in the West has since become relatively invisible in relation to the problem of youth within (non-white) immigrant families. This imperceptibility is due to postwar understandings of race that translate the traditional/modern paradox characteristic of the modern era into East/West — backward East and modern West. In looking at the history of how youth have been seen, it becomes clear that culture clash is not an ethnic phenomenon. Contrary to popular understanding, the conflict is not underlain by ethnic difference per se and degrees of assimilation. White youth have also been perceived and constructed as at odds with the values of modernity. The culture conflict is really about the clash between the cultures of traditional and modern. Youth as a symbol of this conflict has tended to make the source of this tension invisible.

A look at post-1950s panic over white youth shows that notions of delinquency, corruption, and moral and social decay were constructed in relation to, and as dependent on, representations of the non-white ethnic. In the process of registering and containing fears around modern social progress and its possible "dark" side, middle-class Canadians were also defending the meaning of white reputation and the continued dominance of a white nation. While the anxieties around youth were manifested somewhat differently for white youth during the 1950s, there are similarities with the ways in which youth are now positioned as in need of protection and guidance in both South Asian and white communities. There are also parallels between the ways in which youth and the non-white immigrant are positioned and constructed in the modern era. They are both seen as potentially volatile, in need of guidance, development, or protection. These ideas of guardianship around age intersect with ideas of protection of culture for South Asian youth, and women in particular because women have come to represent certain notions of identity, tradition, and culture. In the Western context then, young South Asian women are seen as in need of protection not only because of their age, but also because their culture is seen as threatened by erosion. Ideas of protection have justified various restrictions and forms of social control over women.

The use of notions of womanhood to mark the boundaries of national and cultural identity can be traced back to colonial India. During the struggle for independent India, the idea of women was used by Indian nationalists and British colonialists alike, both concerned about the authenticity and boundaries of their respective cultural identities in a struggle over political rule. The British colonialists were instrumental in making women a central issue in their bid for continued control over India. They used and intervened on the "woman question" in order to position themselves as culturally and morally superior and thereby justify continued rule of a presumably uncivilized indigenous population. Indian nationalists resolved the contradiction between modernization and westernization by allowing women to modernize without giving up what was perceived to be a true Indian identity. Notions of womanhood were used not only to resolve the ambivalence between premodernity and modernity but also to assert the claim to Indian self-rule. In the context of colonial India, concepts of femininity became inseparable from a politics of cultural authenticity, preservation, and Indian identity itself. From this standpoint, the white woman represented everything the Indian woman did not. Indian women became synonymous with the characteristics of innocence, spirituality, and purity and were also positioned as the moral guardians and keepers of a particular brand of Indian culture.

The woman question is also being employed today in the post–September 11 American "war against terrorism." Again, Western concepts of freedom and the right to conquest are being carved out and justified in relation to the treatment of women by the Taliban in Afghanistan. The long-standing complaints about the oppression of women in Afghanistan have suddenly become paramount in mobilizing public support in favour of American intervention. Thus gender becomes a political tool in the formation of strategic alliances and marking of cultural identities.


## ⤷ The Young, Modern, and Delinquent

Franco Moretti argues that in times of great social change, there is a heightened focus on youth, and that particular anxieties about the future are projected onto them. In other words, the more the social perception becomes one of instability and uncertainty with respect to social norms and culture, the more intense is the image of youth used to acknowledge these anxieties.3 For a variety of reasons, post–World War II Europe has been perceived as a time and place of tremendous change. According to Lesley Johnson, although there had been tremendous industrial and economic change in the eighteenth and nineteenth centuries, social and cultural ways of life were relatively unaffected. She argues that in the 1950s these anxieties about change were translated into ideas about "normal" adolescent development in the Western world.4 Similarly, it has been argued that young people were increasingly seen as defenceless against the possible dangers of modernization, not only because of their age but also because old methods of cultural survival were in some ways obsolete in the postwar era. The (pre-industrial) survival tools that generations had relied on and the knowledge they had passed on to their youth about what to expect in adulthood were no longer completely suitable for a changing new world.

Parents and communities began to worry when business interests began targeting teens as a separate consumer market. In Canada, for example, a plethora of magazines, films, books, and other consumer items were specifically geared toward the teenager.5 While the interests of commerce helped to forge the idea of youth as separate from adulthood, so too did new ideas in the fields of medicine and psychology. These professional disciplines generated theories of biological and psychological development to explain why youth needed special attention and different treatment from adults. Biological theories based their analysis on the physiological changes accompanying puberty. The onset of emotional, hormonal, and psychological changes occurring in adolescence due to sexual development meant that persons in this age group were seen as not quite stable, unable to make their own decisions, and easily tempted by the "false promises" of modern society.6 Youth were therefore seen as vulnerable, and in need of protection and guidance in order to adjust and assimilate to the needs and demands of a modern and changing society.

In post-1950s Canada, "family values" were seen as a solution for the dangers posed by modernization. During this time, juvenile delinquency was a great concern. There was panic that youngsters without "adequate parental supervision" were growing up without a proper sense of social responsibility and were therefore vulnerable to committing crimes against authority.[7] There was also fear about the influences of mass media and popular culture on young people, both of which were "at various times, marked as influences capable of corrupting youthful 'innocence,' as threats to young lives and therefore to the future of society as a whole."[8] Youth was seen as a period of innocence and promise which, if not guided or directed properly, could descend into corruption. In this sense, youth were constructed as potentially volatile.[9] Generational conflict was viewed as the friction between the backward (adolescent) and advanced (adult) stages of human development. Any resistance to becoming a modern social being and responsible citizen was accordingly considered abnormal, immature, backward, or unstable. The larger social contradiction between modernity and tradition was made invisible by the idea of the generation gap.

Mary Louise Adams argues that discourses around youth and juvenile delinquency in the 1950s had much to do with regulating young women's sexuality. She shows that for young women, the charge of delinquency most often involved sexual misbehaviour. For women, socially irresponsible behaviour means nonconformity to acceptable sexual standards. There was tremendous concern about women's well-being outside the confines of home. Young women going out late at night led to fears that once they were beyond parental supervision "girls would express their sexuality in a manner dangerous to themselves and their communities."[10] Anxieties around young women's sexuality operate to regulate young South Asian women today in much the same way that postwar discourses circumscribed the lives of young white middle-class women in the 1950s.

While the postwar period reveals an anxiety around growing up for young adults, there was also concern over the influx of non-white immigrants to Canada. White middle classes worried not only about their "own" youth, but also about the threat that non-white immigrants were thought to pose to the developing nation. Questions of modernity were also affected by notions of race, though most conventional analyses of youth make this connection invisible. How did the vision of the "modern human" depend on ideas of race? How did the idea of a new world, with all its modern successes and promises of middle-class material gains, come to be synonymous with whiteness? Middle-class respectability was, in part, supported and maintained through panics about non-white immigrants in Canada.

## ✹ Race: On Your Marks, Get Set, Go

The concept of race as evaluation and separation between superior and inferior can be dated back to mid-nineteenth-century scientific modes of inquiry. Also known as social Darwinism, concepts of biological competition between species were applied to social, economic, and political discussions of friction within a species.[11] David Theo Goldberg explains how notions of progress and advancement were based on ideas of inequality that delegated superior and inferior subject positions:

> Subjugation perhaps properly defines the order of the Enlightenment: subjugation of nature by human intellect, colonial control through physical and cultural domination, and economic superiority through mastery of the laws of the market. The confidence with which the culture of the West approached the world to appropriate it is reflected in the constructs of science, industry, and empire that principally represent the wealth of the period. ... The emergence of independent scientific domains of anthropology and biology in the Enlightenment defined a classificatory order of racial groupings. ... In cataloguing the variety

of racial aliens, however, Enlightenment science simultaneously extended racial self-definition to the West [as superior]. ... The catalog of national characters emerged in lock step with the classification of races.[12]

The categories of modern and traditional, far from being simply descriptive, became evaluative. The former is associated with progress and superiority, while the latter has come to mean primitive and uncivilized. "Modern" has become synonymous with European and North American models of social, political, and economic capitalist development, while non-Western societies have become the markers of "tradition." According to these discourses, the East is backward because it has not fully embraced or entered into the modern world. It is therefore in need of development and Western guidance. The third world, the minority, the racial "other," is associated more with premodernity and is seen as possessing more culture and ethnicity than the dominant first-world majority, which appears to be unmarked in this respect.

The invisibility of whiteness in relation to the ethnicity of brownness was a theme that emerged on numerous occasions in my interviews with young South Asian women. In the following excerpt from an interview with Nina, it is clear how notions of ethnicity and visibility operate. Nina refers to how she feels at school when she is seen with her South Asian boyfriend or her friend Asha:

> Amita: Did you feel kind of embarrassed if you were seen talking to another Indian at school?
>
> Nina: Actually yeah, yeah, 'cause I didn't want people to think that he's my only friend. You know what I mean, 'cause he's brown he's my only friend. Or because she's brown, she's my only friend, and because we're brown we should stick together. I didn't want that impression to come ... I didn't allow myself to become good friends with that [South Asian] person. But I didn't stop myself from

talking to that person if I had a question to ask them. ... I know it's bad, but sometimes even if we're walking, like even if I'm walking with my boyfriend somewhere, like if we're walking in a group, I feel so, I feel like so centred 'cause we're all the same and I feel like people look at us that way and I think that way about Asha too. 'Cause when I see two Indian people I'm like, "Oh yeah, they're just together 'cause they're Indian," but they don't realize that we're together not 'cause we're Indian but—

Amita: [interrupting] But do you think people think that about white people, like if they see a group of white people?

Nina: Yeah, they would think that, too, I guess. Yeah, I think so. But I don't know why but it seems like more, not obvious, but I notice it more though [if it is South Asians]. Like I know even in like movies or whatever, like two best friends — my best friend is Greek and I'm like, "Why don't they show two best friends of two different cultures?" I look at it the same way. Maybe other people don't. But because I see Indian people that way, I see every culture that way, like [in hushed tone] when I see Oriental people I think of them in the same way, like they always have to hang around together. It seems like everything is so racially...

In my research I found that young women were consistently positioned by discourses of East/West, backward/modern, and brown/white. Most of the tension that young South Asian women experience in Canada is produced and constructed through the taken-for-granted concepts of traditional/modern. This either/or opposition generates conflict and contradiction for women who do not comply with the cultural codes of either East or West exclusively. It is when we trespass understood codes of behaviour that the norms, rules, and markers that define and constitute communities as bordered entities become visible.

## ✑  One Little, Two Little, Too Many Indians

I remember well the depiction of India and Indians during countless classes and history lessons from grade one to the last year of high school. The projector would come on, the lights would go off, and a forced hush would descend across the room: "India is a poor nation … India is an overpopulated nation," the movie audio track would say. And I would sit there lifeless, quite separate and far away, hoping to shut out the giggles as people secretly pointed in an effort to indicate a connection between me and the screen.

In Canadian history lessons, South Asians were nowhere to be found amongst the sterile accounts of Loyalists and Confederation. Never during my entire educational process was I taught about the contribution of "ethnic minorities" to the process of nation-building or about the history of racist policies and movements in this country. It was through forums in the black community and through South Asians forums like Desh Pardesh that I was able to piece together a bigger picture of my own history. Over the years, Desh Pardesh brought together artists, activists, grandmothers, and teenagers, each with a generational story to tell, each with some history to share. My historical picture came in the stories and presentations of older Punjabi Sikhs from Western Canada who spoke about the hardships of early settlers who worked in the lumberyards. It came in learning about Port Moody sawmills and how early pioneers settled in worker and army barracks and small overcrowded living quarters in British Columbia. It came in the discovery and sharing of old letters and historical memoirs of those separated from their families, unprotected in winter. It came in reading books like *Continuous Journey,* which documents the early history of South Asian settlement in Canada and includes the following examples of early immigrant narratives:

My first job was for an English farmer in Langley [circa 1907].
I didn't know any English except the day of the week and "I
want work." When I tried my single English sentence on the
farmer he responded in Hindi! He had been the manager of a
tea estate in India, and he took me on.

· · ·

In 1933 I was working in a Vancouver sawmill for ten cents an
hour. Every Saturday I went off to see a show at the Royal
Theatre. I budgeted ten cents for the show, another ten cents
for a milkshake, and five cents to play a game in the lobby. ...
Many older men still didn't know English but this didn't stop
them from going to the movies. In the 1920s it was easier for
them, since the films were all silent. Still, they kept right on
going when sound movies came in. It was one of the few things
that they did for recreation that involved "whites" in any way.
We still were not welcome in many beer parlours.[13]

Whether the story is about early Sikh settlers in British Columbia
working in road and railway construction or a more contemporary
one of South Asian taxi drivers and Sri Lankan dishwashers with
degrees in chemistry and teaching that go unrecognized by Canadian
government officials, the effects of immigration policy are consistent;
the policy has been based on various criteria of exclusion and cultural
difference. A look at South Asian immigration and settlement in
Canada from the turn of the century onwards suggests that moral
panics over immigration and representations of the ethnic "other" as
backward, inferior, or unsuitable helped to construct whiteness and
Canadian nationhood as synonymous.

The attitude toward South Asians in Canada can be divided according to the three waves of immigration. Doreen Indra, who bases her
analysis on research in British Columbia, argues that during the first

wave (1905–14), South Asians were seen as morally and politically unde-sirable. From 1928 to 1937, due to immigration controls, South Asian migration to this country was significantly smaller. Little attention was paid to the South Asian community by the mainstream press during this second phase; although they were still seen as morally question-able, they were not considered to be a threat. Of the third wave of immigration (1967–76), Indra argues that because South Asian immi-grants arrived in greater numbers due to a more flexible immigration policy, and because they had also made considerable economic and political gains, they re-emerged as a threat to Canadian society in dominant and popular discourses. They were increasingly associated with immorality and crime in the popular (white) imagination.[14]

Canadian immigration policy over the course of the last century reveals contradictory and inconsistent practices regarding non-white migration to Canada. This tension stems from the need for immigrant labour in Canada on the one hand, and the desire to maintain (white) cultural authority on the other. Bolaria and Li argue that the inter-secting needs of colonialism and capitalism led to the migration of South Asians to Canada.[15] Colonial circumstances in India, as well as famine and poverty, made going abroad with its promise of new opportunity and a better life (even as indentured labourers in the West Indies) very appealing.[16]

The anxiety about new immigrants in Canada first surfaced at the turn of the century when, due to labour needs, British settlers in Canada began to recruit workers. South Asians first arrived in Canada in 1900.[17] They were predominantly Punjabi Sikhs who settled in British Columbia. Most of them worked in the sawmills and lumberyards, at railway construction, mining, fishing, or as agricultural labourers.[18] Their arrival went relatively unnoticed at first. Canadian public opin-ion was focused on Japanese and Chinese migrants, whose settlement in the second half of the nineteenth century had, by this time, resulted in an outcry in the Western provinces. There was increasing pressure from all segments of the white population in British Columbia against

Chinese and Japanese immigration. South Asians thus entered British Columbia at a time when anti-immigrant sentiments were being manifested in policies that economically, politically, and socially disenfranchised and excluded Chinese and Japanese immigrants.[19] While little attention was paid to the first South Asian immigrants, their increase in numbers captured the province's attention by 1906 (as demonstrated by the rise in anti-Asian sentiment); by 1908, there was a complete ban on South Asian immigrants. Buchignani and Indra summarize the mood toward immigration at the turn of the century: "The kind of person who was a desirable immigrant was a contentious social issue at the turn of the century. The result was a compromising immigration policy that tempered common ethnic and racial biases with practical economic considerations: the 'right kind' of British and Americans were best; Germans and Scandinavians were all right; Eastern Europeans could be tolerated on economic grounds; southern Europeans were to be discouraged; and Asians and blacks should not come at all.[20]

At the time, the British government found itself in a peculiar predicament regarding the position of Indians within the Empire. On one hand, there was the need for agricultural labour in the Western provinces, and on the other, there was pressure from the Canadian colony to limit the spread of Indians in Canada. It was during this time that cultural difference was first used to justify the restriction of South Asians' entry into Canada. In arguing for a ban on further Asian migration, officials claimed that South Asians were not adaptable or suitable for residence in the country. For example, in 1908 the following plea was made in the House of Commons:

> It is clearly recognized in regard to emigration from India to Canada that the native of India is not a person suited to this country, that accustomed as many of them are to the conditions of a tropical climate, and possessing manners and customs so unlike our own people, their inability to readily adapt themselves

to surroundings entirely different could not do other than entail an amount of privation and suffering which renders a discontinuation of such immigration most desirable in the interests of the Indians themselves.[21]

The white anxiety over non-white immigration translated into a racially restrictive immigration policy that was maintained until after World War II. There was no significant migration of South Asians again until the 1960s. Whereas approximately 5,000 South Asians had entered Canada between 1900 and 1908, only 29 South Asians were admitted between 1909 and 1913.[22] By 1931 the census indicated that there were only 1,400 South Asians living in Canada.[23]

A number of official measures were taken to prevent the growth of the South Asian population in Canada during the restrictive immigration period.[24] Most damaging to the growth of the South Asian population in Canada was the imposition of the "continuous journey" stipulation in 1908. It allowed only those who came directly from India to Canada, without any stopovers along the way, to enter the country. Since the main mode of transportation for new arrivals at this time was by water, this requirement was virtually impossible to meet.

The infamous *Komagata Maru* incident illustrates the unwillingness of both the British and the Canadian (Dominion) governments to extend the right of settlement, or even visitation, to South Asians at this time. In this instance, the continuous journey stipulation was tested by an Indian entrepreneur who chartered a ship in Calcutta in 1914. Upon its arrival in Canada, most of the 376 passengers were refused entry. The government used the threat of contagious disease as grounds to issue deportation orders. The *Komagata Maru* sat in the port of Vancouver for sixty days, prohibited from taking food on board, until it was forced to sail back. Upon reaching the shores of India, most of the surviving passengers were arrested and interned under the orders of the British colonial rulers.[25]

The social context of these restrictive policies was a racist panic that immigrants would outnumber the white population. In the United States and Canada, as well as in other Western countries, there was concern over the declining fertility rates of "native-born" residents, and predictions of a so-called race suicide. This anxiety about the extinction of the race was a response to actual shifts in the birth rate, sexual practices, and family structure brought about by modern changes, such as urbanization and industrial development,[26] but the arrival of immigrants — non-white immigrants in particular — was blamed. In the late 1800s, economist Francis A. Walker had argued that immigration posed a major threat: changing social conditions, economic competition, and a weakening of the "moral fibre" of American society, presumably brought about by immigrants, led to a decline in fertility rates for white families. The poverty and wretchedness of immigrants, he wrote, made bringing offspring into the world appear undesirable to whites.[27] In 1904, writer Robert Hunter added credence to this fear by concluding that, if not limited, the growth of the non-white population would replace and obliterate the white population altogether. He also pointed to the class dimensions of this extinction, arguing that the rich were being outnumbered by the poor.[28] The United States was beset by fears that the "Yankee stock," which displayed the lowest birth rates, would be overwhelmed, numerically and hence politically, by immigrants, non-whites, and the poor.

At the turn of the century, while there was a decrease in the population growth of white Canadians, population rates as a whole increased. For example, McLaren and McLaren state that the population rose from 4.3 million to 8.5 million from 1881 to 1920, largely due to immigration, and that there was doubt as to whether the newcomers could be Canadianized or whether they would "overwhelm the young nation."[29] Concern over non-white immigration in the British Empire is best illustrated by John Morley's (the secretary for India) comment to the viceroy in 1908: "The great topic of the hour is the question of Asiatics in the Transvaal ... one of the largest questions concerning the Empire as a whole and indeed not only the empire but all white governments against all yellow, brown and black immigrants."[30] An article by W.S. Wallace, eventual editor of the *Canadian Historical Review*, entitled "The Canadian Immigration Policy" appeared in *Canadian Magazine* the same year. Wallace explained the possibility of "race suicide": "The native-born population, in the struggle to keep up appearances in the face of the increasing competition, fails to propagate itself, commits race suicide, in short, whereas the immigrant population, being inferior, and having no appearance to keep up, propagates itself like fish of the sea."[31]

Immigrants, like the poor sectors of white society, were seen to be of inferior genetic stock. Eugenicists, strongly in favour of immigration control, developed and promoted standard theories about so-called gene pool purity, and what they saw as the consequent purity of race, as the grounds to push for control of the birth rate of undesirables. They encouraged those with "superior" genes to refrain from birth control, and tried to persuade those with "inferior" genes to practise it. The former were WASP and affluent, while the latter included immigrant, poor, mentally and physically disabled, and the "criminal" populations.[32]

A complete historical exploration of eugenics movements is beyond this overview of twentieth century moral panics about race and immigration. In this context, however, I would like to suggest that white, middle-class anxieties about "their" youth and the 1950s discourses of juvenile delinquency were, in addition to reflecting an ambivalence toward social change, about maintaining whiteness. As well as being a sexual construct, delinquency is also a racial one. Crimes against authority can be read as racial misbehaviour. The fears around the corruption of youthful innocence are possibly also about white youth becoming less white. (It is doubtful that youthful innocence was seen to be embodied by black or South Asian Canadians.) Past moral panics about race demonstrate that notions of inferiority, poverty, and wretchedness are obviously raced as non-white. In relation to this construction the white ideal is superior, both biologically and socially (and middle class). Ideas about controlling delinquency and moral and social decay simultaneously inscribed and fortified the essence of white, middle-class respectability and centrality.

## ☙ Conclusion

The concerns over youth and over immigration from the turn of the last century, far from being unconnected, are in some ways integral to each other and historically related. Both are products of modern capitalism. Moral panics about youth in the postwar era have operated as a diversion from the failures of modern social progress and the promises of capitalist growth. Guidance and protection (of youth) have been offered as the solution for tensions inherent to growing up in the modern world. Similarly, social panic about the non-white ethnic has distracted from examination of class disparities in the power structure of this country. One of the ways to justify inequality in the era of progress and advancement is by scapegoating non-white immigrants as the source of disparity and resulting social strife. Limitation, restriction, and preventing the "spread" of non-white immigrants have been presented as solutions to economic and social tensions within Canada. The arrival of non-white immigrants and the concepts of racial and cultural difference that position them obscure the clash between the desires to embrace modern social change and to contain it.

Race and age work together in positioning young South Asians as particularly vulnerable to the dangers of modernity. The dangers of modernity are perceived by the South Asian community in the form of the threat of westernism, and by mainstream Canadian society they are seen as a threat to Canadianism. The fears characteristic of the modern era, and certainly embedded in twentieth-century concerns around social change — fears of degeneracy, delinquency, and social decay — are racial constructs that have secured notions of white, middle-class respectability. This respectability is accomplished by comparison with and distinction from its racial opposite.

# CHAPTER THREE

# Modest and Modern:
## Women As Markers of the Indian Nation State

In my interviews with young South Asian women, conflicts with parents emerged as the most salient and persistent issue. All of the women spoke about the restrictions on their lives and tied this into the expectations around being a girl. While some were able to escape these confines, others, because of limiting family circumstances and lack of networks, were unable to risk committing any significant acts of disobedience.[1] Although I experienced my adolescent years fifteen years prior to them, I was struck by the degree to which I could relate to the issues and concerns they were raising. There was almost an immediate understanding over how parents and community work to regulate young women's lives. For instance, parents used a particular brand of disciplining with their daughters, and during the interviews we often laughed at the identical phrases of chastisement, which usually focused on an unstated effort to protect women's sexuality.

For South Asian women, negotiating their femininities doesn't just affect their sexual reputations; it also reflects their degree of allegiance to an ethnic collectivity. Rupinder, for example, spoke extensively about how her recent backtalk to her parents in reference to the "unreasonable" restrictions they were placing on her raised concerns not only about her rebelliousness but also about the extent to which she was South Asian.

> Rupinder: You say, "Well, you don't let me do what I want to do, so why should I do what you want me to do?" They're like, "Well, we're Indian, we're not white."
>
> Amita: What do you think they mean by that? What do they see as Indian and what do they see as white?
>
> Rupinder: I guess Indian means being wholesome and not being able to talk back to your parents, do whatever they say and just go to school and home and home to school and work and have no social life. And being white, I guess they see people being as like sluts and rebels and just a lot of rebellionism I guess.

"Rebellionism" here is challenging parental authority. This concept of authority, however, draws on understandings of "Indian" and "white," as well as on generational differences. The dictates around appropriate femininity are maintained through labelling transgressions as "Western" or "white": challenging parental restrictions makes Rupinder "white." Crossing the boundaries of appropriate behaviour not only signifies a gender transgression but also a cultural one. A real Indian girl would not talk back to her parents and would not want to go out, and so Rupinder's desire for self-determination puts into question her cultural allegiance.

Looking back to history as a way of understanding this dynamic has shown me how women, in the context of larger political struggles, become positioned as representative of cultural, ethnic, and national identities, and how ethnic boundaries depend on notions of gender. Notions of women's sexuality are used to mark the boundaries of cultural and ethnic identity, preservation, and authenticity.

During the nationalist struggle for independence from British rule, for example, certain notions of womanhood, tradition, and culture were used by both British colonialists and Indian nationalists to forge a distinction between East and West, as discussed in Chapter 2.[2] The female body became the site for testing out the modern way of life, and this is still the case: the modern is often presented as a sexual threat for women, and women continue to be the site of an East-West cultural battle.[3] As a result, current questions of cultural authenticity and cultural preservation are inextricably tied to the history of regulation of women's sexualities.

Lata Mani defines colonial discourse as "a mode of understanding Indian society that emerged alongside colonial rule and over time was shared to a greater or lesser extent by officials, missionaries and the indigenous elite, although deployed by these various groups to different, often ideologically opposite ends."[4]

Colonial understandings of women, tradition, and culture persist in the Canadian context in situating young South Asian women. The positioning of South Asians vis-à-vis a dominant white/anglo population continues to be accomplished by drawing boundaries around notions of tradition, culture, and women related to those that operated in colonial India. In fact, "South Asian" is a meaningful category because it is continually marked and distinguishable from the dominant norm.

While youth can be understood as symbolic of both fear and anticipation of modern change, women have come to represent the flip side of modern civilization and the possibility of being outside the effects of modernization. Women are associated with the memory of all that is seen to be good from premodern times. In this sense, they could provide the antidote to the anxieties associated with modern social progress — namely the possibility that limitless freedom might bring about moral and social disintegration.[5]

The question becomes how to preserve women's innocence without sacrificing modern social progress. Indian nationalists fashioned a feminine identity representative of the nation that was modern and Eastern. In colonial India, notions of spirituality, innocence, and purity were enmeshed in a debate about culture and cultural difference. Women became synonymous with these characteristics and were also positioned as the moral guardians and keepers of a particular brand of Indian culture.

## 🪶 Protecting the Khan Dhan[6]: It's All Relative

Much of what is considered fixed, natural, and objective ethnic and national identity is actually based on changing political, economic, and social goals. Certainly, what it is means to be an American today is markedly different from what it meant before September 11, 2001. The boundaries around America have literally and figuratively changed, as have the passion and sentiment behind protecting what is perceived to be the American way of life. At this moment of history it is clear that the American sense of identity is very much in reference to the external world. Joseph Levenson argues that there has been a shift from culturalism to nationalism. The former, which he locates in premodern history, based its notion of community in a natural belief of cultural superiority; it did not seek approval or justification outside of the collectivity itself. Only when cultural values had to seek legitimation in relation to an outside threat in the late nineteenth century, according to Levenson, do we begin to see a disintegration of culturalism and a swift transition to nationalism.[7] Similarly, the Asian historian Duara Prasenjit argues that the notion of ethnicity and its association with the nation-state are modern phenomena. Nationalism, here, is understood as culture being protected by the state or as the politicization of culture.[8] Prasenjit explains how notions of community and nation are mobilized:

> Nationality is formed when the perception of the boundaries
> of community are transformed, namely, when soft boundaries

are transformed into hard ones. This happens when a group succeeds in imposing a historical narrative of descent and/or dissent on both heterogeneous and related cultural practices. ... The narrative of discent is used to define and mobilize a community, often by privileging a particular cultural practice (or set of practices) as the constitutive principle of the community — such as language, religion or common historical experience — thereby heightening the self-consciousness of this community in relation to those around it.[9]

Both Levenson and Prasenjit perceive power struggles between communities as having an important impact on community consciousness. Awareness of identity is seen to be heightened in relation to an outside threat.

The power struggle between East and West, and the construction of their respective identities, is based on their relationship to one another; the meaning of each is constructed through the marking out of symbolic boundaries. Women are central to this boundary. This East/West relationship is, of course, not an equal one. In constructing its own oppositional narrative as a marginal community, both currently in the West and previously during the colonial era, South Asian Canadian and Indian nationalist discourses use (or used) certain symbols of community identity as a strategy to assert their own right to cultural (self) determination from a marginal location. Nations can be understood as imagined communities that are built on certain cultural and historical symbols.[10] South Asian community identity in Canada is accomplished by mobilizing certain discourses around ethnicity and cultural preservation. The community imagines itself by using certain historical (colonial) notions of tradition, culture, and gender.

Historians have sought to uncover how gender has been used as a political and ethnic marker in times of change, resistance, and revolution, both in liberal and conservative discourses. Floya Anthias and Nira Yuval-Davis argue that the boundary of ethnicity is inseparable from notions of gender. They contend that women are responsible for upholding the norms and consequent identity of an ethnic collective:

> The boundary of the ethnic is often dependent on gender and there is a reliance on gender attributes for specifying ethnic identity: much of ethnic culture is organized around rules relating to sexuality, marriage and the family, and a true member will perform these roles properly. Communal boundaries often use differences in the way that women are socially constructed as markers. Such markers (for example, expectations about honour, purity, the mothering of patriots, reproducers of the nation, transmitters of ethnic culture) often symbolize the use of women as an ethnic resource.[11]

In the early 1990s, my partner in crime Vinita Srivastava and I put in a proposal at a community radio station (CKLN 88.1 FM) for a bhangra show. [12] We were inspired by the female British Asian DJ Ritu, who hosted the BBC's "Bhangra in Bed." The bhangra explosion in the U.K. was unprecedented. While the explosion included groups such as Alaap and Apna Sangeet who maintained a traditional Punjabi folk style but exchanged "back-home" content for a longing for "back home," it also included the likes of Bally Sagoo and Apache Indian who mixed or blended old classical songs with a ragga backbeat rap and reggae-style vocals. What emerged as a central question about music fusion was also the question that underlies the kind of conflict that Rupinder and her parents had: the issue of authenticity and what is truly Indian. The feeling was that this fusion would offend cultural authenticity. Whether the music was played eight years ago in Toronto or for the first time in the new millennium in Trinidad and Tobago, the response was the same: what will the parents think? Won't heads of the community be upset and/or offended? The battle here was between viewing culture as fixed and unchanging and seeing it as always forming, in flux and in fusion.

The idea of tradition as fixed, static, and synonymous with certain notions of Hindu Indian femininity can be dated back to colonial understandings of Indian culture and tradition.

## 🕊 India's Struggle for National Independence

The genesis of the Indian nation-state provides a good example of how gender and ethnicity worked together to carve out notions of national identity. British colonialists used women as a yardstick to measure the extent of modernization in India: the low status of Indian women indicated to the British the backward condition of the entire country. Arguing that the prevalence of certain cultural practices involving women proved that Indians were unfit to rule themselves, British colonizers relied on a distinction between "civilized" and "uncivilized" to justify their continued occupation of India. In response, women were used by an Indian (male) nationalist agenda that set out to prove the validity of Indian cultural practices through relying on notions of authenticity and the right to cultural difference. A look at colonial history shows us the instances in which women and tradition became synonymous.

Lata Mani's work on sati (widow burning) provides an excellent unravelling of the various understandings of tradition and culture during British colonial rule in India. She has shown that debates around sati, while seemingly about women, were more about what constitutes authentic cultural tradition; there was a struggle over the meaning of Indian culture and its boundaries. For both Indian nationalists and British rulers, women became the battlegrounds on which to test notions of tradition. Mani contends that the ideas of tradition in operation during British rule, which continue to operate today, are colonial in nature.[13] These interpretations of Indian culture have understood tradition as invariable, culture and tradition as Hindu, and women as synonymous with the boundaries of Indian cultural identity.

In their effort to manage India, British colonialists used religious texts, and interpretations and translations of these texts, as a means of understanding Indian custom and practice. They relied on these texts as the ultimate authority on Indian custom and practice and coded indigenous law accordingly. This law was used as a vehicle of administration and a means to establish rule.[14] Mani suggests that the centrality of religious texts was itself a colonial creation. For example, she argues that British colonials, in an effort to regulate sati in a way that would not appear overtly interventionist, relied on Brahmanic scriptures[15] and positioned themselves as protagonists interested in returning the Indian masses to the original and authentic practice of sati. Colonialists in favour of abolishing certain kinds of sati did not intervene on the grounds of the barbarity of the practice against women, but on grounds that sought to reinforce their interpretation of tradition. This interpretation then became part of arguments justifying their civilizing mission in India.

Privileging Brahmanic texts as the mainstay of Indian society had several consequences. Tradition was made synonymous with non-change because the source of information about tradition was fixed and unchanging, namely religious texts. This ignored any possible bias of translation and interpretation and advanced the idea of cultural tradition as being fixed according to the written word rather than as being a dynamic process of practice and interpretation. According to Mani, colonial constructions view tradition as ahistorical and change-less and synonymous for the most part with religion and culture.[16]

Indigenous discourses on sati also tended to rely on scriptural texts in order to safeguard ownership and self-determination of this practice and to deflect British intervention into personal Indian matters. In both discourses, religion became synonymous with tradition and rigidity, and women came to signify tradition for both colonial rulers and the indigenous elite: "For the British, rescuing women becomes part of the civilizing mission. For the indigenous elite, protection of their status or its reform becomes an urgent necessity, in terms of the honour of the collective — religious or national. For all participants in nineteenth century debates on social reform, women represent embarrassment or potential. And given the discursive construction of women as either abject victims or heroines, they frequently represent both shame *and* promise."[17]

The exclusive use of Brahmanic texts also helped to privilege Hindu notions of tradition and culture, and to forge the construction of Hindu and Muslim as oppositional and distinct heritages. Treating religious texts as the basis of the entire legal system in colonial India ignored totally the "secularism, rationalism, and non-conformity [of] pre-British Muslim ruled India."[18] It also led to the fixity of religious identities that were hitherto nonexistent.[19] Creating Hindu and Muslim as oppositional and internally homogenous categories meant that people were now forced to construct and conduct themselves only according to these colonial religious categories of law.

Women became the focus of a struggle for national independence that was integrally linked to a politics of cultural authenticity: for Indian nationalists, the category "woman," and more accurately, certain notions of the Hindu woman, became emblematic of an Indian national identity.[20]

## Indian Femininity as Virtuous and Chaste

For young South Asian women in Canada, nose piercing is a way of calling attention to their ethnic/racial identity. While it has also been associated with the (white) punk rock movement, the nose ring in a Western context indicates a link to South Asian heritage. It is also a gendered performance of ethnicity in a predominantly white context. In Punjabi it is referred to as *koka, nath,* or *long,* and the symbolic meaning of this fashion accessory has changed with each generation depending on the cultural and political context. I have witnessed these changes in my own lifetime. I first remember the nose ring on the face of my grandmother. For my mother's generation of middle-class, educated Punjabi women, the nose ring represented a backward (unmodern) practice. Some modern women growing up at the dawn of modern India did not wear one. The absence of this accessory helped to distinguish a (middle-class, educated) modern femininity from a traditional one. When I began to wear a nose ring, my mother saw it as an act of rebellion. For me it was an act of (cultural) asser-tion, a way of marking difference in the Canadian context that acknowledged and reclaimed to myself and others the idea that being different from white was not necessarily negative.

In interviews with young South Asian women, I found that there was a definite understanding of how certain feminine behaviours were linked to and defined being Indian, while others were associated with being un-Indian. Nina, like all the other girls, spoke to me at length about conflicts with her parents that she saw as having to do with both her gender and culture: "Like if you want to drink, Indian girls can't drink, Indian girls can't smoke, Indian girls can't do this, you can't date."

These concepts of Indian femininity can be found in Indian nation-alist visions of Indian identity. During the late nineteenth and early twentieth centuries, Indian nationalists sought to differentiate them-selves from both the idea of past tradition and from the West. During "the entire phase of national struggle, the crucial need was to protect, preserve, and strengthen the inner core of national culture, its spiritual essence."[21] Women, substantially, became the sign of this inner iden-tity that was in need of protection and preservation. Indian national-ists attempted to preserve the innocence of women while simultaneously meeting the needs of modernization. They proposed a new kind of woman, one who could enjoy the freedoms of the modern world, such as education and paid employment, while at the same time attending to the responsibilities of the home and upholding cultural norms and the virtues associated with spirituality. Keeping up with modern progress would keep India on par with the British. This nationalist project promoted a notion of civilization which, while rooted in post-Enlightenment understandings of progress and modernity, sought to set itself apart both from a disgraceful past that the British pointed to as a mark of inferiority, and from the West.

What developed, Patha Chatterjee argues, was

> a dominant characteristic of femininity in the new construct of "woman" standing as a sign for "nation," namely spiritual qualities of self-sacrifice, benevolence, devotion, religiosity, and so on. This spirituality did not, as we have seen, impede the chances of woman moving out of the physical confines of the home; on the contrary, it facilitated it, making it possible for her to go into the world under conditions that would not threaten her femininity. In fact the image of woman as goddess or mother served to erase her sexuality in the world outside her home.[22]

Chatterjee maintains that Indian nationalist discourse can only be understood in relation to the dichotomy between the private and the public, or what he calls "the home" and "the world." Indian nationalists asserted that the essential identity of the East "lay in its distinctive, and superior, spiritual culture" (the home) which had not been and did not have to be colonized, yet they also saw keeping abreast with the modern material world as imperative.[23]

The nationalist agenda based its vision of woman on certain assumptions about femininity, about woman as closer to nature, nurturing, and spirituality. Mahatma Gandhi, the influential national leader most strongly associated with his nonviolent strategy to overthrow British rule, also espoused prevailing notions of masculinity and femininity. He wrote in the 1920s: "The female sex is not the weaker sex; it is the nobler of the two: for it is even today the embodiment of sacrifice, silent suffering, humility, faith and knowledge."[24] Women were seen to be inherently sacrificing and to possess the virtues of innocence, purity, and suffering. They were best suited to symbolize civil disobedience, because according to Gandhi, "women optimally embodied ... a dual impulse for 'obedience and rebellion against authority' primarily within the family" that he felt he could mobilize for a revolution against colonial rule. These qualities were glorified as the standard that women should uphold in the nationalist struggle.[25]

This vision of spirituality affects significant aspects of female sexuality. For women, when spirit and body meet, the female body — bearing the mark of the sexual and in this sense overdetermined by it — contains the threat of sexuality. As the active agent of her sexuality, woman is powerful. The only way to make the body-spirit union unthreatening for men is to completely subsume woman's sexuality into the spiritual realm, leaving behind "the realms of the psychic, of desire, of pleasure."[26]

Women therefore became desexualized in the process of nation-building. The idea of the new woman was advanced in the interests of the nation. Her sexuality became the marker of virtue and a symbol of what differentiated her from the Western woman. Modesty, as a code of dress, behaviour, and the proper use of the body (refraining from smoking or drinking), became the symbolic marker of this cultural difference. Chatterjee explains: "A woman identified as westernized, for instance, would invite the ascription of all that the 'normal' woman (mother/sister/wife/daughter) is not — brazen, avaricious, irreligious, sexually promiscuous."[27] The new Indian woman was forged on the grounds of her difference from her Western counterpart. This narrative represented the white woman as everything the Indian woman was not. There are also ethnic and class dimensions of the nationalist project that promised "superiority over the western woman for whom, it was believed, education meant only the acquisition of material skills to compete with men in the outside world and hence a loss of feminine (spiritual) virtues; superiority over the preceding generation of women in their own homes who had been denied the opportunity of freedom by an oppressive and degenerate social tradition; and superiority over women of the lower classes who were actually incapable of appreciating the virtues of freedom."[28]

The Indian identity also became inseparable from a notion of Hindu femininity. The Hindu woman, her fasts and prayers, became the object of aspiration, the symbol of morality and national identity.[29] "Woman" in this process is commissioned as carrier of the nation, the marker of national distinctness symbolized in the specificity of certain cultural practices. I am suggesting that by extension, women are also seen as the carriers of culture. British colonialists contributed to establishing links among woman, tradition, and national identity by refuting the interpretative nature of religious texts and advancing their own civilized notions of practices involving women. This intervention was a show of superiority in order to justify the rightful place of British colonial rule in India.

##  East, West, and Sexual Difference

Laura Ann Stoler adds to colonial historical analysis by exploring the ways in which white women's sexualities have also been regulated through colonial discourses. She argues that "the very categories of 'colonizer' and 'colonized' were secured through forms of sexual control that defined the domestic arrangements of Europeans and the cultural investments by which they identified themselves."[30] The European sense of identity and the inclusion and exclusion of members within the definition of the European community "required regulating sexual, conjugal, and domestic life of *both* Europeans in the colonies *and* their colonized subjects."[31] Stoler argues that European empires also used certain notions of femininity which fluctuated according to colonial needs. For example, she points out that between 1600 and 1900 the emigration of European women to the colonies was virtually prohibited.[32] During this period, European men cohabited with local women. This, Stoler maintains, worked just fine for colonial rulers; it met the needs of the white settlers, and actually saved on maintenance costs for the empire. Assumptions about femininity, namely that women are whimsical, unwise, predisposed to the fancies of middle-class consumerism, and unfit for the hardships of living in the settlements, were used to exclude European women from the colonies.

Stoler argues that these notions of femininity changed, however, when concubinage threatened the boundaries of European community. As children were born from these mixed unions, the line separating rulers from natives became less clear. How were these children to be categorized? Mixed-race children created a crisis in the definition of European identity. In the first half of the twentieth century in the Western world, anxieties around race purity were translated into a panic about white race degeneracy and cultural contamination in the colonies.

The entrance of white women to the colonies, Stoler claims, helped to undermine the image of a deteriorating empire. White prestige, which colonial women helped to restore, was a significant feature of colonial mentality, and women emerged as the hallmarks of respectability and civilization. White women were, in the 1920s and 1930s, called upon to restore moral order to the colonies and became exemplars of devoted and voluntary subordinates to, and defenders of, colonial men. European women's presence in the colonies helped to shift public opinion, invoking sympathy in favour of colonialists when needed, and served as a justification for certain regulations of the lives of natives.33 These restrictions also affected white women, who were expected to conform to rigid codes of dress and sexual conduct — they were not to mingle "too closely" with "native" men or dress and act in "alluring" ways. Stoler concludes that a "defense of community, morality, and white male power was achieved by increasing control over and consensus among Europeans, by affirming the vulnerability of white women, the sexual threat of native men, and by creating new sanctions to limit the liberties of both."34

By revealing the construction of gender divides, analyses by historians such as Stoler and Jenny Sharpe help to break the assumption of a homogenous colonial community. They also explore the ways in which gender operated in relation to white as well as non-white women. For both European rulers and native nationalists, colonial notions of women demarcated boundaries of cultural difference that helped to attain specific, if conflicting, political objectives.

## ﾒ Conclusion

Identified with nature and the act of procreation, women have been relegated to the task of upholding the virtues associated with all that modern change is said to reject. They, like youth, are associated with purity and innocence, which, if left untouched and protected from the ills of the modern world, could help to preserve some vestiges of a past golden age and thereby alleviate the downfalls of rapid change. However, in nationalist Indian discourses women were placed in a position of having to preserve premodernity in a way that was not at odds with modern change, but distinguished itself from Westernism.

Women are markers of ethnic difference and nationhood. Both Indian nationalists and British colonialists were concerned about the authenticity and boundaries of their respective cultural collectives in the struggle over political rule. Indian nationalists resolved the contradiction between modernization and westernization by allowing women to modernize without forsaking what was perceived to be a true Indian identity. Notions of womanhood were used not only to resolve the ambivalence between premodernity and modernity but also to assert the claim to Indian self-rule. Concepts of femininity in the context of colonial India became inseparable from a politics of cultural authenticity, preservation, and Indian identity itself.

The relationship between East and West is interconnected in this respect, each responding to the perceived threat of the other. In the following chapter I will examine how a sense of nation or belonging is created in the South Asian diaspora and in the East-West contest that continues to play itself out in contemporary Canada. Colonial understandings of women, tradition, and Indian identity (as Hindu and middle class) persist in communities that have migrated from the subcontinent and settled in the West. South Asians in Canada have tended to view tradition and culture as fixed and rely on concepts of femininity as standing in for true Indian identity.

CHAPTER FOUR

# Fusion or Confusion?
## Multicultural Doublespeak

In colonial India, the dominant sense of identity and nation that Indian nationalists constructed was, in essence, a middle-class Hindu one. Numerous other Indians such as tribal, lower class and caste, and Muslim peoples, were excluded by the dominant definition of the ideal Indian. Like the nation-state, diasporic peoples also rely on the work of imagination to maintain, reconstitute, and reproduce a sense of community and culture beyond those territories presumed to belong to specific national or ethnic groups. The South Asian diaspora both imitates and challenges the exclusionary norms of the nation-state system.

In the diasporic context as in the colonial context, the power struggle between communities is pivotal. While non-white diasporic communities in the West continue to imagine national and community identity, this imagination takes place within the context of racism. In order to understand the relationship of South Asian communities to dominant cultures of Canada, we need to look at the ways in which Canada has attempted to come to terms with its cultural diversity and the ways in which culture has been conceptualized. Canada's policy of multiculturalism has helped to create and maintain a particular narrative of

Canadian nationhood. The official discourse of multiculturalism, intended as a way of managing cultural diversity, has in essence constructed a fragmented identity for Canada, one that is hierarchically organized, producing insiders and outsiders. This fragmentation is played out in the lives of the outsiders, who experience an everyday racism hidden by a public discourse of tolerance and multiculturalism.

Race is a significant feature in the lives of the young South Asian women I interviewed. Young South Asian women receive mixed messages about what "Canadian" means. On the one hand they are told that there are two dominant cultures in Canada; on the other hand, that their culture is just as important as the two primary ones. The message here is, you can be different but not too different from the dominant culture(s). The narrative of Canadian-ness is based on often invisible boundaries marking the difference between the dominant cultures and "others." This invisibility is linked to the fact that the dominance of white anglo norms appears natural and commonsense to those who embody them. The tensions between assimilation and multiculturalism produce a dichotomy of too Indian versus too Canadian. The second-generation South Asian women I talked with continually attempted to negotiate these two identities and face the tension between sameness and difference, in two senses. First, identity is negotiated in relation to "white" as the normative reference point, which means not being too different from the white norm. Second, identity is negotiated in relation to "brown" as the point of reference, in that there is a desire not to be perceived as stereotypical South Asians.

I found that the girls contest the internal homogeneity of the category "South Asian." The following passages from separate interviews with Rupinder and Nina illustrate this point:

> Rupinder: I was mostly like with the Indians, 'cause people just see you as being who you're hanging around with. Like they think just because you have like mostly white friends you're like anti-Indian. And if you're

hanging around with Indians they think you're racist and you don't want to be with anyone but your own kind. So just ... I don't know, subconsciously I guess [we] just train ourselves just to be with our kind.

. . .

Nina:     It's sort of like I'm considered like a white person. 'Cause all my friends are white ... and like I don't consider myself different from them as a whole but I don't consider myself the same. I realize I'm different.

Amita:    Than?

Nina:     Than, like, my friends. I don't want to be considered like "you guys," like "you white people." Like, I don't want to be considered like that but I don't want to be considered like the "white people and [me]." I don't consider myself different in that way but I don't consider myself totally into their, like make myself white or anything. But that makes me angry when they're like "you [are] this."

Rupinder and Nina each discuss the relationship between friends and identity. Here, the racial makeup of friends becomes implicated in the marking of an individual's identity. Race then becomes an important factor in mediating one's perceived identity with, affiliation, and loyalty to an ethnic collective. Rupinder chooses to hang around with her "own kind" in order to resist being labelled "anti-Indian." In the second passage, Nina is referring to a group of black kids in her school and to her brother, who see her as "whitewashed." She does not want to be seen as either the same as her white friends or as merely a differentiated appendage to her white friends ("white people and me"). Her dilemma illustrates the fluidity of identity constructions and the contradictory ways in which power operates.

## ✌ Diaspora: Travelling Cultures

The idea of diaspora attempts to account for what happens to community identity when people migrate.[1] Diaspora not only engages with the ways in which people imagine their sense of community and belonging when they are displaced from the geographical territory associated with home, but it also has the potential to account for the displacements that take place within "home." In other words, because diasporic peoples often make a claim of national allegiance to both their country of residence and their original homeland, diaspora has the potential to unsettle the assumption of homogeneity associated with "back home."[2]

While there is disagreement over the direction of causality, most historians would concede that ideas of nation and nationalism are profoundly connected to understandings of culture and identity. Indeed, so tied are they that it is difficult to think about ethnic identity outside the parameters of a nation. Floya Anthias and Nira Yuval-Davis argue that the nation-state system assumes a correlation between political geographical boundaries and national collectivities. The idea that people from the same ethnic backgrounds inhabit one and only one geographical space, however, is erroneous. No such pure nation-states exist. There are always people settled within nation-states who do not share the dominant national identity, and historically there have also been national collectivities that have never inhabited a nation-state, such as the Palestinians. Anthias and Yuval-Davis assert: "The fact that there still exists this automatic assumption about the overlap between the boundaries of the state citizens and 'the nation,' is one expression of the naturalizing effect of the hegemony of one collectivity and its access to ideological apparatuses of both state and civil society. This constructs minorities into assumed deviants from the 'normal,' and excludes them from important power resources."[3] There is, furthermore, an assumption that all affinities to a nation or to belonging are homogeneous once they are contained within the same geographical boundary; that all people living within that boundary share a sense of allegiance to the same collectivity, and that there are therefore no internal boundaries of exclusion.

There are several problems with mobilizing multiculturalism as a way of managing cultural difference. Each ethnic collective is seen as essentially different from the norm and yet internally the same, and there is an assumption of separate components of culture, which are fixed, changeless, and unambiguous.4 In this sense, multiculturalism and assimilation are representative of the sameness versus difference debate I spoke about earlier in this chapter and in Chapter 1. My interviews with young South Asian women revealed both the prevalence of whiteness as the norm, and the ways in which they challenge and negotiate the idea of fixed cultural boundaries. Narratives of multiculturalism have generated a contradictory and fragmented Canadian identity which positions young South Asian women in paradoxical ways.

## ⟫ "Multiculti" for Whom?

Canada's official response to the demographic reality of its diasporic communities has been the adoption of a policy of multiculturalism. According to the 1978 document *Multiculturalism and the Government of Canada*, several developments led to this policy. One of these, wrote Norman Cafik, the minister of state for multiculturalism, was "the large number of newcomers and the varied countries they represented [which] seemed to be leading to growing tension among immigrants, native born Canadians and various established ethno-cultural groups."5 The Canadian government set up a Royal Commission in the late 1960s to suggest the steps needed to implement an equal partnership between the "two founding races,"6 namely the English and the French. During the course of the Royal Commission's investigation, a number of concerns were raised by immigrant groups and minorities who argued for the full acknowledgment of Canada's cultural diversity.

The multicultural policy arose as a response to public pressure by minority groups to be included in the community of Canadians, as opposed to restricting the definition of Canadian identity to biculturalism. Despite its consideration of diversity, in 1969 the Royal Commission concluded, "Although we should not overlook Canada's 'cultural diversity,' this should be done keeping in mind that there are two dominant cultures, French and English."[7] It was at the commission's suggestion that Prime Minister Pierre Trudeau opted for an official policy of multiculturalism within a bilingual framework in 1971.

Canada's official adoption of multiculturalism was predicated on an interest in national unity, and that idea of unity is dependent on a singular national identity. While there is an acknowledgment of cultural diversity, it is conceptualized only within a framework of duality, at most. Ironically, this duality is constantly being tested by the nationalist movement for an independent Quebec. As a component of the nation-building process, multiculturalism was adopted by the Canadian government partly because it did not threaten the idea of the original founding fathers, namely the division of the country between English and French bourgeois men. Despite multiculturalism, the daily reality is that an anglo identity continues to dominate the cultural norm in Canada and to be synonymous with Canadian national identity. Racism is woven into the ideology of multiculturalism through notions of cultural tolerance.

Writing about Western Europe, Philomena Essed has pointed out that modern-day racism operates through a discourse of tolerance. Tolerance in a culturally pluralistic society presumes that people of colour and other immigrants "accept and internalize the norms and values of the dominant group" while at the same time having "permission" to retain their cultural identity, so long as it does not conflict with the dominant way of life.[8] As a discourse of culture has (apparently) come to replace a discourse of race as a means of understanding difference, so too has cultural tolerance been substituted for racial tolerance in Canada.[9]

Brown Schools and White Schools

Going through school in Toronto during the 1970s, I confronted a lot of isolation. I was a teenager at a time when there were fewer South Asians in the city, and attended a school where there were almost no other non-white students or teachers. The issues I encountered then are somewhat similar to what I found, fifteen years later, in my interviews with young women. Being accepted by both peers and parents is extremely important, and yet often the behaviours and lifestyle of both groups are contradictory and unacceptable to each other. While this is common to most teenage/parent/peer relationships, for minority youth and their parents the issue of race and culture figures prominently in the equation. I spent most of my junior and high school years attempting to hide my South Asian identity and being ashamed of it because, on many levels, I knew that my parent's culture would not be accepted by my white schoolfriends. The difference between my own experience and the experiences of the young South Asian women I interviewed is that most of them attend schools that they described as ethnically diverse and multicultural. Their "cultural esteem" seemed remarkably higher than my own.[10]

In the interviews we spent a lot of time talking about school, peers, and family. Drawing from memories of my own experience, I asked all the participants whether they had ever felt ashamed of their culture in relation to their peers. Some of them could not relate to questions about cultural shame, or interpreted questions about racism by using brown rather than white as the point of reference. Pinki and I had the following exchange:

> Amita: Was there ever a time when you were ashamed of being an Indian?
> Pinki: No, never!

Amita: You know, because of the racism?

Pinki: No, maybe when I was younger I felt a little bad. I remember in grade three, this girl who sat beside me she got lice and—

Amita: She was Indian?

Pinki: No, she was West Indian,[11] and ahh, you know, everyone found out that she got lice. You know and they all looked at me and they said, you know, "You gave her the lice," and they checked my hair and it was fine. Just because she has it doesn't mean that it came from me. And that was the kind of times I remember but otherwise, you know, when people say things, you know, I just ignore it and it doesn't bother me. I'm proud to be Indian.

Amita: So you never felt that you wanted to try and be white?

Pinki: Oh no.

Pinki's experiences of racism stem from the early years of her schooling. During our conversation, she made a distinction between racism and cultural shame. Although she says that she experienced a lot of racism in her elementary school, she does not extend this to the experience of low cultural esteem. She explains that she attends a "brown school," a term used commonly among South Asians to describe schools that are predominantly comprised of South Asian students. Most of her friends are Punjabi and she speaks this language both at school and at home.

Zarah, who is fifteen years old, made similar comments about racism and cultural pride:

Amita: Okay, would you say there has ever been a time when you have been ashamed of being...

Zarah: Ahh, well no, I haven't.

Amita: Like you felt that maybe you wanted to hide the fact?

Zarah:    Well when I was younger, because everyone used to say, "Oh my God, they're so disgust—, they're so dirty," whatever, right? And then that kind of gets your self-esteem down, right? So I kind of, I'm like why, why me?

Amita:    So how old were you when that was happening?

Zarah:    I was in grade eight, so I was thirteen.

Amita:    So how do you feel now?

Zarah:    I feel really good to be a Pakistani, and I live up to that.

Zarah also describes her school as multicultural, with the majority of the population being brown and Chinese. While she remarks on the connection between racism and self-esteem when she was younger, a few years later, surrounded by a mostly non-white school population, she comments on her cultural pride. When I asked if she had experienced anything more recently at the school she was now attending she said, "No, no. Or else everyone would back up that person, right? Our school is like that. They like everyone. They wouldn't ever say anything like prejudice." Zarah draws a correlation among the lack of racism, the school's diverse composition, and the idea that prejudice would not be tolerated.

I was struck by the interpretation of my question about cultural shame by a few of the participants. For example, when I asked Alka, a sixteen-year-old Hindu girl, the very same question, she responded, "Yeah, there was a lot of times when I questioned our beliefs and why the girls had to fast and not the guys. I had major difficulty with that idea. Like in our school when the rozay [ritual during Ramadan] went on for like the Muslims, the entire community from guys to girls from young to old, everyone fasted and I used to get mad. Like why isn't there a day in our religion to say that everyone can fast?"

Alka described her school as "brown." She explained that when it first opened, 90 percent of the students were South Asian. At the time of the interview this had dropped to 70 percent, with black and

Chinese students comprising the rest of the school's mix. Because of the majority–South Asian context, she interpreted the question about cultural shame in relation to an inside and not outside reference, that is, in relation to differences among South Asians. A little later in the interview, I attempted to ask her a similar question about racism. My assumption was that a question framed around racism would automatically imply white racism:

> Amita: So, do you have any memories either at this school or the one before of racism at school?
>
> Alka: Ahhm, no. Actually I can't say that I've ever been really a victim of racism so to say, but I can tell you that you feel it because of such a segregated society, that being close friends with only Muslims, you never have that feeling of having a close friend. You can never have a best friend...

Alka went on to talk about divisions between Hindus and Muslims and parental warnings about Muslim people. Although most of her friends are Muslim, she nevertheless holds stereotypical perceptions of them. Even a question about racism, an inquiry that intended to explore the exclusion of South Asians from white dominant culture, resulted in a response about exclusion and difference among and in relation to other South Asians. This seems directly tied to her school environment, in which brown and not white constitutes the dominant culture.

Two of the girls attended schools that were predominantly white, and their experiences were remarkably different from those of most of the other young women. Nina, an eighteen-year-old Sikh girl, recounted a story of her childhood in response to being asked if she could recall an instance of racial shame:

> Nina: Not really, I mean like I've had little incidents happen like ever since I was younger, but I never really thought

to associate it with... I never really thought bad of who I was because I guess it hasn't really on a general... 'Cause it's not like it happened every day and I was being like discriminated or isolated because of my... So it doesn't like affect me or it doesn't really bug me. But I've had little things happen to me, like when I was young. Things just like, I remember I was five or six or something and this girl that I met... I remember one time I came to her house and I remember her mom like telling me to get out of her house.

Amita: Because...

Nina: I was, yeah.

Amita: She said that?

Nina: Yeah, she said like... and I just remember all a big blur. But all of a sudden, I was like in her house on the couch, and all of a sudden I was being kicked out of her house. And it was just like, you know. But I never really thought of like, you know, to associate to my... in that way I haven't really been... It hasn't been bad in that I haven't always looked at myself and said, "Oh my God, I'm so different."

Nina uses various descriptors that downplay racism as a factor affecting her experience. She describes the event of being kicked out of somebody's house as "little" and argues that because these kinds of occurrences do not happen on a daily basis she is not affected by them overall. Although the incident involves an adult who ousts her from the house because she is not white, Nina does not identify this event and others like it with the fact of difference. What is also interesting here is that she never actually attributes the difference to skin colour or culture. And yet there is a level of conversation going on between us where we understand what is being named without actually naming it.

Philomena Essed asserts that one of the features of racism in the context of tolerance is the denial of its existence. Denial can be partly located in the fact that practices of racism have become so routine, repetitive, and familiar as part of everyday life that they are unrecognizable (especially to non-marginalized groups). Supported by commonsense notions that confirm accepted opinion, the new racism conceals the ideologies and practices that legitimate and support it.[12] The fact that Nina does not name race or culture as the points of exclusion, and our shared mutual comprehension of what is not being identified, support Essed's arguments about commonsense understandings of racism and the sense of shared experience they can generate.

In the above quotation and in the interview generally, Nina did not position herself as a victim of racism. A conventional reading could regard her refusal to see how she is positioned as a denial of the existence of racism, but I would argue that it can also be read as an example of resistance, a refusal to accept being positioned by others. The victim narrative would mean having to accept the taxonomy of difference. Her choice is between accepting the label of difference or asserting herself as no different from the norm. Further on in the interview, when asked if she feels accepted by her white friends, Nina did comment on the notion of difference. While she sees herself as different from white, she rejects the totality of difference:

Amita: Do you feel totally accepted by them [your friends]?

Nina: Yeah, I do. Like I mean we get into little things, like I mean as far as I'm different, like because of being Indian and everything. They say little things, you know, like, "Ah yeah, stupid Indians," and like they know that I'm there. But as far as like, I mean, I've never been rejected by them or anything like that. They know that I'm Indian. I make them know. Like I'm not, I don't flaunt it, but I don't let them, not that I don't let them forget it but you know — not that

> they should — but they're aware that I am Indian
> 'cause they, I mean, I feel like I constantly have to
> explain to them why I am Indian, because of the way
> my parents are. I have to explain that I can't do this
> with you, I can't do this with you. Why? Because my
> parents are Indian and that's why I can't.

Nina describes her friends, primarily "white jocks," as the "in" group
in the school. The above passage suggests that part of the negotiation
around racial identity involves divesting from one's ethnic/racial location. In relation to her friends at school, Nina argues that it is because
of her parents' culture that she cannot participate in certain social practices. Here her sense of belonging to the category "Indian" rests on her
parents' association to it. By locating her parents as "Indian," and the
source of her difference, it is her parents' inflexibility to change and
not her friends' racism that becomes the problem. This also becomes
a way for her to relinquish any responsibility for being Indian, although
at no time does she reject this as an identity altogether.

G. Tsolidis argues: "Ethnic minority adolescents, who are already
questioning so much about themselves and their environment, are
also being told that their parents are socially unacceptable and inadequate. Their parents' status is diminished and insulted because of
cultural dissonance, linguistic factors and economic dislocation.
Messages about parents are also messages about their children.
Clearly dissociating oneself from the family, under these circumstances, is to raise one's own status."[13] For Nina, aligning herself with
her parents in this case not only means choosing her parents over her
friends, but takes on the added meaning of choosing her parents'
culture over the culture of her white and westernized peers. An affiliation with white culture in the context of a predominantly white
school, where the point of reference is white, increases Nina's status.

## ✑ "Refs," "FOBs," and "Typical"

I found many similar examples of young women resisting stereotypical representations of South Asian-ness while simultaneously seeking to maintain a higher status in relation to other South Asians. Many of the girls I interviewed differentiated themselves from what they called the "typical Indian" and described themselves as "normal," "cool," or "neutral." In some cases a typical Indian was identified as someone "fresh off the boat" (FOB) or a "refugee" (ref). While "fresh off the boat" and "refugee" were used interchangeably, one person noted that the former referred to newly arrived immigrants, while the latter was reserved for those who had been here for some time, but stayed "typically Indian." In the following exchange about the composition of her high school, Rupinder, an eighteen-year-old Sikh girl, remarked:

Rupinder: It was predominantly South Asian, but like fresh off the boat ones — and a couple of them like us who have been here for a while. But I don't know, again, it was like no one really like mixed with anybody.

Amita: So what was the view of the people who had recently arrived by the ones who have been around for a while?

Rupinder: I think our view of them is, like, they're not cool enough for us. Like I'm not trying to be snobby about it, but... And they perceive us as being like sluts, and you know what I mean? And they think we're trying to be too westernized if we don't like have our hair in braids. And I guess the way they talk. I guess we don't really want to associate with them, 'cause we don't have the accent and they do.

The conversation reveals both a certain representation of newly arrived immigrants and the separation that Rupinder makes between them and herself. While Rupinder holds a stereotype of more recent South Asian immigrants, she perceives them as holding a stereotype of her. In this discourse "West" and "East" become fixed categories, so that the differences within each category aren't as important as the perceived commonalities that hold each together, thus creating the stereotype. In the preceding passage, people from the "homeland" are viewed with caution and seen as possessing certain views about sexuality. Again this points to the centrality of sexuality and gender as markers of national and community identity. This cultural difference is also described in terms of bodily markers, such as hairstyle and accents. What remains unspoken is that the new immigrants are different because they aren't conforming to Western hairstyles and accents typical of this country.

In the following conversation, Nina mobilizes notions of normality to understand the diversity of the South Asian experience:

Nina: We have a few Indians [at our school] but not what people would consider normal Indians...

Amita: What do you think people mean when they say "normal Indians"?

Nina: Well right now, in this day and age, I see a lot of people see normal Indians like, I guess, cool Indians. Like normal Indians, like you and me sort of, rather than with long hair. I guess I can't describe it on the recording [laughter].

Amita: Keep going.

Nina: You know, like with long hair and, you know, like in accents.

Amita: Is it just in the way that they dress?

Nina: Yeah, and then their accent and just the fact that they're right from India or Sri Lanka or wherever they're from.

Here, "uncool" becomes the signifier for "new" South Asians and "normal" represents second-generation South Asians. Nina positions herself as Indian while simultaneously distinguishing herself from the stereotype Indian, whose accents and long hair not are representative of a "cool" degree of assimilation. Interestingly enough, she invites me in along with herself as part of the cool Indian group, even though we both have long hair. The South Asians to whom she refers display cultural markers that are visibly different from the Western norm and point to their recent migration. Of course, what she is not explicitly stating is that anglicized accents, modes of dress, and hair are normative. Mary Louise Adams argues that normalization is accomplished through taken-for-granted and commonsense notions of difference that need not be continually mentioned. Normalization works as a self-regulating discourse where the subject actually comes to desire what is seen as "normal."[14] But, as these conversations demonstrate, this desiring of the "normal" is a tremendously painful and conflicted experience.

Rupinder and Nina both speak to a eurocentric notion of normality and difference. The hidden narrative in this framework points to the conditionality and relationality of difference; the notion that being different is "cool" so long as it remains within an acceptable limit relative to the norm. They reveal threads of a discourse that locates difference as arising from individuals rather than being constructed in and through social, political, and historical relations of power and struggle. Nina bases her perspective not so much on direct experience as on a commonsense notion of what is normal, and she alludes to "people" and "in this day and age" to lend credibility to her claim. She uses "people" as a universal category, although it is clear that she is not referring to the beliefs or practices of the people she is describing, but rather to those of long-term inhabitants of this country.

While long-term inhabitants of this country have more status than newly arrived immigrants, they are not automatically included in the definition of the acceptable Canadian. The following conversation between the two sisters, Tina and Pam, shows that "Canadian" is not inclusive of South Asian cultural practices:

Tina:  Montreal is a cosmopolitan city, but the brown people there are spread out and they're also Canadianized more.

Pam:  Like you wouldn't catch an Indian person or an Indian child over there, let's say a teenager, listening to Indian music, at all.

Tina:  Not at all, they don't do that there.

Pam:  It's embarrassing for them.

This comparison between Toronto and Montreal suggests that Toronto is a city that has a higher concentration of South Asians in particular areas. But what also emerges is the observation that the definition of "Canadian" is not inclusive of "other," in this case South Asian, cultural practices. The girls explain that what makes Montreal South Asians more Canadian is an absence of overtly "Indian" signifiers, such as music.

Nina revealed the desire on the part of second-generation South Asians to be seen as different from "other" South Asians, namely those newly arrived, "not as assimilated as us" South Asians. But there was also a need to be seen as more Canadian through a distancing from South Asians in general. I would say that this is an example of resistance to the idea of internal cohesion as well as a means to maintain and negotiate higher status in relation to the dominant community. For example, in relation to internal cohesion, many girls felt self-conscious in the context of an all-brown space. As previously mentioned in Chapter 2, Nina revealed:

Amita:  Did you feel kind of embarrassed if you were seen talking to another Indian at school?

Nina:  Actually yeah, yeah, 'cause I didn't want people to think that he's my only friend. You know what I mean, 'cause he's brown he's my only friend. Or because she's brown, she's my only friend, and because we're brown we should stick together. I didn't want that impression

to come ... I didn't allow myself to become good
friends with that person. But I didn't stop myself from
talking to that person if I had a question to ask them.

This portion of our conversation suggests a desire to escape the association that all South Asians should stick together. There is an interesting assumption that friendship with a white person would be
based not only on skin colour. What is not being named is that this
desire is forged in relation to the white gaze. This point is further
illustrated when Nina discusses her relationship to her close friend,
Asha, and her boyfriend, both of whom are South Asian:

Amita:   Do you think when people see you and Asha together
         that they must think that...
Nina:    Yeah, yeah, and sometimes we even worry about that.
         We go, "Don't you think if people saw us together..."
         Like I worry. I know it's bad, but sometimes even if
         we're walking, like even if I'm walking with my
         boyfriend somewhere, like if we're walking in a group,
         I feel so, I feel like so centred 'cause we're all the same
         and I feel like people look at us that way and I think
         that way about Asha too. 'Cause when I see two Indian
         people I'm like, "Oh yeah, they're just together 'cause
         they're Indian," but they don't realize that we're
         together not 'cause we're Indian but—
Amita:   [interrupting] But do you think people think that about
         white people, like if they see a group of white people?
Nina:    Yeah, they would think that, too, I guess. Yeah, I think
         so. But I don't know why but it seems like more, not
         obvious, but I notice it more though. Like I know even
         in like movies or whatever, like two best friends — my
         best friend is Greek and I'm like, "Why don't they show
         two best friends of two different cultures?" I look at it

the same way. Maybe other people don't. But because I
see Indian people that way, I see every culture that way,
like [in hushed tone] when I see Oriental people I think
of them in the same way like they always have to hang
around together. It seems like everything is so racially...

Several important themes emerge from Nina's talk. First, as with the
previous quotation, Nina shows how she is positioned in relation to a
white reference point. Although she views all people of the same
culture who hang out together as cliquish, for her, white people in a
crowd are not as noticeable when they are together. This points to how
white ethnicity in her context is normative and therefore has the privilege of appearing invisible. This conversation can also be interpreted
as a resistance to the stereotype of internal homogeneity. This is
presented in a line of reasoning that suggests that "just because we're
South Asian does not mean we are all the same, or have the same interests, or should be friends." Part of what is being expressed by Nina here
is a desire for the same anonymity that white people are seen to experience. South Asian people are more conspicuous as a group because
of their difference from white. Nina unsettles the assumption that the
only important features in friendships among brown people are ethnicity and race. Her argument in support of interracial and cross-cultural
friendships is a means to break the stereotype of internal cohesion and
unsettle a seemingly fixed racial boundary.

I found that the young women I interviewed did not describe the
"typical Indian" just in relation to a stereotype, but also in relation
to a host of traits which they perceived as negative. "Typical Indian"
was thus described as "gossipy," "snobby," and "not very nice," or "It's
in the way they act, they ... have an attitude" and are "ignorant." The
following conversation with Ratna illustrates the ways in which the
"typical Indian" is represented and how she places herself in relation
to this construction. Ratna explained why she did not like going to
South Asian dances:

Ratna:  I didn't like the atmosphere, I didn't like the people there, and I don't like to be with a whole bunch of Indians, 'cause I like a mix.

Amita:  What don't you like about it?

Ratna:  I don't like the way how all the Indian people were, how they were together, just the way they acted, it wasn't me, 'cause I'm not like typical typical Indian Indian. You know what I mean?

Amita:  How do you define a typical Indian?

Ratna:  Gossipy, I don't know, they just, like, I can't stand when people talk Indian all the time, like Punjabi or whatever, that makes me sick. I don't know, just the way they act you know, you can tell, they act a bit different.

Amita:  Could you try and define what that is?

Ratna:  'Cause they're so, sometimes they're really stuck up, they think they're too good and they're not very nice, you know they have an attitude. Like that.

[a bit later]

Amita:  So if you don't see yourself as typically Indian, like how would you describe yourself?

Ratna:  I don't know, I guess I'm neutral, kind of... One thing I don't like is if you're Indian people believe you have to stay with Indians. I don't like that, I find that, you know, you should go around and talk to everyone else too. That's what I don't like, like I don't stop myself, I talk to everyone, I don't care, I don't want to be known as, oh okay all my friends are Indian and I'm just — you know what I mean?

Ratna identifies "typical Indian" as dependent on markers of ethnicity, such as language (Punjabi). However, she and many of the other girls also described "typical Indian" as anything that they wanted to distinguish themselves from, and it seemed to stand in for any behaviour or practice that they disliked. While this construction resists the outside (white) stereotype of internal cohesion, it also contests inside pressures to remain within the group boundary of "South Asian." So strong is the desire to resist expected norms around group loyalty and internal homogeneity that Ratna's statement that people speaking Punjabi all the time "makes me sick" can be read as resistant in part, rather than solely as a form of allegiance to a white anglo norm. Both Nina and Ratna are attempting to move outside what they see as a parochial notion of community.[15] For Ratna, growing up with three older siblings who are identified with South Asian signifiers, popular culture, and friends, the idea of a brown space is neither novel nor subversive. For her, moving out of "brown" into the realm of interreligious and interracial social spaces is an act of subversion and breaking of norms.

While this construction of the typical Indian can be read as part of a process of racialization that has fixed "Indian" so that it is associated with the negative, or as an example of internalized racism, I also began to see it as a form of negative identification: the young women seemed to be more at ease in describing what "Indian" was not or the type of Indian they did not want to be associated with. In a study of Puerto Rican "gang girls" in New York, Anne Campbell describes a similar process of self-definition by rejection. In her research, Campbell found that girls'

> sense of self as gang members is derived from their rejection of various aspects of membership of three interlocking societal identities: class, race, and gender. They arrive at a female gang identity by default rather than by affirmation. The fragmented and reactive nature of their self definition helps to make sense of many of the contradictions which are present in the social talk of the gang girl. By "backing away" from one aspect of an assigned role, she may run the risk of being cast in another unacceptable

role from which she must also extricate herself ... The point is that not all components of a given role are rejected.[16]

These girls' sense of individuality is partly achieved through a rejection of certain aspects of identity that are associated with their social position. While they do not reject their ethnicity or womanhood altogether, they attempt to articulate that they are not "that kind of woman." Campbell explains that "the words and typifications we use to characterize our enemies are often an important guide to the ascriptions we most reject in ourselves. By extension, our self concept may evolve from our rejection of such negative personal attributes rather than from the active construction of a social identity."[17]

Campbell describes the relationship between Puerto Ricans living in the United States and Puerto Ricans living in Puerto Rico in terms similar to how these young South Asian women distinguish themselves from those "back home." Most of the girls she interviewed termed the moral values of "back home" Puerto Rico old-fashioned in comparison to those of Puerto Rican New Yorkers. They emphasized their "American" status and its "superiority over other more recently arrived immigrants."[18] Equally, the distinction between "refs" or "FOBs" and "cool" or "normal" Indians makes a bid for a "Canadian" status that is superior to that of recent arrivals.

I found that the rejection of behaviours associated with a certain group is embedded in sets of meaning that evaluate white dominant culture as more desirable and superior. It is because of this relationship between status and behaviour that these young girls reject certain aspects of behaviour associated with Indian-ness.[19] The discourse around "typical Indian" is a response to the white dominant norm. In this sense, it constitutes a resistance to, or rupturing of, assigned (stereotypical) identities. Even though the girls engage in some behaviours and practices that they label as "typical Indian," what they are resisting through the construction of typical Indian is the association of certain behaviours and practices to a totalizing identity. In other words, the only means by which they can reject a stereotypical Indian identity is by distancing themselves from "that kind of Indian."

 Multicultural Do's and Don'ts

Even young women attending brown schools reveal the normative construction of whiteness. Although their schools are racially diverse, the girls who attend them are positioned in a discourse that tells them that they can be different but not too different from the white norm. Part of the invisibility of white as the norm has to do with a discourse of multiculturalism that emphasizes tolerance. The limits of this tolerance, however, are enmeshed in commonsense notions of race, culture, and difference.

Reading and rereading through the transcribed interviews brought my attention to how the young women took up notions of multiculturalism in the context of their schooling environment. All but two of the girls described their schools as "multicultural," but their use of the term tended to be descriptive of the school population rather than referring to actual practices of multiculturalism. Most of the girls described their schools as multicultural in terms of the cultural mix of the school, the organization of official "multicultural" days, and the use of space within school premises. Faiza, an eighteen-year-old Muslim girl, explained multiculturalism in the following way:

> We have multicultural weeks each year, and they have like a few displays, and they've got a few things in different locations, like a karaoke machine for like Japan, and last year they had in the gym belly dancers and some guy who walked on glass, like from Jamaica or Brazil. I don't know, something like that. He was West Indian. They had Indian girls doing classical dancing, Bharat Natyam, just so everyone is aware of different cultures, which I think is really good 'cause I don't know of any other

school that does that. So it's not in the curriculum but [it] does make you more aware of things.

Through Faiza's description we can trace the dominant construction of multiculturalism as a positive strategy in the promotion and sharing of differences. Here, exposure to other cultures is seen as pivotal in the creation of good feelings and racial harmony. Faiza equates culture with curiosity and exotic entertainment worthy of display precisely because of its difference. It is a break from the ordinary, banal aspects of everyday, normal culture. That non-white culture and history stand outside the norm of whiteness, without even naming whiteness as normative, is testimony to the subtle and powerful process of normalization that is taking place here. In her account, multiculturalism in school is reduced to a "show and tell" version of culture and amounts to nothing more than the sari samosa syndrome. Multiculturalism becomes synonymous with a celebration of the cursory manifestations of culture, such as food and dance, permitted at designated times and spaces within the official and otherwise white context.

What is interesting, however, is that Faiza and others who identify multiculturalism as positive also claim that the curriculum does not reflect the cultural mix of the school. Responding to the question about whether she feels her school (70 percent of whose students are South Asian) has taught her anything about the Indian subcontinent or her history, Alka said, "No, not really, I don't find that at all, it's just normal." In this one sentence she exposes the limitations in formal education and the notions of multicultural exchange. "Normal" signifies instruction that is predominantly based on a eurocentric curriculum. Similarly, Ayesha, an eighteen-year-old Ismaili Muslim, said the following about cultural exchange: "I try to get more into my religion, like being Indian and stuff, just to, you know, I never experienced being with Indians and stuff so I try to get more into it. So I found my religion more, I try and learn about it. And I try and learn about other religions, like I always ask Ratna about hers and like about Sikhs, and I ask her about her religion, and you know I look at everything, everything as a whole."

Her remarks are as suggestive about her own culture as they are about the culture of other non-white groups. Ayesha's perspective of cultural dialogue and sharing indicates that she cannot rely on school-based systems of learning, and needs to seek out her own sources of information. Learning about other cultures stems from a sense of individual choice and responsibility. This particular brand of multiculturalism contradicts governmental rhetoric, which claims that removing discriminatory attitudes and misunderstandings is to be achieved in part through muticultural education.[20]

The young women's talk provides insight into how multiculturalism comes to be seen as a positive development, despite its marginal position in relation to the official school curriculum. In fact, some actually attributed a decrease in racism to the advent of multiculturalism. Rupinder explained that she no longer experiences racial name-calling like she used to, and reflected on why she thinks this has changed: "I guess it goes back to that, you know, how they usually never publicized multiculturalism back then and it felt like we were in the melting pot then, I guess. That and just everyone telling you, 'Speak English,' and you know, it was like you were pressured into it."

While examining the interviews, rather than focusing on whether the young womens' accounts documented an actual decrease in racism, I began to look at how they were naming, and not naming, racism. All of the women seemed to downplay racist events and often produced a preferred reading of cultural miscommunication rather than one of racism and power. Seeing their schools and their larger social context as multicultural seemed to foreclose any possibility that discriminatory acts toward them were actually racist. Many women started with the statement "No, not really" in response to my question whether they had ever experienced racism, but then would recount various racist incidents. I use the word *incidents* quite purposefully to indicate that these young women defined racism very much in terms of events, rather than subtler ongoing or systematic daily practices. The above example of Nina being kicked out of a white family's house because she was South Asian, and her description of this as a "little" incident, illustrate the invisibility of racism and perhaps even her difficulty in acknowledging that she is a target of racism. This suggests that the discourse of multiculturalism makes racism invisible.

I found that young South Asian women's relationship to clothes also reveals hidden norms with respect to multicultural tolerance. The following discussion with Alka about clothing shows some of the invisible discourses around race and multiculturalism:

Amita:  Would you at your school feel comfortable wearing a salwar kameez?

Alka:  Yeah, at our school, we do, we do feel comfortable.

Amita:  Would you feel comfortable wearing it outside of school, say a restaurant?

Alka:  Yeah, but what I don't like is, ahm, I still don't like going shopping with it on.

Amita:  Do you know why?

Alka:  I don't know, I think it's more, like, indirectly it's more like a personal thing, but you think of excuses, like it's harder to try on clothes and so forth, but ahm I think... Yeah, I think it's like from the beginning, I never liked... I can go anywhere with a salwar kameez, I can go to a little plaza, I can go anywhere but still sometimes when I like go to see a movie or something I don't want to go in a salwar kameez. I'd rather go in Western clothes just to fit in.

Amita:  But at school, there's...?

Alka:  No, there's no problem.

Amita:  So when you're outside then, do you feel that if you wore a salwar kameez that you'd be made to feel embarrassed, that people would look at you in a certain way?

Alka: I think it's more if, ahh, people look at you and you know there's no need to be different at this point in time, you know I'm not making a statement or something by wearing a suit [salwar kameez] and it would be more comfortable if I wear something, you know. It's not like I don't wear Western clothes and I can't wear it, so ahm... It's not saying it's a hard strict rule, you know, not to wear it but, you know. I prefer not to and, you know, there's no point and I feel comfortable within myself.

Amita: So do you wear salwar kameez to school?

Alka: Yeah, like on Diwali, and like we had a whole project on India and we all dressed up in suits, so there's no harm in our school, like on multicultural day everybody gets dressed up, so.

There are several interesting moments in this conversation. She begins by identifying her school as a safe place in which to practice her ethnic identity. She feels comfortable wearing a salwar kameez on multicultural day and Diwali, and yet the fact that she wears it at these particular times gives her the sense that it is permissible more generally. The designated specific times and days are not presented as exceptions to normal school protocol but rather as reflective of the school's tolerant atmosphere. She says, "Yeah, at our school we do, we do feel comfortable," suggesting that at other schools people may not feel that way.

Alka makes visible how assimilation organizes her practices in the public sphere. She maintains that Western clothes are important to "fitting in" and that the salwar kameez carries the marker of difference. She reveals the desire for a certain kind of anonymity that is part of fitting in. She describes wearing a salwar kameez as "dressing up" and says that "Western clothes" promise a sense of normality and anonymity that South Asian clothes do not. Feeling comfortable in Western clothes in certain spaces at certain times is presented as a matter of individual choice and preference, thereby hiding the discourse of assimilation and integration. This perspective also hides the power that this particular discourse has in constructing difference as "other" and as less desirable. Alka indicates that time and space are important indicators for the permission of difference. She suggests that there are certain times and places when being different does not make sense because it is seen to overplay difference. In the context of sanctioned and appropriate times and spaces, such as multicultural day, difference is seen to be part of the appropriate statement, when non-white race and ethnicity is expected and allowed to accentuate itself.

Norms become so taken for granted that their presence as a standard of measure actually becomes invisible, even to the person who is governing herself according to them.[21] It is not so much that permission to practise non-white ethnicity is overt, but that this display of culture is only "normal" at designated times and places (and thus can be safely contained). It is only when we are reminded that Bharat Natyam and glass-walking are not part of the daily school protocol that we are able to see that there is in fact a constructed "normal" that such practices fall outside of.

## Indian/Canadian Dichotomy

While the young women all identified themselves as "Indian," they had great difficulty in defining what this was, and most of them were full of contradictions. They relied on essentialist notions of race, such as physical traits, as well as notions of ethnicity. Often the attempt to define "Indian" was forged in relation to what it is not, in other words, "Canadian." For example, two sisters, Pam and Tina, described their father:

Tina:   My dad's honkified.
Pam:    Totally. He can't even speak Hindi properly.

Tina:  He's very, very Canadian, English. He lived in England. You know the only part of him that's Indian is his religion.

Their father's Indian-ness is conditional on his religious affiliation. Pam and Tina categorize their father as Canadian because his retention of the Hindi language is poor. Because the girls discussed "Indian" in relation to "white," I asked them to define what they meant by the two:

Pam:  Indian values, I'd say, like activities. You know, like the typical going skiing every winter and going camping every summer, I think those are, those are white values. Do you know what I mean? A typical Indian couple or family would not think of going skiing or, I mean, sure they would take it up as a hobby, influenced by a white person.

Tina:  It's not a value, it's just a hobby.

Pam:  I know, but most like... that's the thing, most... The hobbies, you know, like it starts from there and then from there it's sort of like the lifestyle. Would be... ahm... like basically doing what white people would do. Like going at Christmas time. Church every Christmas, Easter, church. But that has something to do with the fact that my stepmother's Christian. But even before my father married my stepmother, we would go to church.

Amita:  But what do you see, like when you use the term "typical Indian," what is that to you?

Pam:  A typical Indian would be a person who would live in India but is living in Canada, like living Indian morals and values.

Amita:  Which is?

Pam:  Which is subzi [cooked vegetables] every evening like, more or less that, temple every Saturday and Sunday.

Both of the sisters draw on stereotypical views of Canadian-ness and Indian-ness. Here, religion, food, and particular activities are important markers for both Canadian and Indian identities. "Canadian," however, is very much defined in relation to "white" activities, hobbies, and lifestyles and is not inclusive of "Indian" food or language or non-Christian religions. Both Tina and Pam, on several occasions, emphasized that they were not "typical Indian." What I found interesting is that although they defined this label partly in relation to temple visits, later on in the interview, Pam and Tina had the following to say about their white friends:

> Tina:   They don't understand. Like when I do something like go to temple or something like that. There's a lot of things that you do within the community that brings you closer as friends. It's like we're doing something together, and we're doing something within a small group and that's what makes it more important, you know.
>
> Pam:   Like white people, like going roller skating or going to a movie or something like that.
>
> Tina:   Their interests are different.
>
> Pam:   While I would prefer to go to a club, or going to see an Indian movie or something like that, or doing something that is not typically white.

Here the same temple that was presented earlier as a "typically Indian" activity from which they saw themselves as distinct is now presented as a means of consolidating group identity. The temple, a brown space, provides a sense of belonging.

## ☞ Day Dances, Bhangra, and Worries

Newspaper articles and other mainstream media play a significant role in constructing a perception of culture conflict and representing young South Asian women as victims of this conflict. These representations draw heavily on a subtext of backward, restrictive parents and confused, uncontrollable, and oppressed youth — a subtext that is best understood in relation to a backdrop of demographic changes in Canada and continuing white anxiety over their cultural, political, and economic place within the power base of this country. Teun van Dijk argues that the media play a crucial role in the reproduction of racism. News in most Western countries consistently represents ethnic relations in ways that replicate stereotypes. Media coverage of immigration, for example, often emphasizes "problems, illegality, large numbers, fraud, and demographic or cultural threats."[22] Accordingly, the subtext is the construction of the non-white ethnic as "different, problematic, deviant or threatening."[23] Through this kind of representation of the ethnic "other," the media reinforce the prestige, superiority, and respectability of whiteness. As van Dijk writes: "Whereas other cultures are routinely derogated as backward or primitive, western culture and its values are either taken for granted or positively presented as modern, rational, and humanitarian."[24]

Media coverage of immigration and the South Asian community certainly supports van Dijk's analysis. The media, of course, are not autonomous from the white dominant social relations of which they are a part. They can reproduce dominant perspectives and representations of race relations while all the while appearing to be neutral and tolerant towards difference.

The terrain of music received a lot of attention in the 1990s from both the mainstream Canadian media and segments of the South Asian community. For the most part the media explored the explosion of South Asian fusion music and dances as a site where the clash of cultures between South Asian teenagers and their parents is most evident. South Asian dances began to receive media attention with the advent of day dances, which started as an alternative to night dances in 1990. In particular, they were brought to public awareness in 1991 when promoters known as Punjab Culture Shock planned a dance just before Christmas holidays with popular bhangra star Apache Indian. The night before the dance the Mississauga venue was firebombed, causing minor damage. This received a lot of media coverage, and it was suspected that conservative members of the South Asian community were involved in the firebombing. This incident served as a catalyst, bringing to the forefront a variety of issues concerning second-generation youth in Toronto and dances in general.

The media predominantly described the day dance controversy as being between strict, traditional parents and teenagers wanting to enjoy the freedoms of Canadian society. The CBC's *Fifth Estate* did a special report on day dances in November 1993. Journalist Trish Wood described these dances as a rebellion against traditions and parents and argued that young women in particular were caught between the "strict traditions of parents on the one hand and the temptations offered by Canada's liberal, youth-driven society," on the other. She claimed that young South Asian girls "sneak out to do what most teenagers do all the time." Among the people she interviewed was Mr. Pandoori (head of the Malton Sikh temple), who is well-known in the South Asian community for his conservative beliefs. He said that the dances must be stopped, that the teenagers that go to these dances are "pigs," and that only girls who want to "smoke, drink and get pregnant" would go to these places.

Wood used the dances as a backdrop to explore attitudes towards childrearing, violence, and abuse among South Asians. Her report showed how parents' strictness with their teenage girls was in some cases leading to violence. She also focused on the history of South Asian migration to Ontario. She explained, "Thousands of South Asians emigrated in the late 1960s and '70s," especially a large Sikh population, and said that there are 30,000 students of South Asian descent in the Peel region, which in some schools accounts for over 50 percent of the student body.

Currently, a renewed controversy over visible minority immigrants is emerging forcefully in popular discourses in many Western countries. Christopher Husbands has examined the underlying anxiety over national identity and nationhood in the United Kingdom, the Federal Republic of Germany, and the Netherlands.[25] He maintains that the rise in these countries of right-wing factions who oppose multiculturalism and immigration indicates a moral panic over immigration. Lurking beneath white anxieties about immigrants is the fear of being outnumbered demographically by "foreigners," as well as a perceived threat of cultural dilution. There is a renewed emphasis on national identity and ascertaining the boundaries and definition of nationhood. This emphasis has particularly increased since the incidents of September 11, 2001. While each of these countries has an official rhetoric of flexibility and tolerance, the idea of nationhood and identity continues to be challenged, especially in what Husbands refers to as a time of economic and moral barrenness. Building on Stanley Cohen's definition of "moral panic," Husbands claims that a moral panic is easily recognizable in reports that focus on "regular polling data, the 'difference' of certain social groups (in this case non-white, 'ethnic' groups, with a post–September 11 emphasis on Arab-looking communities)," and reporting that suggests a particular group or migrants from a particular country are a problem.[26]

I briefly reviewed the *Canadian Periodical Index, Canadian News Index,* and the *Canadian Index* to survey news items around immigration from 1990 to 1995, around the time of the mainstream media focus on bhangra, day dances, and culture conflict within the South Asian community. These indexes list most of the prominent newspapers across the country, such as the *Calgary Herald, Winnipeg Free Press, Globe and Mail, Montreal Gazette,* and *Halifax Chronicle Herald.* In mid-September 1992, all five newspapers reported the findings of a survey by the Canadian immigration department. The *Globe and Mail* reported that Canadians are "in their most hostile mood in years toward immigrants."[27] Receding to "minority" status was among the fears that Canadians had, according to this poll, and one-third of those surveyed wanted to exclude from Canada "people who are different than most Canadians." Three months later the paper ran an article entitled, "Immigrants' origins increasingly diverse: Demographers fear racist backlash." This article assuages the fear that white people will be outnumbered but emphasizes the threat around difference. It begins by reporting that, proportionally, the percentage of immigrants has remained almost identical since World War II.[28] However, it also explains that while in the early 1960s 90 percent of migrants were from Europe (e.g., Britain and Italy), now arrivals from Hong Kong and India comprise almost half of all new immigrants. Stating that the immigration policy is meant to "bolster" birth rates because since the 1970s "Canadians have not been bearing enough children to replace themselves," the article had a motif similar to the more blatant race-suicide appeals a century earlier.

More recently, in 1995, the *Globe and Mail* printed a front-page article headlined, "Population crisis feared as billions enter fertile years: Failing to address impact on immigration, economies may be 'ultimate global blunder.'"[29] The article draws attention to the "billions" of young people in developing countries who are now entering their reproductive years, and draws a direct link to their impact on the West. This fertility is not only "threatening to worsen economic distress in developing countries" but will "stimulate even greater immigration." The article stands as a warning of further ethnic siege.

In the *Montreal Gazette*, Harvey Schachter focused on the changes confronting the city of Toronto in 1994. "Change," he argues, "provokes tension. Massive change can provoke massive tension. And this has been massive change." The change he is referring to is the inflow of non-white immigrants. He starts off with the following reflection about commuting on the public transport system: "I'm beginning to feel that I'm a visible minority on the Toronto subways. I'm white." In an attempt to understand the growing backlash toward non-white immigrants, he contends, "It's not a question of racism. ... it's a question of comfort levels, of not feeling alien in your own city."[30]

Around the same time, the *Globe and Mail* ran a three-part series called "Suburbs in Transition." Ads for the series read, "Some of Canada's burgeoning regional municipalities have become laboratories for the government's policies on immigration and multiculturalism."[31] Lila Sarick focused on the Peel region in part one of the series, treating the area as a microcosm and consequent reflection of Toronto and other Canadian urban centres. The final article was headlined, "A region grown like a gawky adolescent: Many Peel residents accept, if not enthusiastically embrace, its multicultural nature," which is interesting for its metaphoric connection of adolescent development and the development of a racially diverse urban community. The predominantly non-white ethnic community is thus constructed as being immature and in need of guidance.

Sarick begins her first article with a "reality check" forecast for Toronto residents, warning them to expect "more traffic, more portable classrooms, and more immigrants."[32] She argues that Brampton and Mississauga are no longer "traditional" suburban communities because the region's 700,000 population is now largely constituted by visible minorities: "By 2001, the region's population is expected to be almost a million people, 40% born outside of Canada and 1/3 members of a visible minority group." The article makes an implicit link between violence and the growing "ethnic" population, explaining that for some residents Peel's rapid multicultural growth has "brought unpleasant side effects" such as concern over a recent shooting in a nearby mall. Sarick reports that residents worry about a decrease in property values, overdevelopment, the possibility of urban slums, and non-English speaking neighbours.[33] And some, like Norman Fishbein, worry about their own displacement: "Four or five years ago you got on the bus and the ethnic population wasn't very evident. ... I'm a born Canadian and I always feel now they're trying to push us out." [34] People like Mr. Fishbein are reassured with a reflection from Peel Regional Police Chief Robert Lunney, who says, "We don't experience a lot of ethnic crime. ... The process of assimilation is well under way."[35]

In May 1995, the *Montreal Gazette* reported the findings of a poll commissioned by the Immigration Association of Canada. This survey found that three out of five Canadians desire a five-year moratorium on immigration in order that "the country absorbs newcomers already arrived." On the same day, the *Calgary Herald* announced, "Close doors, speak English, majority tells pollster" and reported that the poll "found more people in favour of Canada being an English-speaking culture than a multicultural society."[36]

These are only a small portion of the newspaper articles written on immigration issues between 1990 and 1996, but all demonstrate some of the trends that Husbands discusses in relation to the media's role in the construction of moral panics: an emphasis on demographic changes and the possibility of being outnumbered, the difference of certain social groups, possible cultural dilution, and a construction of non-white migrant populations as the source of economic and social problems in Canada.[37] These articles are also valuable as an indicator of public opinion. The media do not conjure up, but rather play up, various aspects of popular opinion at the same time as they work to constitute and create public opinion.

These newspaper articles frequently reference polling data that emphasize both numbers and cultural difference. Even the use of language such as "influx," "population crisis," "billions," "close doors," and "flux" conjures up images of numerous immigrants clamouring to break into the country. The *Globe and Mail* reports that the "percentage of Canadians who are immigrants has remained almost exactly the same since the Second World War but their cultural backgrounds have not."[38] However, in media reports, the size of the immigrant population continues to be emphasized, playing on the (white) fear of being outnumbered. Some of the articles also touch on urbanization and the influx of immigrants as indicators of rapid and unmanageable change. The emphasis on numbers and references to cultural difference divert anxieties about a rapidly modernizing society onto immigration. Moreover, a focus on immigrants as the source of the nation's problems helps to mask socioeconomic changes and class tensions.

I believe that concern over immigrants in Toronto and across the nation during the early 1990s reflected, in large part, anxiety over a faltering economy. In 1992, the *Globe and Mail* reported that the national unemployment rate was 11.8 percent, the highest in a decade, increasing fear over job security.[39] And although there is no evidence that new immigrants snatch jobs from Canadian-born citizens, in Toronto and Vancouver, cities with the largest inflow of immigrants, in an economically depressed climate the resentment toward newcomers is greater.

The media's focus on immigration and on the resulting tensions can also be read in terms of concern about the boundaries of Canadian identity. Despite an official Canadian rhetoric about tolerance, flexibility, and acceptance, these articles demonstrate some of the ways in which the tensions between assimilation and tolerance continue to be played out. They also reveal the continuing negotiation of national identity and definition of Canadian nationhood. From these clippings we get a sense that immigrants bring crime (now possibly terrorism), increase tension, are violent, decrease property values, and make you (read: white Canadian) feel uncomfortable. Implicit in the reversal is that white, English-speaking Canadians are peaceful, are a more lucrative investment because they do not decrease property values, and make you feel comfortable. White Canadian parents don't beat their kids and are not strict with their daughters. There is a familiar colonial East-West tone to this discourse. How South Asian parents treat their daughters, for example, in the stories on *The Fifth Estate* and in *Toronto Life* becomes emblematic of the entire backward condition of the

South Asian community.[40] The treatment of women within "their" community serves as an indicator of the extent of modernity, that is, assimilation. It is because the boundaries of white ethnicity are threatened, both numerically and culturally, that the narrative of the backward and problematic ethnic immigrant is useful.

# CHAPTER FIVE

# The Hall of Shame:
## Lies, Masks, and Respectful Femininity

*I had taken some time to prepare myself for the wedding reception of an old family friend I had not seen in seven years. I showered and scented myself so that I looked as freshly pressed as the printed shawl that draped my body. As I entered the house, I saw that most people were involved in exchanges of greetings with those they saw only on such occasions. I headed straight for the samosas and kebabs, food being one of the only attractions of this kind of event. I busied myself in chit-chat with old family friends hovering around what was left of the appetizers.*

*Politely excusing myself, I walked through the groups of chattering people to the kitchen, where men were helping themselves to alcohol. Festivities had started and people slowly cleared the room. When it seemed that no one was looking, I quickly poured a glass of red wine into a Styrofoam juice cup that promised to hold my secret. For fear of being discovered, my lips tugged quickly at my first and then second sip of wine. Just as I started to feel a tinge of smoothness to movements and thoughts, my stomach dropped a few miles down and my eyes widened at the sight of my uncle. My hands frantically glided through the contents of my purse in an effort to find some gum.*

*"Uchah, beti, so tell me what are you doing standing alone when everybody else has gone for food?"*

*"Uncle, I was just trying to avoid the rush." As I spoke, I became aware that my bra strap was not as neatly tucked under my kameez as it should be, and it began to fall over my shoulder in slow motion. Yet to remedy the situation would only draw more attention to my shamelessness. Uncle and beti stood entrapped in an awkward moment. Placing my hand on my stomach, I faked sudden hunger pangs and quietly excused myself.*

*As I was reaching for a second dip of imli chutney, a group of aunties encircled me.*

*"Doesn't she look lovely?" one said.*

*"So, when is your turn coming?" another one asked.*

*"Well, Auntie..."*

*"Come on, it's time a girl of your age got married," a third one remarked.*

*"You know, it's such a shame, a lovely girl like you going to waste..."*

*"Yes, but she's going to be busy studying to be a doctor, isn't that right?"*

*I bit into my samosa in an effort to buy time. I was a painter and a dancer, a spirit traveller and a car mechanic, a sitar player and a pot smoker, a yoga teacher and a lawyer, a swimming instructor and a mother of two, a driving school teacher and a magazine writer, a quilt maker, an avid reader, a closet salsa dancer, a restaurant owner and a CEO with a drawer full of Cuban cigars... I smiled apologetically, indicating my mouth was too full to speak. I caught the gaze of a woman dressed in a blue silk sari who stared at me disapprovingly. She was the only one who had not spoken as yet.*

*"Yes," I muttered, "pre-med."*

*Blue sari auntie looked at me as if she knew all my secrets. And seemed to follow me wherever I went: at school, in the privacy of the bathroom, on a date, in the midst of celebration, in my dreams while I slept. And no matter how hard I tried to fit the image of goodness on the outside, inside my heart skipped away with beats of anxiety, defeat, and swallowed feelings of shame.*

*My world was about the constant negotiation and changing of masks —*
*being able to do what I wanted to do while all the time appearing different.*
*I feared the external discovery of who I really was. Who I really was did not*
*fit into any expectations about Western teenagers or good South Asian girls.*
*It was about being me.*

In my interviews with young South Asian women it became apparent
that parental and community regulation of women's sexuality was tied
into protecting young women from the ills of Western society. All the
women in my study knew how they had to behave in order to be
accepted as "good" daughters and community members. They were all
concerned about their sexual reputations in one way or another and
were very aware that their behaviour has an impact on how their family
is viewed by the rest of the community. In their experience, their reputation, and the resulting family reputation, was closely monitored by
community members: relatives, family friends, and acquaintances.
What struck me as familiar and noteworthy were the lengths to which
we would go to protect our reputations, and the extent to which our
lives were experienced as fragmented. This fragmentation meant that
the codes of femininity we observed outside the home were completely
different to those observed within the family and community. Our
good reputations were always ultimately based on our sexual reputations, although much of the discourse around reputation was embedded in taken-for-granted notions of feminine codes of behaviour;
hence its sexual subtext was often implicit.

## Mis-Uses of the Body

The debates involving women in colonial India are not only a historical example of how women come to represent and maintain cultural
boundaries but the illustration of a process of contestation over

cultural difference. There are continuities between this earlier period of colonialism and nationalism and the present diasporic context. A similar struggle over cultural difference is taking place in Canada. The discursive elements of the struggle over tradition and culture in colonial India, and women's place in that discourse, are comparable to the construction of the culture conflict debate and issues of cultural preservation in the Canadian context. Particular meanings of tradition and culture continue to be mobilized in what can be called a neocolonial context. Specifically, there are parallels between colonial racism and Canadian racism, and the South Asian diaspora mirrors, in significant ways, the Indian nation-state. In the diasporic context young women continue to mark boundaries of cultural difference. These boundaries are maintained through notions of femininity that regulate the body in how it is adorned, what it consumes, and where it goes (meaning women can go only certain places at certain times).

Leslie Roman has argued that the body is a primary site on which notions of femininity are constructed.[1] She shows how bodily consumption and adornment are tied into sexual reputation, and how control of the body is an expression of social control. As a mechanism of social control, "dirtiness" is linked not only to health but also to prevailing cultural norms around order and propriety. Individuals who transgress these are seen as vulgar and bad.[2] Roman applies this theoretical framework to her study of girls in a Catholic high school. She points out that for women, smoking is associated with "low" behaviour, such as alcoholism, and "provocative" dress. It suggests a "looser construction of the body; a body freed to its desires, so to speak, as well as a rejection of the 'little girl,' the niceness, the willingness to get along, the softness" that often characterizes dominant notions of femininity.[3] Roman found that the "'price' of freedom of the body — freedom to be at ease in public arenas, to wear comfortable and casual clothes, to smoke cigarettes — was the loss of a good reputation."

For the young women I interviewed, maintaining a notion of difference from white Canadians is also contingent on notions of appropriate femininity. Like most girls, South Asian teenagers face community sanctions if their conduct does not conform to expected feminine behaviour. Regulations and sanctions are strategies of identification and a means by which community is imagined and produced. It is through the sanctioning of those who transgress the boundaries that communities are constituted as bounded entities. By observing specific norms of conduct, "we" come to feel identity with each other and see ourselves as different from "others."

Most of the women I spoke with defined normative feminine behaviour by things they were not supposed to do: drinking, smoking, doing drugs, and dating boys. What they were expected to do included studying hard, going to family and community gatherings, and helping with domestic duties. For South Asian women, negotiating their femininities doesn't just affect their sexual reputations — it also indicates their degree of allegiance to an ethnic collectivity. The danger of engaging in immoral activities is associated with the outside world. Nina explained that much of her life outside the home was hidden from her parents and that they did not understand or accept many of the things that she wanted to do: "Indian girls are not supposed to drink or smoke or go out, you know. My parents think, well you know, if you go out so much, if you're going to clubs and stuff, it looks so bad on you. Like I know friends whose parents think, well you know, if you go to a club nobody's going to marry you, because you're always going out all the time and you're doing this and that."

Nina shows how the East/West dualism is embedded in codes of feminine behaviour that regulate drinking, smoking, and social (potentially sexual) affiliations. A woman's failure to comply with these codes brands her with an unscrupulous sexual reputation and will eventually inhibit her marriageability. Nina explains how restrictions on freedom of movement and bodily expression are synonymous with being South Asian. Her ethnic identity depends on complying with these restrictions around femininity. Notions of South Asian-ness and femininity are integral to each other, so that transgressing the norms of one category simultaneously destabilizes the other. Later, Nina said about her friends: "They're aware that I am Indian 'cause they, I mean, I feel like I constantly have to explain to them why I am Indian, because of the way my parents are. I have to explain that I can't do this with you, I can't do this with you. Why? Because my parents are Indian and that's why I can't." Here, the restriction of social activities by parents becomes part of what actually defines being South Asian.

The girls I interviewed all explained that most conflicts with their parents revolved around their lack of freedom in general, and going out in particular. What I find most interesting here is how discourses about freedom are constructed and how the girls themselves understand freedom. Nina's comments below substantiate how difference is constructed and used in order to regulate freedom of movement in the public sphere.

> Nina: The big thing I'd say [regarding] conflicts between my parents and me, [they] were always about going out, about going out late at night... It's just the whole thing of the Western culture that [my parents say] "We're not like them, why do you want to be like them?"
>
> Amita: Why do you think that they, your parents, don't want you to go out, is it just because...
>
> Nina: A big reason is that they don't want me drinking. I think the big thing is the guys. They don't want me meeting them and that's what my mom said. Like lately we've been arguing a lot about going out and stuff, and she goes, "If you're going to these like dances, clubs, or whatever, you're going to meet guys and everything." And she doesn't realize that that's never where I meet guys. Like people come up to me in gurdwara [Sikh temple]. Like some guy started phoning from gurdwara. I told her, "You think just because I'm out of your sight means something bad is going to happen."

Nina relays the message that her parents present to her about being different and the importance of maintaining that difference. The public sphere, especially when it is associated with white, Western society, becomes a dangerous space for South Asian women. South Asian spaces are portrayed as innocent while the public realm of white/Canadian/Western becomes a place of impurity. Nina, however, addresses the mythology of this construction. While she does not argue that the non–South Asian spaces that she visits are completely safe, she does point out that South Asian spaces are not as innocent as their parental or community construction suggests. This is an example of mythology functioning as a means to justify regulations around women's freedom of movement outside of community gaze and protection.

Public debate about tensions between parents and children in the early to mid-1990s focused on attending dances. Dances represent a median where adolescent sexuality, culture, femininity, and East-West contestation over cultural difference intersect. I use dances, then, as a point of exploration, an illustration of how these discourses come together and how gender and race work together to regulate and monitor women's sexualities. The day dance discussions about women and sexuality are about an East-West battle. Both white Canada and the South Asian community, in their struggles to assert and maintain cultural boundaries, are enmeshed in discourses about cultural difference that utilize certain notions of women. It is only by identifying the operation and context of these various concepts around femininity and ethnicity that we can begin to understand the complex subject positions that are made available to South Asian adolescent girls, and the processes through which they take up, refuse, or negotiate these positions.

The firebombing of the dance venue already referred to in Chapter 4 served as a catalyst, bringing to the forefront a variety of issues in the South Asian community concerning second-generation youth. For Mr. Pandoori, head of the Dixie Gurdwara, day dances were a direct rebellion against what he perceived as Eastern values. He viewed day dance goers as wanting to adopt the worst of Canadian values, such as "people drinking on Yonge Street, people picking food from the garbage, topless dancers ... they [youth] want rights without fulfilling their duties and obligations that go with them." He also explained: "You think a 14-year-old girl just wants to go to dance? That's not true. When Sikh parents open the *Globe and Mail* or *Star* or the *Sun* and they read that in the Western world 85 percent of students by the age of 18 have had sex, they say my daughter is never going to any goddamn dance, no matter where it is."4

Alka, whose school was most notorious for its day dance goers, explained how the crisis over these dances came about:

> This is what happened. They did articles left, right, and centre. They first did a special on Indian TV which hit off really well. I mean they did a *whole* hour special on daytime dance in which they got video footage of people, and these people obviously got caught ... The program said that these kids lie, skip school, they go out with guys, they go everywhere in miniskirts and they go with makeup and they all look like whores. You wouldn't believe the stuff they did. This went out in every Indian newspaper... all Indian newspapers, *Pakistani Times, India Times, India Today,* Markham paper and they stressed [the schools where] there are more Indians ... It was on local news and stuff and what happened was the parents just went crazy. A lot of people stopped going to daytime dances, people got caught like you wouldn't believe and they even got in more trouble, more troubles at home. Like if our parents called the school and said they want to see our [attendance] records, they had to show the records. So people got caught for all sorts of things just because of that stupid thing. The school got in trouble because they didn't take attendance. You know, like why wasn't attendance taken? But then again, they [the schools] can get themselves out of it but at home you can't.

The day dance controversy represents a locus of various struggles: South Asian youth became the battleground between the family and school in conflicts about authority, accountability, and guardianship. Large numbers of kids, especially from brown schools, would skip classes to attend these dances a couple of times a month and could do so without their parents' knowledge. This was certainly enabling for some girls, who because of particular discourses around freedom and culture found it difficult to go out at night. The day dances emerged as a means to accommodate young heterosexual women and a means to attract young heterosexual men. They served as a good marketing technique for dance promoters who were looking for a way to tap into the youth music market. But the central issue in this controversy was who had the authority to regulate and monitor the daily activities of South Asian youth.

Some schools attempted to take a non-interventionist stance in relation to day dances. While skipping classes is not tolerated by official school policy, it seems that in the case of South Asian youth, administrators, teachers, and truancy officers have tended to overlook unattended classes — particularly in the brown schools. The young women interpreted this lax attitude as stemming from the school authorities' understanding of how strict their parents were, and young people's need for enjoyment, so that a different standard around class attendance was applied to them. School authorities attempted to position themselves on the side of their South Asian students in an effort to protect them from overbearing and traditional parents. For their part, parents felt that the schools were not fulfilling their responsibility to guard and protect their teens from unwanted outside ills.

My interest here is how these concepts of protection operate. The positioning of South Asian girls in Alka's account, for example, demonstrates that the outrage of community members centres not on the safety of the young women, but rather on an erosion of their moral (read traditional) values and conduct. We don't hear about the young men, but rather about "miniskirts," "makeup," and "whores." A subtext of Alka's account is that it was young women, not men, who got caught. The public sphere not only poses a sexual threat for women, but it also provides a space where women can possibly engage with their sexuality and threaten categories of appropriate femininity.

Angela McRobbie points out that because dance is "a popular leisure activity where the female body has been allowed to break free of the constraints of modesty, it has aroused anxiety about sexual play."[5] Salimah told me that the first time she went to a bhangra dance, she was exhilarated. It was the first time she had danced to bhangra music outside her home and in such a large space. She also explained that dancing had become a private act after she entered puberty: "When I was younger and we used to go out to family things, we used to do bhangra in the house. But he [my father] started saying, 'No, you are not allowed to do it in front of men,' so I was not allowed to do it in front of men ... Because I was getting older and he didn't want me dancing in front of men he changed his mind and saw that I shouldn't be dancing in front of them."

Bhangra music and dances stand in opposition to dominant white culture in the struggle for cultural space, as we will see in the next chapter. They also assert girls' resistance to parental attempts to control their sexuality. As Salimah explained: "Most of the girls go to the dances to find guys, Indian guys, 'cause that's the only place to see them. That's the only place where they can do what they want, where they can act the way they feel without their parents lurking over them, watching them."

 Geography of Gender

As mentioned previously, the boundary of ethnicity is often dependent on gender. Characteristics that have become associated with gender serve to carve out ethnic identity and what most often distinguishes one ethnic collective from another are "rules relating to sexuality, marriage and family ... and a *true* member will perform these roles properly" (my emphasis).[6] Gender and ethnicity work together in establishing definitions of identity, and notions of cultural authenticity help to maintain regulations around "appropriate" femininity. This became apparent during the course of these conversations.

My interviews often began with an exploration of school environments, and I used these discussions to explore the young women's sense of ethnic identity vis-à-vis their sense of belonging in relation to other cultural groups. In all of the interviews it was often implicit that they had to be different from "Canadian women," by which they meant white women. I observed the contest between East and West in the various discourses that construct white and South Asian women's sexualities in contrast with one another. I spoke with Salimah, for example, about the various cultural groups in her school, and we began to tease out some of the ways in which South Asian women were located differently from white women in relation to sexuality. In a discussion of stereotypical representations, Salimah said: "Okay, when I see white girls, I can generalize here, most white girls are more giving, like fast sexually, you know. Even though Indian girls aren't [fast], well not all, but I'm just saying they're taught not to be. But I don't think that's enforced in, in you know, white families. I know of this one girl whose mother bought her the pill. That would never happen in an Indian family."

The East-West dualism operates as an organizing category in her talk and she points to the oppositional relationship between brown and white women. Here, brown/white stands in for East/West. Part of what differentiates South Asian and white girls are codes around sexual behaviour and family acceptance of (heterosexual) sexuality: Salimah shows that in order to be seen as good girls, young South Asian women must conform to sexual norms that are not associated with what white girls do.

Within modernity, unresolved fears about modern social progress, anxieties about social change, and the possibility that unregulated freedom could cause moral and social disintegration have been projected onto both youth and women. We have also seen how the West has become synonymous with modernity, while the East is associated with tradition or premodernity. The young women in my study suggest that fears about modern change are manifested in fears about westernization. Within South Asian communities, in the sexualized discourse of East as pure and West as temptress, women are often positioned as sexual by the mere fact of living in the modern West. Salimah talked about how diasporic sexuality is viewed by those "back home."

I'll tell you, I've had one comment made about me by this guy who's seen me at a few places. Guys get scared when they start realizing, oh this girl's kind of cool, and she might know a few people and stuff. And he told someone not to hang around with me 'cause I was a bad influence. And I'm not allowed to turn around and say, "What the hell did you say that for?" and, "You don't know crap about my life." ... Just because I wasn't what he wanted me to be, that typical Pakistani girl. 'Cause *he came from Pakistan but he now lived here and was in an American school, so he wasn't like every Pakistani but he knew about things.* [There's] definitely a double standard. 'Cause I want to meet a really nice sweet guy kind of thing, but once you get them, *they don't want the modern girl, they don't want that girl who could be smart or anything.* They want that girl who's going to do everything for them, whose going to be that typical Indian girl. You know, and that's not what Canada's producing at the moment, I'm not lying. That's another thing, the Pakistani cricket team was here and one of the guys met this girl and phoned her and said, "Oh I want to get with you" and this and that. And she's like, "What do you think I am? *Just 'cause I'm from Canada I'm a slut? Just 'cause I'm from Canada, I'm not your typical one,* so you can turn around and do anything with me?" That's what a lot of Indian girls are getting slack for, just 'cause they're from

Canada, they're modernized and they're not what people want them to be. [my emphasis]

Salimah begins by commenting on how men are threatened by women's independence and popularity. For her, the typical Pakistani girl fits modern colonial notions of South Asian womanhood: servitude, docility, and chastity. A typical Canadian woman, on the other hand, is seen as sexually active and associated with modernity. Modern is defined as both intelligent and sexually promiscuous. There is also a subtext of cultural authenticity; living in Canada makes one less Pakistani than living "back home."

I have quoted this passage at length because it points to several important themes. Salimah's comments indicate that the discourse around sexuality is not just about the relationship between white and brown. Even within the category of "brown" some forms of sexual behaviour are seen as more authentic than others. Let us refer back to Yuval-Davis's claim about the boundaries of ethnic identity being dependent on gender. From Salimah's account we can see that the definition of South Asian is contingent on the degree to which it is associated with the non-West. The non-West is not defined just geographically, however; it is also contingent upon certain sexual codes, whereby women become the territory upon which East is constructed as pure and West as degenerate. This moral discourse views the modern/West as a sexual threat to notions of South Asian femininity and thereby constructs women on a modern terrain as sexually available to men. Salimah's passage maps out Canada as a modern terrain. This terrain is gendered and thus a South Asian girl's mere residency in the modern positions her as a sexual object.

Most of the young women I interviewed commented on how their parents often referenced "back home" as a standard of measure. Statements such as "In Pakistan (or East Africa, or India), women don't behave like that," or the threat of being sent "back," operated as methods of control over women's behaviour. Alka shows how the myth of "back home" works in regulating young women's sexualities. She addresses this myth in relation to upper-class youth culture in India:

> I went to boarding school in India for six months ... And I go back there every year and I know. I mean, Indian girls are far worse than we are. I mean Indian students right now, they are horrible. I mean it's a whole generation of chaos over there ... They've moved on so rapidly that, I mean, we seem primitive to them. I mean girls go out left, right, and centre. Where they go out? To clubs and you name it. The only happening thing right now is big clubs and nice hotels and whatever. They go out for coffee, they come home late nights, even. I'm talking about even in the most decent homes they go out, they go out guys and girls. I mean you should see New Year's, it's a blast there ... But the really funny thing is that when I go back it's like freedom like you wouldn't believe. I get freedom like you wouldn't believe and I enjoy it. That's why I like India a lot, 'cause I get freedom like you wouldn't...

Alka explodes the "back home" myth by revealing that the worst fears about women and the West are actually occurring in the East. The strictness and sexual propriety associated with the homeland are displaced by her account of experiencing more freedom in India itself than she does here in the Toronto diasporic community. Why, then, maintain the fantasy? Because this myth serves as a means to hold on to a notion of protection, purity, and propriety associated with the East. This protection from modernity may be all the way back home, but it serves as a distant standard to aspire to. This myth also justifies the regulation and protection of women on diasporic terrain by giving permission for the reproduction of "Indian" (from India) in Canada.

## 〜 White Lies, Brown Parents

All of the girls I interviewed admitted that they lied to their parents. While most teenagers do not share everything with their parents, I was struck by how instrumental lying is in maintaining the next-to-impossible status of the good South Asian girl. Salimah told me she "had to lie," although she had mixed feelings about it. She explained that her parents viewed her as an innocent, good daughter and that it was very important for her to maintain this image: "I lie to my parents a lot, and if I started thinking that I feel bad about lying then there wouldn't be much to my life. It's kind of like living, doing what you have to do. I do feel bad about lying, but I want to keep my parents happy. If I didn't lie I wouldn't get anywhere. And I do feel bad about lying that much but I'd feel more bad if ... I want to keep my parents happy. I really do. I really look for their approval."

I recall learning about concealment as central to ideas of respect in my own family, when I found a pack of du Maurier cigarettes in my older brother's room. He was smoking but hiding it from my parents. Later that evening, my father lit up a cigar with some friends, a habit he indulged in occasionally. My grandparents were not at home. He was smoking but hiding it from his parents. The next day, I saw my grandfather come inside from an afternoon walk, and I detected the smell of bidis (Indian cigarettes) on his breath. He realized that his secret had been found out. "Shhh, please don't tell anyone," he said. He was smoking but hiding it from everyone! Over time I realized: it was not that nobody knew about each other's smoking, but that not openly engaging in a behaviour that was deemed negative was enmeshed in notions of respect.

For the women I interviewed, lying is used not only to negotiate freedom, but also to uphold the good girl image in the eyes of their parents and the larger South Asian community. Even when family members are aware that their daughters are engaged in activities deemed inappropriate by family and community members, they participate in maintaining the lie. To speak about these activities honestly is considered to be disrespectful. In addition to upholding the image of goodness for family and community, however, with their peers the girls had to negotiate another set of expectations. With friends, they often lied about lying, because they found those who were able to participate more freely in the social world often did not understand the necessity for masking. Lying, it seemed, conformed only too well to the stereotype of the South Asian girl. For example, Nina explained that she could not be open with her white friends about the extent to which she lied to her parents:

> It is easier to turn to them [South Asian friends] than to my other friends sometimes, when they don't understand and I, I feel like I'm being put down, like my own character is being put down... They go, "Why can't you argue with your parents?" And I tell them that I try to. But I feel like they're putting me down... They go, "But why don't you be stronger?" and they don't realize that I'm trying to be really, really strong and they don't understand that and I get really defensive... They go, "Oh but if I was your parents' daughter, they would die, they would-n't last," and I go, "If you were my parents' daughter then you wouldn't be like the way you are now."

In relation to her friends, lying represents not being rebellious enough. Acquiescing to authority is equivalent to docility and does not measure up to the carefree, heroic rebellious image of the west-ernized teenager. And yet for Nina in relation to her parents, telling the truth risks the loss of a good reputation.

Although most girls crossed over the boundaries of proper femi-ninity, many of them did not feel that they were "bad" girls. Yet they knew that in the eyes of their parents they would be seen as disobe-dient or immoral and therefore un-Indian. Defining South Asian femininity as synonymous with the restrictions around self-determination that I have spoken about leaves very little room for a self-definition that describes the reality of the young women's lived experiences. I found that young women were able to negotiate their freedom and sexual reputations through the use of clothing. Lying, in this case, takes the form of masking and manipulating femininity. Salimah described her relationship to clothing:

> They [parents] don't mind me wearing normal clothes and everything. The only thing they don't like is ripped jeans, anything that is tight. I'm not allowed to wear shorts, all that kind of stuff. One story, it was in the summer, I was in shorts and all of a sudden I see my dad at the end of the driveway and I started waving to my dad [instinctively] and he started driving by and then I realized. So I jumped into a bush and I changed and my friend's just watching me and watching my dad driving by, and I changed in the bush, in the mud and everything, and I got up and she said, "Ahh, he's gone," and I'm like, "Oh shit, oh well" [laughter].7

In her study of working-class girls in England, Susan Lees showed that young women walk a tightrope in order to negotiate their reputations.8 She argues that both "good" girls and "bad" girls stake out their femininity through clothing. Good girls must negotiate the next-to-impossible line between adhering to the ideals of beauty and attractiveness and appearing too sexual. In my conversation with Tina and Pam we talked at length about their parents and the issue of freedom. They described their parents as less strict than most, explaining that because their parents were separated they had more freedom than many South Asian girls. They lived with their mother, who was "more reasonable" and "tolerant" than their father. In talking about sexual reputations, they pointed to how dress conveys certain meanings around traditional and modern, good girls and bad girls:

Tina: Well okay, you have your modern Indian girl and the traditional... Okay, if you see like the traditional Indian girl, they're more like, okay, study well, do what your parents say, and there's lots of them. I'm talking the traditional Indian girl.

Pam: Okay there's this girl... We went to Square One one day, I saw her walking into the mall with her father, plain face okay? When we saw her in the mall later on, she left her father and she was wearing bright red lipstick and makeup and everything, and I bet she like washes her face by the time she goes and sees her dad again, and goes home like nothing happened. And I see this girl go to dances and...

Tina: Ahh, she's pretty, ahh, promiscuous.

The sisters indicate how girls manipulate their femininity through fashion in order to suit the dictates of a particular context. For the girl they discuss, the mall represents a public space where she negotiates contradictory codes of femininity. Her dilemma is similar to Salimah's description of changing clothes in the bushes. The fear of getting caught by her father translates into getting caught for wearing makeup that transgress the boundaries of appropriate femininity. The trouble is, of course, that appropriate femininity is defined differently in other social spaces, to which these young women also wish to belong.

Pam and Tina negotiate the good girl/bad girl framework by masking parts of their identity:

Tina: And I don't even have respect for girls who do that [wear something provocative], especially being Indian, because being Indian you're not supposed to do that. Like my dad, right, he doesn't say anything, he doesn't say much about anything, but with clothes and stuff

if he really doesn't like what we're wearing he'll be, like,
you know, "Why are you wearing that, take it off. You
know you're not supposed to wear things like that."

Amita: Like, do you sometimes feel embarrassed wearing
certain things in front of your dad?

Tina: Yeah, I don't, yeah, we change later that's what we do.

[later in the interview]

Tina: Well not every, like, okay, Indian, Indian values for a
girl, okay, not boys, boys can do whatever they want,
right? But the girls, the girls first of all they have to
dress properly, second of all they have to speak properly, they have to do well in school.

Amita: What is dressing properly?

Tina: Respectfully, conservatively, like not totally, completely
wild or anything like that and...

Pam: And you know they have to act, it's also the way they act
and keep their reputation good, and I think it's important for a girl because when time comes for her to get
married, then, you know, she has to have a good name.

The contradictions inherent in these two sets of expectations around
femininity can be seen in the discrepancy between Tina and Pam's own
behaviour and the judgment they place on other girls for doing the
very same thing. They described the woman in the mall as promiscuous because, as well as wearing makeup, she also visits forbidden public
spaces, such as dances. They tie in their discussion about proper feminine behaviour with a comment about cultural boundaries: "being
Indian, you're not supposed to do that." Yet, they too admit to changing their clothes for their father. Later, they reveal the double standard
between permissible feminine and masculine behaviour. They define
traditional/typical Indian women as studious, compliant, respectful,
and conservative. Several times they made it a point to emphasize that

they were not "your typical Indian girl," a category that excludes them from possibilities of teenage rebellion and defiance.

Sexuality has been central to discourses around adolescence. According to Christine Griffin, medical and psychological discourses reflect the uniquely sexualized nature of adolescence as a construct, and historical analyses demonstrate that sexuality has been established as "a social institution in which heterosexuality was defined as normal, compulsory and a mark of maturity, resting on the representation of femininity and masculinity as complimentary opposites."9 From the girls' comments above, we can see how notions of sexuality are tied into concerns about securing heterosexual relationships. Reputations affect future access to the institution of marriage. The discourse of the good South Asian girl is, of course, similar to most prescriptive discourses about "good girls" — listening to your parents and doing well in school — yet here part of the message about feminine regulation is hidden under a message of cultural preservation.

Some young women saw marriage as an escape from parental regulation. Alka, when asked what advice she would give to South Asian girls about how to deal with the lack of freedom in their lives, said, "For all the experiences that I have been through for being sixteen ... the one thing I can say is that, and this is truthfully, I really think that either if you have the guts and if you had everything set up for you I would run away... I would never run away to the streets or anything but like if you have another home to go to or so forth or you should plan to get married." Interestingly enough, in an interview a year later, Alka confided that due to pressure to get married to a boy she had originally liked but then began to dislike, she ran away from home a week before the wedding. The events in her own life led her to question the idea of marriage as an escape from parental control.

While lying helps young women gain more freedom, it also helps them negotiate their reputations. Lying gives them some control over their reputations at home and school. While the emotional cost of "living lies" is extremely high for these young women, for many

South Asian women honesty is too high a price to pay. It carries the risk of exclusion from the definition of "South Asian." Walking this tightrope of upholding community identity in a white dominant context brings with it a tremendous amount of emotional stress. Constantly masking or hiding parts of the self which are not accepted either by the world of peers or parents has a serious negative effect on self-esteem and self-worth. It is seldom that all the parts of the self can be celebrated, approved of, and accepted.

Defiance of adulthood is manifested for youth in terms of challenging and defying authority. For young women this takes place on the sexual terrain, manipulating their femininities and transgressing expected codes of behaviour. In its narrative of womanhood, the South Asian community draws on nationalist constructions of femininity that are in direct opposition to discourses around teens in the West. While white girls may defy social norms around growing up through dress and "sexual deviance" (i.e., sexual expression), for South Asian girls rebellion against the responsible adult citizen narrative is also seen as a defiance of cultural identity and a disloyalty to ethnic membership. South Asian girls in Canada have to negotiate contradictory messages about their sexuality. On the one hand, they "get slack" because they are modernized; not being "typical" makes them open to assumptions about their sexual availability. On the other hand, being South Asian in Canada automatically sets them up as sexually unavailable in relation to dominant white culture. According to the latter, the typical South Asian girl is a patriarchal construction of docility and passivity. Her subjectivity is depersonalized and disregarded by a discursive construction that locates her as a victim within a cultural problematic only. While these narratives regulate and limit the lives of young South Asian women, I would like to place them within the wider context of Canadian racism. An allegiance to certain authentic notions of tradition and culture is also a means by which to articulate a standpoint against a racist and assimilationist white Canadian society. In this sense diaspora is a complex and overlapping space: it disrupts some normative categories while simultaneously reproducing others.[10] In the context of negative or absent representations, notions of South Asian cultural authenticity also serve as a powerful site of resistance.

Parental discourses of authority with respect to young South Asian women are culturalized. Colonial notions of South Asian femininity, characterized by chastity, domesticity, and docility, persist as a standard of measure that actually defines the boundaries of what it means to be South Asian. While Partha Chatterjee argues that nationalist discourses during the colonial period sought to mark a distinction between modernization and westernization, in the diasporic context this distinction is less consequential.[11] Modernization within the West is in essence westernization. Within the diasporic context, then, the need to protect women from the "modern/Western" is heightened by its proximity. The modern/West is not just a theoretical threat or a relationship that comes out of global international economic and political ties. For the South Asian community, residing in the lap of the West brings new dimensions to the fears associated with modern change.

# CHAPTER SIX

# A Patch of "Indian":
## Music, Fashion, and Dances

*A*fter some time, my cousin from India and I bid farewell to parents and family friends. "We have to do some homework at a friend's house," I explained calmly. In my excitement to leave I forgot I had to take the subway home. Halfway down the street I felt the dread of public transport in a salwar kameez. I stopped, wondering if I could go through with it, but decided I had to snatch the bit of freedom that was now at my disposal. I waited on the platform and made myself invisible by making those around me disappear. I stood enveloped in my own shield, keeping my eyes away from any human contact. The alarm of the subway doors closing snapped me out of my statue-like position and I jumped on. I felt the weight of stares on me and my chunni fell. But this time, the falling garment accentuated my brownness. My shield did not seem to work, there were too many eyes to dissolve. My cousin moved freely. She did not grow up with glares as a form of measurement in the same way that I had. As we stepped off the subway, someone shouted, "It's not Halloween!"

I reached home and changed my clothes, replacing the outfit with a tight tank top and pants. At school, every one of my friends had been asked out on a date except for me. But tonight I was going to a South*

*Asian dance. At these dances, I felt noticed the way I wanted to be. My friends and I had been planning for weeks, working like bees, buzzing on the telephone line, networking and planning. Chipping away. Slowly convincing mothers and fathers to let us go. Some lie, some are able to tell the truth.*

*We take over the old basement of a school or community hall. The dull surroundings are overcome by sparkling anticipation. In the background plays the latest Michael Jackson hit. Someone serves pop, or samosas and alcohol if they are lucky. The boys sit on one side of the room, the girls on the other. The room is full of us — all South Asian teenagers.*

Except for the community hall and the music, most of it seems the same in 2001. Crowded, loud tunes, and lots of young people hanging out. In the more recent version, the venue is a two-storey club. The latest Michael Jackson hit is still in the background, but with it you will hear Punjabi folk, Pakistani qawwali, and the most recent Hindi film soundtrack, mixed to the backbeats of reggae, hip-hop, house, or R&B. The dance movements differ, however, from the ones I remember. Young men climb on the shoulders of others. Young women dance in bunches, swirling their arms and bodies like Hindi film heroines.

I remember being in Ferozepur in 1970, at age seven. Sitting on the lap of an unfamiliar relative, dizzy, I watched my grandmother twirl with grand-aunts in a circle, arms in the air. My Mataji, the one with the most energy, danced in the middle of the ring surrounded by the other women. Traces of what I saw thirty years ago in a small town on the Indo-Pakistani border are visible to me in the movements of the young women in the big clubs of Toronto.

While I was growing up, the sense of community we celebrated existed within an enclave that was separated from the public sphere. Functions and cultural celebrations were commemorated among a small group of friends at somebody's home. This, of course, has greatly changed over the years in form, content, and venue. The first time I heard bhangra music in a mainstream club downtown was in 1992.[1] I was awestruck by the memory of old Hindi film soundtracks that I grew up listening to at home or in the homes of my parents' friends. During my teenage years, my relationship to this music was far from harmonious. The music represented the kind of environment that separated me from my (white) friends, the kind of sound that, if I could, I would erase from every corner of the house, along with all other cultural markers that reminded me of difference, backwardness, and inferiority. But it was also part of my psyche, my memory bank, my background noise, imprinted with home, family, and childhood. When British DJ Ritu played at the Rivoli in Toronto in 1992, hearing this music brought with it an inner stir I cannot quite describe. The club was crowded with "mis-timers" like me, those who grew up without any South Asian signifiers. This place was saturated with desis[2] and there was an indescribable solace in numbers, a silent celebration and anguish for all the years when this overt merrymaking was not possible. Part of this celebration also came from the intermix of sounds, sounds that were also part of my nostalgic fabric: rock, disco, and R&B. For a moment all the separate parts and fragments of self seemed to merge.

South Asian popular culture represents both a possibility and a limitation: possibility, because the terrain of popular culture grants us the prospect of negotiating subject positions that assert their racial identity and resist colonial notions of tradition and culture; limitation, because this terrain is problematic for its reproduction of universalistic notions of community. While the eruption of South Asian music in the West has helped to create a brown signifier for second-generation youth, this signifier tends to fall within a unifying framework because it remains predominantly Punjabi, Sikh, or Hindi/Hindu.[3] Asian fusion music provides a space of resistance, but it also reproduces nationalist notions of identity and obscures the dynamics of gender.

For second-generation immigrants in Canada, the problematic of Canadian identity is often manifested in the overlap between inclusion and exclusion in both the community and the definition of "Canadian." I, for example, while having for the most part grown up in Canada, did not give up my Indian citizenship for Canadian citizenship until I was thirty-six. India does not recognize dual citizenship. Not exercising my right to Canadian citizenship in some ways grew out of not being included in the image of the community of Canadians.4 I was never assumed to be Canadian and I never felt Canadian, whatever I imagined that would be. Similarly, Chandra Mohanty explains her contradictory relationship to "home" in her refusal to relinquish her Indian passport. This refusal opens up questions and reflections about home and belonging: "What is home? The place where I was born? Where I grew up? Where my parents live? Where I live and work as an adult? Where I locate my community — my people? Who are 'my people'? Is home a geographical space, an historical space, and emotional, sensory space?"5

On the issue of identity, Mohanty writes, "Obviously I was not South Asian in India — I was Indian. What else could one be but 'Indian' at a time when a successful national independence struggle had given birth to a socialist democratic nation-state."6 She explains that her succession of labels have included "Indian," "foreign student," "student of colour," "resident alien," and "expatriate Indian citizen."

In the past few years, unravelling the concept of home and problematizing my association to "back home" has made me rethink my connection to Canadian-ness. Part of this has come out of visits to India, where a glorified notion of home and community was supplanted by the reality of disturbing class disparities and increasing Hindu fundamentalism. Added to this social and political awareness has been the personal experience of disconnection as an outsider, a foreign-born expatriate Indian living in Canada. When I went to renew my Indian passport recently, I was informed by a new passport officer that I was not eligible for renewal until I renounced my British citizenship. I looked across at a man dressed in a grey suit shuffling papers on a big desk and explained, "I have never been a British citizen."

He held on to his fountain pen, slowly removed his glasses and emphasized, "It doesn't matter, Madam, you were born there and that gives you the right to be one. You need to renounce this right before..." At this point, I was frustrated and shocked.

"You have always known I was born there. I have had Indian citizenship my whole life."

The officer began taking a call, covered the phone piece and said, "I'm sorry, Madam, the rules are the rules."

Having held on to my Indian citizenship for many years out of a sense of loyalty, despite the fact that it made worldwide travel more difficult, I became stateless. I was neither Indian, British, nor Canadian. It became clear in that moment that my allegiance and loyalty to Indian citizenship was irrelevant. My sense of belonging (or lack thereof) was reduced to a matter of arbitrary bureaucracy.

As I have previously discussed, the East-West battle over cultural difference is manifested and (re)produced in the Canadian/Indian dichotomy. For second-generation South Asians living in Canada, this binary is emblematic of a series of misnomers. Mohanty, as a first-generation migrant to the United States, writes that in relation to the "home question," she is still unsatisfied with her own response. For second-generation South Asians, even more than for their parents, who can claim an identity based on at least some notion of birthright and nationality coinciding with geographical location, the question of naming is onerous. The answer is even more complex for those whose migration may have begun from the subcontinent (in generations past) but whose contemporary route to North America is via Africa or the Caribbean. For me, the question "Where are you from?" was further complicated when I began to share my home between Canada and the Caribbean. After taking a big deep breath, I often found myself answering, "My parents are from India, I was born in London, England, I grew up in Canada, and I now live between Toronto and Tobago, between here and there." This was often too much information for a question meant for quick referencing and usually lost the interest of the seeker. I have realized that for second-generation immigrants, the question "Where are you from?" follows no matter where we go, where we choose to reside, or where we claim allegiance to. Neither Canadian nor South Asian adequately describes our identity. Nisha attempted to explore her association to being Canadian:

Amita: Back to the identity. So if someone asked, "What are you?" what would you say?

Nisha: I'd say I'm Ismaili Muslim. I wouldn't be ashamed to say it, like a lot of people think I'm Spanish, Portuguese or something. They look at me and don't know what I am. But I tell them, I go, "Yeah, I'm Ismaili Muslim," and they ask me where I'm from [and] I say East Africa. Like I'm not ashamed to say it, like not at all.

Amita: Do you see yourself as Canadian, Ismaili Muslim, East African?

Nisha: If someone said where are you from, I'd say East Africa. I wouldn't say Canada. Even though I'm born here I'd say East Africa 'cause that's like where we're from, and if they asked the religion I'd say Ismaili.

Amita: So would you under any circumstances call yourself Canadian or do you feel that doesn't really describe who or what you are?

Nisha: I don't. I think if I was like in India or something. Like when I was in India I said, "Yeah, I'm Canadian." But if I'm here I wouldn't say, "Yeah, I'm Canadian," 'cause to me, like, everybody's Canadian, but like, there's different parts of being a Canadian. Like I'm a Canadian, but I'm from East Africa. That wouldn't help them much. Like when I went to India, about a month ago, people would ask, "Where [are] you from?" And I'd say, "Yeah, I'm from Canada, I'm Canadian," and that would help them more see who I am.

Nisha shows that being Canadian is relational. Because it is a raced category, being Canadian for her makes sense only outside of Canada, in much the same way that being South Asian for Mohanty makes sense only outside of India. Nisha points to the complexity of her identification: the term *Canadian* does not reflect "the different parts" of who she takes herself to be. Its definition is not inclusive of "Ismaili Muslim East African." She recognizes her difference and feels a need to be specific about her Canadian identity. While "Canadian" is constantly contested for second-generation South Asian youth, so is "Indian." Take Rupinder, for example — while she does not relinquish her Indian identity altogether, her attempt to hold on to it creates contradictory subject positions:

Rupinder:    Well, when I answer [the question of my Indian identity] I might be contradicting myself, but it's just, well, being Indian, I guess it just goes back to what I said about how your parents bring you up. And if you go by their beliefs or rules: like I believe in a lot of things that my parents say but I don't, like, you've got to compromise. Like being Indian is, see it's hard to explain, like being traditional but not being too traditional, like you've got to bend your back sometimes. You've got to know who you are but where you're living.

Amita:       So what do you mean by traditional?

Rupinder:    Well, being religious. But not to the point like... Being traditional. Knowing what your roots are I guess and where you're from and being able to do your paht [prayers] and your prayers and just knowing your customs and knowing your mother tongue too. 'Cause if you're talking to your aunts and uncles they're going to think you're stupid, you know. Is that deep enough?

Amita:      Just say someone came to you who didn't know Punjabi or Hindi and wasn't religious, but still said they were Indian. What would you say to that?

Rupinder:   I'd say yeah, you're Indian, 'cause I guess, your skin colour. But no one, even if you're in India, I don't think anyone is a pure Indian, Indian, Indian, you know what I mean? Again it just goes back to, yeah, I'd say you're Indian but I guess I'd consider them obviously first generation... And just how much you're influenced by Western society that makes you... I'd still consider them Indian. Being Indian isn't all just being religious, you know what I mean, 'cause I consider myself a religious person but I don't show it. Like I'm not going to try to prove something just to make my point, like if I know I am, I am. And if I do what I'm supposed to be doing the way I was taught to do it, then I know I'm doing it and I guess it's just for me to know.

Rupinder moves from a definition of "Indian" that equates it with "traditional," to a sense of tradition that acknowledges her diasporic location, to a definition rooted in the knowledge of language and observance of religious rituals, to, in the final instance, being the autonomous subject who fashions her own Indian identity. She positions herself as traditional but then quickly realizes that her cultural practices are different from those of her parents, who set the standard for what "Indian," "religious," and "traditional" mean. (Earlier in the interview, for example, Rupinder had explained that she was religious but not a vegetarian like her mother.) She then retracts her statement equating traditionalism with religion. Her dilemma is that she identifies herself as Indian, equates this identity with tradition and then realizes that she falls outside of the very definition that she has created. The contradictions here in part reflect the inadequacy of binary categories in accounting for her sense of identity. Rupinder ends up negotiating between them in order to locate a different notion of traditional, modern, and Indian.

In the last chapter we saw how the kind of femininity that has come to represent ethnic identity in the South Asian context leaves very little room for a self-identity that adequately describes the complex reality of young women living in Canada. Notions of womanhood are enmeshed in an idea of cultural difference that defines culture as fixed and unchanging. According to this construction, change or modification in "normal" cultural practices precludes an allegiance to South Asian identity. Since the early 1990s, many second-generation South Asian youth have been challenging this notion of cultural authenticity through the production of music and dances. Expressions of popular culture created by South Asians, especially in the U.K. and Toronto, have helped to negotiate a brown signifier in a Canadian and British context that is predominantly saturated with a white aesthetic. For example, Pam talked about the absence of brown in the public sphere:

Amita:  How would you compare going to one of those [bhangra] dances to a rock 'n' roll bar downtown?

Pam:    Now if we were to go to a bar, we wouldn't go to a white bar, 'cause we wouldn't get noticed. See the problem is no matter what, we are brown, okay. We do not fit in with white people. I don't think I find myself comfortable in a bar, like a white bar, instead of like a brown dance. I mean what's the point in going to a club where you don't know anybody and you feel like an outsider, when you can go to a place where you walk in and people will say hi to you when you say hi to them, and you enjoy yourself, you know, like good friends, you know.

In many ways, the second-generation diasporic population is invisible and unidentifiable in relation to existing definitional categories of "Canadian." Their representational quest is about strategies of self-identification that account for the complexity, rather than homogeneity, of human identity. The terrain of popular culture is one place where this negotiation of specificity is taking place.

## Bangles and Bhangra Bashes

In the early to mid-1990s, bhangra music exploded into the Canadian market. The public visibility of bhangra dances and music goes hand in hand with the public visibility of what some have referred to as a South Asian youth culture, a distinct fashion and style. This particular cultural production in some ways mirrored the bhangra explosion in England that began in the late 1980s and has captured the attention of both the South Asian community and the white mainstream.

Leading the way into the mainstream was Apache Indian, who in 1990 released his single, "Movie over India" and then in 1995, the album *Make Way for the Indian*. While earlier U.K. groups like Alaap, Premi, and Apna Sangeet consisted of first-generation migrants singing about displacement and alienation, the 1990s collection of music in Toronto, dominated by disc jockeys and the art of remixing rather than an ensemble of musicians, conveys a message about placement. DJ names, such as Asian Empire, Asian Boyz Club, and DJ Guru, suggest an in-your-face racial presence. Cassette and CD titles sometimes reference the subcontinent, as in *Bollywood* or *Bombay Dance,* and include names like *The Empire Strikes Back, Stardust: An Asian Scandal, Judgement Night,* and *One Nation Equals Justice.*[7] If you look closely at the back of one of these cassettes, you just might find the legend "Made in Brameladesh" (i.e., Bramalea). In reference to regions of greater Metropolitan Toronto, you may also hear an occasional Brownton for Brampton and Singhdale for

Springdale. Along with the music also came what some referred to as "gangs": PM (Punjabi Mafia), PWA (Pakis with Attitude), and Khanda Queens. The music, like the generation, is not easily classifiable and not "pure" anything — not quite black nor white nor brown. Asian fusion has incorporated the influence of black musical sounds and at times mimics its trademarks — MC Hammer becomes MC Rootz and Naughty by Nature is recast as Punjabi by Nature.

A subtext to this scene of music and fashion is, of course, a valiant celebration of racial identity. Most young South Asians have participated in this new fusion of music, which speaks more directly to their sensibility as "hybrid" than the music of their parents' generation. In the 1990s, bhangra captured the attention of South Asian community members, many of whom disliked the fusion, which they saw as tampering with authenticity in its remixing of classic Hindi film and Punjabi folk songs.

Fashion, along with music, has become an important marker of identity for South Asian youth. Salimah explained the complexity of negotiating between different ethnic symbols:[8]

> Salimah: Well I've noticed that Indian guys, most of them dress hip-hoppy. They all wear hats, a lot of them have goatees. And a lot of them, all the Sikhs, all wear karas, like silver bracelets, and most of the Hindus will wear something around their necks. Like they want people to know, this is who I am. Or Muslims, like me, wear the Allah sign, but I've been wearing this since I was a kid though. Or they will wear, like, things drawn on their jackets. Like there's one guy who has "Pure Punjab" written on the back of his jacket. Like a lot of Indians do do that just to identify them. Especially in the Indian crowd they want people to know, I am Indian, you know, that I'm not, you know.
>
> Amita: What about the girls?

Salimah: The girls, most of the girls dress, like the younger ones dress a certain style, like wide pants and nice suede jackets or plaid jackets, and nose rings. They all have nose rings, to let people know they're Indian. But most of the Indian girls wear clubby kind of stuff, they're just dressing cliquey or houser kind of.

The terrain of fashion and appearance for South Asian girls is a contested one because it oscillates between multiple meanings and contexts. For example, Pinki described the difficulty in negotiating her own identity:

He [her father] said, "Well, are you going to come home with me or stay at the dance?" And at that time I had the khanda [a Sikh symbol] on my jacket and he told me to take it off, you know [because I wanted to stay at the dance and am therefore not respectful enough to wear the khanda]. But I can't take it off because it doesn't come off. But you know I'm proud to be a Sikh, but there's other things, like, as you can see, my bangs are cut. But you know religion is something totally different than your nationality. Like my father was saying that Sikhism is more religious, and that a true Sikh, you know, they pray and their lifestyle is much more different. You know Punjabi should be more appropriate because that's what you are, you know, Punjabi not Sikh, like I guess Christians and Catholics, which is true. But, you know, I'm proud to be Indian and everything, but to me what I do, because I cut my hair and you know I have a nose ring it doesn't mean that I'm trying to put my religion down. But it does seem like I am. It just means that that's the way I feel comfortable. And its not because you know other kids are teasing me. You know in junior high a lot of kids have teased me about "your hair," oh you know, "Your hair is so long, chop it off." You know sometimes I felt bad, but then other

times I thought, oh, they're just jealous. And nowadays I get a
lot of compliments and stuff [about my hair].

Wearing the khanda places Pinki in the midst of a struggle over meaning. In the eyes of her father, the khanda is a religious text alone, not
meant for secular public display. His argument rests on an understanding of authenticity and essential meaning. Placing the khanda symbol
on a jacket transgresses a religious boundary. Here the struggle is between
her father's context and the context of a predominantly Christian society. For Pinki, articulating her own meaning and subject position in
wearing the khanda emphasizes her difference from white dominant
culture and is a prideful assertion of Punjabi Sikh identity. Pinki articu-
lates her own meanings and subject position as she negotiates between
a white context where she says, "I am proud," and another where she
says, "Just because I apply this symbol in a non-religious context does
not mean I am not respectful of where it comes from."

Pinki also explains that cutting her bangs is not because of shame.
While in the past she was teased about her long hair (long hair being
one of the tenets of Sikh tradition), she now chooses to modify her
hair in a way that mixes religious representation with her own brand
of femininity. Pinki's statements also indicate the contradictions
between religious and ethnic identities. While the two are almost
inseparable in the case of Sikh identity (there are few non-Punjabi
Sikhs, except for the denomination of white Sikhs in parts of North
America), she attempts to forge a distinction between them. She
explores the idea of a non-religious identity that does not, in her
mind, foreclose her affiliation to being Punjabi.

South Asian dances, like fashion, also serve as a means of asserting
racial identity and claiming cultural space. Salimah described how she
feels dancing to South Asian music: "I have so much fun dancing to
bhangra. I can't even explain this one feeling inside, that you're dancing and nobody else understands what you are saying — it's just this
feeling of pride. It's just the same I guess for Jamaican people when

they hear reggae. Bhangra, I just cannot get enough of it. I love dancing to it. I mean in English it's fine and everything, but when you hear an Indian song it's just like, yeah, I want to get down to it and bhangra just makes you do it, I mean you just go crazy to it." Part of the feeling of pride comes from the act of exclusion, which in the context of white dominant culture says, "This is something *you* can't understand." The reversal of exclusion provides a sense of power. Thus this space is not about segregation alone, but also an act of celebration, a moment of cultural self-identification, a marking-out of *our* social territory.

Similarly, Alka explained why she likes bhangra: "Yeah, you can relate to it better. I mean I call myself a freak child sometimes because I'm an extraordinary Indian than I am any other way. I mean I love Indian music, Indian movies, and I know everything, you know the stars and everything. I follow Indian movies, I don't follow English movies, so I'm really, really Indian. For me to hear that [kind of music] relates to me more than me hearing Western music because I wouldn't know the difference from the next one so I can relate to Indian music more [laughter]." Alka shows her reference point to be brown rather than white. She reverses the stereotype of ethnic difference that treats non-white ethnicity as homogeneous. For her it is white music that seems all the same. She places her affiliation to bhangra music in a wider context of South Asian signifiers, which to her largely consists of Indian pop icons. The authenticity of her Indian identity rests on the consumption of popular culture. For her, listening to Indian music and movies makes her more Indian.

Tina explained that feeling "very comfortable and very, like, popular and powerful" was one of her reasons for liking bhangra dances. Part of what makes these brown spaces more desirable is the contrast to white spaces, which many of the young women experienced as unfamiliar and uncomfortable. The level of comfort is seen as contingent upon knowing people and feeling accepted. It is the context of white dominant culture and these girls' exclusion from it that makes brown dances a relatively more comfortable space. I am using the word *relatively* quite deliberately here, because brown spaces were also fraught with tension, at times, for these young girls.

The eruption of bhangra music and dance can obviously be read as a reaction to a predominantly white aesthetic. It can also be understood, however, as a disruption of a homogeneous reading of South Asian identity. It calls attention to the diversity of subject positions, thereby accounting for diasporic locations which reflect the "cut 'n' mix": destabilizing Canadian national identity by drawing on Western popular music, mixing in "back home" references and African-Canadian traditions. In its public visibility as well as its unsettling of stereotypical representations of South Asian-ness, bhangra challenges the definitions of both "Canadian" and "South Asian."

Ali Rattansi has described the music of Apache Indian as an illustration of postmodern rap. He argues that Apache Indian breaks essentialist notions of (South Asian) identity by pulling on African diasporic sounds and by challenging the cultural practices of his own community. Rattansi substantiates his claims by referencing three songs: "in songs like 'Arranged Marriage,' 'Sharabi' (alcoholic) and 'Caste System' [Apache Indian] challenges cultural practices among the British South Asian communities which subordinate women, valorize hard-drinking and displays of masculinity, and reinforce boundaries of caste, class and ethnicity."9

In many ways Apache Indian has all the trappings of a postmodern rapper. He combines Punjabi, patois, and English and sings to a reggae backbeat that sometimes merges, briefly, with a segment of South Asian classical tabla (drums), or the Punjabi dhol (drum). He positions himself as an educator (in "Come Follow Me") and his songs often start with a revelatory invitation to a multiple audience: South Asian youth or community members, white, or black, depending on the content of the message. He is one of the few South Asian artists who has referred to marginalized segments of the South Asian community, such as the Sri Lankan population (the "Tamil Posse," for example, in the song "No Problem") as well as including all the religious groups that comprise the diaspora. His songs often begin with a salutation in the various languages to the Sikh, Hindu, and Muslim communities. Apache Indian has also dealt with issues that are often publicly ignored. In "Aids Warning," he addresses young South Asian men in a message that advocates "safe sex" (and monogamy) rather than the usual rhetoric of abstinence. In "Drink Problems" he makes direct connections between male alcoholism, the neglect of family responsibilities, and the mistreatment of women. Most recently in 2002, he has publicly aligned himself with issues of racism and the failures of the justice system in his song "Free Satpal Ram." [10]

However, some of his messages in relation to women are stereotypical. In a plea for an understanding of the tradition of "Arranged Marriage," Apache Indian summons his audience (presumably a non-Asian one) to learn about the workings of an arranged union. While he attempts to break stereotypical representations by enlightening his listeners about the process of arranged marriage, he also reproduces certain normative notions of womanhood, playing into archetypal female images in his desire and search for the perfect female. She is pretty, like a "princess," knows Punjabi, has the "right figure," is adorned with Indian eyeliner and is wearing "traditional" Punjabi dress. She will also serve him, look after him, and make him roti.

Bhangra, the music and the dances, is a male-dominated cultural production and space. The youth culture that surrounds it remains largely reflective of a male/masculine aesthetic. Pragna Patel argues that "youth activity generates a culture which appears autonomous from the rest of the community. Yet, as the experiences of women indicate, that culture is a mirror reflection of values sanctioned in the family and the community at large." [11]

The young women that I interviewed described the contradictory nature of this cultural space. While many of them like the music and dances for their inclusion of racial/cultural location, their sexualities continue to be monitored and regulated. For example, Zarah explained why she didn't go:

Zarah:    I'm really scared. I've had so many chances and I have a ride home, a ride there, but I would never do it.

Amita:    What makes you scared of it?

Zarah:    It's just rumours you get, right? You go to one club and you get what, forty rumours. Because I haven't even been to a club and I've got so many rumours otherwise and that, right?

Amita:    Oh, about your reputation?

Zarah:    Yeah, but it's all lies, right, so...

Tina elaborated on the kind of reputation women who go to these clubs develop: "There are a lot of guys, like, if they see a girl — this is not every guy, some guys, you know, like the ones that want a long-term relationship — they'd never have a long-term relationship with somebody that they met at a club 'cause they think she's, like, a slut. You know, she goes out at night."

The dances are largely promoted and organized by male DJs who hold them in the daytime or offer free admission to women in order to attract women to the space for the predominantly male clientele that attend them. As Tina points out, however, the women who do frequent these clubs acquire the stigma of being too sexual. The movement of women in the public sphere at night leads to assumptions about the looseness of their sexuality. In this sense, this space reproduces dominant notions about South Asian femininity, whereby good South Asian girls are supposed to follow the dictates of modesty and chastity.

In addition to sanctions and normative modes of feminine conduct, young women also confront various forms of sexual harassment in these spaces. Salimah revealed this kind of male-female dynamic: "[My friends and I] were walking by a club and these guys are like calling out to us. It's embarrassing, like I don't find it flattering at all. I'm the kind of person who doesn't put up with shit, though, like what guys do. 'Cause I've had guys come up to me and go, 'Hey baby I'd like to rub my thing.' Fuck off, I don't need to put up with shit like that, I think it's disgusting." Groups of young South Asian men have sometimes used their collective power to control and threaten women in these spaces. When violence erupts, it is usually between men as an expression of male contestation over female "territory" (as in, "You were looking at my girl"). Sometimes, however, women themselves become the targets of sexual violence, as in Pam and Tina's story:

Tina: What happened was, there were no bouncers there, so all the Punjabi guys lost control, and from what I heard guys were going around grabbing girls and stuff like that, and girls were like crying 'cause they didn't know what to do. You know, like they had no control and that's the scary part, when a girl does not have control. But the thing is that nobody blamed the girl or the guy. They just go, "Oh well, they got the power to do it so they can do it."

Amita: So no one questioned it or said that obviously something's wrong?

Pam: Nothing. It happened once. The fact that they had control over that dance 'cause basically they were PM [Punjabi Mafia] guys and they can do it and get away with it and nobody can stop them. Like nobody could even say anything to them, otherwise they get punched out.

Tina: If PM is ever involved, they usually get blamed for everything.

Pam: Because it usually is them.

Tina: There's nothing anybody can do about it, 'cause that's what they do. I mean I dated a guy that was part of that group and he's not anymore and they're like, they mean business, you know. If they really want to hurt somebody, they can kill somebody. Absolutely seriously, they can kill somebody. And that's the scary part of it because they represent... nobody. I don't think white people look at it

|        | as if, oh they're Punjabis, or they're Sikhs, or whatever. They're Indians, you know, so we all get a bad name even if you're Muslim, even if you're, whatever you are. |
|--------|---|
| Pam:   | You're brown, that's the colour of your skin, and that's what goes, you know. That's why I don't like going to Punjabi things, 'cause they, they put our name down for no reason and I don't want to be looked at like that. |
| Tina:  | That's the thing about Mississauga, to top it all off. 'Cause my dad lives there and every single Indian person in Mississauga is Punjabi, Sikh. You know [we] really don't fit in at all. |

This conversation raises a variety of interlocking themes. First, it suggests that there is a connection between the use of male violence and the control of women in the public sphere. Second, it mobilizes certain monolithic assumptions of male Punjabi identity, which reproduce stereotypic images of the Sikh community: male violence becomes the principality of Punjabi/Sikh men. Third, Pam and Tina touch on the ways in which violence in the South Asian community is viewed by the dominant white society. Ethnicity, in the Canadian multicultural context, constructs each ethnic group as a homogenous entity. These are not just any guys; these guys come to represent all South Asian men and are seen as reflective of South Asian culture as a whole. And finally, Pam and Tina describe another kind of exclusion, one that is rooted in religious and ethnic difference. As non-Punjabis, they are not included in a definition of South Asian that speaks largely to a Punjabi/Sikh aesthetic, both musically and spatially. Tina explained to me that she had made a decision not to attend these dances, "Because I don't look Punjabi, you know? And they know that. And they're not exactly too welcoming."

Similarly, Nina explained to me that there is a popular preference for a Punjabi Sikh identity among South Asian youth: "My cousin was telling me that she asked this one girl, 'Are you Sikh or something?'

and she said, 'No, I wish.' She's like Hindu, and she [the girl] says, 'Are you?' and she [my cousin] goes, 'Yes.' And she [the girl] goes, 'Oh my god! My god, can I see your kara? Can I wear one?'" Nina reveals the desire for a Punjabi/Sikh identity and the symbols, such as the kara [silver bracelet], associated with it.

Continuing on this theme, in the context of a discussion about cultural esteem, Nina told me a story about a young woman who attempted to hide her Indian identity because of the shame associated with it. This is particularly interesting not for what it conveys about internalized racism and a desire for whiteness but for the way in which "Indian" is constructed — certain understandings of "Indian" displace others.

> I asked one girl, "What are you?" And she goes, "Oh, I don't want to say." And I go, "Are you Indian?" And she goes, "I don't want to say." And I go, "Why, you're not Guyanese or something?" And she goes, "Oh please!" And I go, "I guess you're Indian then, so why are you so afraid to say it?" And even in my yearbook she goes [wrote], "You're the first person that I told that I am Indian," in tiny tiny letters. And it's not like she looks white, she's darker than I am. She looks totally Indian, and I go, "Well, it's not like you can hide it."

In relation to a predominantly white context, here an Indo-Caribbean identity emerges as even less desirable than an identity from the subcontinent.

This kind of reaction to South Asians from outside the subcontinent and those who are external to the Hindi- or Punjabi-speaking community has also been reflected in my experience as radio host for a South Asian music program, "Masala Mixx," for the past ten years.[12] While the show focuses on music spanning the entire South Asian diaspora and includes both the classical, traditional variety as well as more recent fusion, the audience is dominated by Hindi- and

Punjabi-speaking South Asians from India. There is a lot of resistance to Sri Lankan Tamil and to Indo-Caribbean music, such as chutney, calypso, and soca, from these listeners. In an informal interview, DJ Jithen, one of Toronto's most popular South Asian DJs, told me in 1996 that while he is renowned in the Toronto scene, he was constantly aware that as a Gujarati his acceptance in this Punjabi-dominated context is tenuous at best. He began his career with the onset of bhangra dances and has now branched out to play R&B, old-school, and funk. However, "When the PM [Punjabi Mafia] rolls into a club and demand that I play a bhangra set or announce their arrival, I know that I better, to keep the peace."[13]

Many remixers and DJs focus on remixing Hindi film and Punjabi music, although they themselves do not have diasporic Punjabi or Hindi roots. It is because of its market value, because this variety of music sells, that they continue to produce it. While those who fall outside of the Punjabi- and Hindi-speaking belt will listen to bhangra and Hindi-film mixes, the reverse is not true. There is very little openness on the part of Punjabi- and Hindi-speaking South Asians to other music, despite the fact that bhangra and Hindi film music held this very same status of "otherness" not too long ago in the Canadian context.

While the bhangra eruption in Toronto in the 1990s brought with it a hype around dances and music, the end of the decade saw a decline in the bhangra scene. South Asians in Toronto began to demand more R&B and less home-grown music. The day dance phenomenon came to an end largely due to "people getting caught" and the issue of skipping school. And local remixing also declined due to pirating and the enforcement of copyright laws. In 2001, DJ Jithen explained, "It's not worth it anymore, with the Internet and the capacity to download any song you want. You don't make any money on remixes. Back then, they didn't care if you sampled a Hindi film song. Now they are clamping down."[14] While things quieted here, parts of America have witnessed a Bollywood flashback similar to what was experienced in the U.K. and subsequently in Canada. But, as Jithen explained, "As far as the bhangra scene, it's like a second coming now. For a few years, nobody wanted to hear any bhangra, they wanted strictly R&B. But like any scene, there are always peaks and valleys." Asian fusion music has now become more accepted. It is played widely at weddings and other social functions and there is less social hype about the dances and the music. And DJs are once again witnessing a demand for South Asian music at parties and dances: "People didn't want to go to the Indian dances because of the fights. But now it's like the PMs are grown up, they have kids and responsibilities. People want bhangra music again," Jithen said. While the music is less novel, the social organization around it is much the same. Most of these dances are dominated by North Indians, Punjabi- and Hindi-speaking youth in particular. Indo-Caribbean and Tamil youth, however, have created their own separate social scene and remixes. Equivalent to bhangra is the popularity of traditional dubba music and dance within the Tamil community.

##  Afro-Desiac: The Politics of Brown and Black Musical Fusion

A more acceptable alternative to mainstream white music for some youth is the black urban scene. In relation to the popularity of R&B music among South Asians, DJ Jithen remarked, "Definitely a mild identity crisis. Indian isn't as cool."[15] This suggests the need for outside approval, that "cool" must be sanctioned first by white or black, rather than being created by South Asians themselves. Some remixers, DJs, and musicians have taken advantage of the profitability of blackness and adopted marketing strategies that obviously associate them with popular African-American rappers, music artists, and themes. Like the musicians, many club-goers easily slip into black urban space for its music and dance without making the links between colour and cultural expression, or challenging the racism towards black people that they grew up with. While there is a history of South Asian resistance and revolution, most South Asians in North America are unaware of this tradition and are taught to aspire to the ranks of the "model minority."[16] Associating themselves with the Western way of life also distances them from what represents its opposite. Blackness, as it has come to be represented, is a reminder of the failures of the Western middle-class dream. Rather than locating the roots of this despair in the structures of inequality, South Asians have tended to hold on to the dream by embracing the promises of materialism and the Protestant work ethic. As Amarjit Singh explains, "The new Asian immigrants cannot become 'white,' so they seek overcompensation in real estate and material goods. ... many Asian Americans make up for the lack of whiteness by acquiring a consciousness that is often as 'white' and assimilationist and 'mainstream' as that of most whites."[17]

Some South Asian musicians, however, have aligned themselves with a political platform and a politics of race that makes connections with racism towards the black community. Apache Indian and Fundamental, for example, make political alliances between black and brown and are forthright on the issue of South Asian racism towards black people. For some South Asian youth, the identification with blackness is an act of rebellion and a means of distinguishing themselves from much of their parents' generation, who bought into and benefited from colonial notions of blackness and "divide and conquer." Black cultural production is much more overtly associated with a politics of resistance and asks questions about a system that is unable to address social inequalities. For youth making similar interrogations, the black African and Caribbean voice offers a space for identification with issues of race and injustice. (For more on Black and South Asian relations, see Chapter 7.)

## Oms, Allahs, and Khanda Clashes

Through my research, I found a connection between developments "back home" and in Canada with respect to tension between the

Hindu and Muslim communities. I spoke with three young women attending the same school, all of whom mentioned that one of the most significant fights of the year, involving a sizeable portion of the school's population, was between Hindus and Muslims. These young women did not know each other and all described the fight in different ways. For example, Reema, a young Hindu woman, did not see the outbreak of violence as having anything to do with religious tensions, but as an act of male bravado and machismo, "a bunch of guys getting out of hand." Alka, also Hindu, saw the incident as a reaction to what she saw as Muslim favouritism in the school:

> Alka:     We have so many Muslims in our school that it's incredible. I mean they have everything. They have whole groups of people who during their special time, they actually get off school early Fridays just because they pray in school. They have a huge group, like clubs, so there's a Muslim club sort of thing where you get off Fridays early for jumma namaz [prayers] so they can pray.
> Amita:  Do they pray in the school?
> Alka:     Yeah, they have a place where they pray, they celebrate Eid. But we also celebrate Diwali too, but you know, we don't go through those dramatic things, like to get off school early and so forth.

In contrast, Ayesha, who is Muslim, saw the fight as directly related to the communal violence occurring in India. The incident at the school happened around the time of the demolition of a historic mosque in Ayodhya, India, by members of the Hindu community who claimed that it was the birthplace of an ancient Hindu deity.[18] Ayesha described the fight among the South Asian males in her school as a result of mounting religious tension: "Yeah, I think so, it was mainly because of the, the fights in India and how the Hindus and the Sikhs were against the Muslims and, ahh, I guess there were tensions building up in school because we're all different religions. Like half of the school's like Muslim, and half of the brown population I'd say is Muslim and Sikh. So obviously there was going to be some tension between the two, so that's how it all started."

When I provided her with the other perspective, that some people in the school had suggested that there was a reaction on the part of students to what they saw as Muslim privilege, she responded: "I don't think it's really because of that, that the Muslims are favoured. I don't think people were looking at it in that way, but because of all the fighting everywhere else, like everybody was fighting, all the religions were just fighting against each other. And I think obviously you're going to be on your religion's side. Yeah, obviously you're going to be influenced by what you are, and people were going on their own religion's side and that's just how everything just came together."

One of the most striking observations that came from all the young women in my study was around the use of space in their schools. Alka, for example, referred to her school as "multicultural" and then proceeded to describe it in the following way:

> What our school is split up into is, ahm, racially. Like within the South Asian community the Muslims are with the Muslims, the Sikhs are with the Sikhs, and the Hindus are with the Hindus... So we basically, we're segregated that way. West Indians, they stay separate, blacks stay separate, and actually the whole entire school is set up in cliques. Everybody has their designated position: the back of the stairs, that's all the black area; next to it, the far right corner, is all the West Indians; and on the far left corner is all the Indians; and in the cafeteria is the Chinese; and in the parking lot is the white people. This is exactly how our school is set up.

Part of this racial organization has to do with familiarity. Alka indicates that notions of familiarity are racialized and work to mark out "us" and "them." How students take up and mark out space as racialized territory, as well as the existence of culturally diverse groups, is seen as evidence of multiculturalism. Her description of segregation was not unique: all the women that I interviewed described a similar organization of space, and all of them also described their schools as multicultural. Hearing these accounts I began to wonder whether difference in the context of Canadian multiculturalism was producing a kind of segregation and separatism.

 Separate Schooling

In Chapter 4, I suggested that celebration of racial identity and cultural esteem appears higher among the young women attending brown schools than for those in high schools with a predominantly white population. Brown schools, and the kind of celebration and assertion of racial identity that is being demonstrated, have far-reaching implications in terms of the debates around separate schooling.

Since the late 1990s, both the Muslim and Sikh communities in Toronto have been fighting for the right to government-funded separate public schooling.[19] The demand for separate public schools is not unique to Canada; it has a long history in the U.K., for example. The movement for separate schooling, in some sense, can be understood as a response to an educational curriculum that is unable to be inclusive of cultural and religious needs, as some members of the community define them.[20] Members of the Muslim and Sikh community have argued their case on the grounds of universality, claiming that the same right that has allowed for separate Catholic schools should be extended to other faiths.

While this is a seemingly legitimate and progressive demand, it has brought with it contradictory alliances. Muslim separate schooling, for example, has also been supported by those outside the Muslim community who argue for a return to traditional social and moral values. The racial subtext to their demand comes out of a perspective that views multicultural schooling and the "mixing" of students as threatening to the boundaries around white ethnic identity. Some members of the Muslim community have argued against separate schooling, claiming that opting out of the public, multicultural school model could disadvantage ethnic minorities, who will not be properly prepared or equipped to compete in mainstream society. This perspective constructs multicultural education as a means of positive assimilation.[21]

## "Refs," "FOBs," and Indian Snobs

Indocentricity and the current popularity of Punjabi Sikh and Hindu identities are not an inherent or a natural prerogative of these particular ethnic communities, but are part of an historical process of privilege. Sikh Punjabis were amongst the first South Asians to migrate and settle in Canada, and the majority live in Vancouver and Toronto.[22] Partly due to numbers, this part of the South Asian community has been able to develop a cohesive infrastructure and sense of community. Similarly, the Hindu/Hindi-speaking community also has a long history in Toronto.[23] In Chapter 3, we saw how discourses of nationalism were predicated on the assumption of Hindu middle-class universality; the centrality of Hindu/Hindi-speaking as a dominant identity in the Canadian context mirrors its prevalence within the Indian nation-state.

As we have seen, in moments of political contestation, markers around ethnic identity become paramount. While it is beyond the scope of this book to make any substantive conclusions, I would suggest that the Khalistani movement for a separate Sikh state has in part informed the trend of cultural celebration and nationalism among Punjabi youth in Canada. Similarly, developments in favour of Hindu fundamentalists in India have affected a sense of pride in Hindu identity among Toronto youth and heightened the need for a more visible Muslim identity. The resurgence of symbols such as the Sikh kara,[24] the Hindu Om, and the Muslim Allah are cultural resources, if you will, mobilized in response to contestation over ethnic/religious identity. These cultural texts, indicating religious identity, are now common among second-generation South Asian youth. Most of the young women attending brown schools that I interviewed were accessorized with their respective markers. While there is an overt marking, however, of ethnic identity, the construction of refs and FOBs as discussed in Chapter 5 serves as a reminder that there are limitations to conspicuous shows of ethnicity; it is okay to be ethnic, but not *too* ethnic.

The Hindu, Sikh, and Muslim communities have all mobilized their own discourses around community cohesion, and the reassertion of religious identity is instrumental to these discourses. Parts of the Hindu community in the West have direct links to right-wing Hindu fundamentalist organizations in India; they are influenced by, and in turn support, influence, and maintain these factions on the subcontinent, through funding and political allegiance.[25] This also holds true for the Sikh community. Punjabi Sikh youth are able to draw on a narrative of cultural and racial pride that in some ways already exists in the form of a nationalist sentiment seeking to assert itself in a struggle with the Indian nation-state for an independent Sikh state.

Inderpal Grewal, writing about the United States, argues that "ties to India are being actively maintained by the middle-class and upper-class professionals who constitute a substantial portion of Indian immigrants. ... what has changed now in India is the opening of doors to outside investment, the need created for the rupee to be traded on the international market, and the emergence of a wealthy professional class of Indians in the US."[26] This reveals an economic and political motive for the return to tradition and loyalty to "back home." While the Canadian immigration trajectory is different, Grewal's analysis certainly applies to the South Asian professionals who flowed to Canada in the 1960s, who continue to maintain a strong and influential stronghold within the South Asian community.[27] The exclusionary narrative of "Indian-ness" intersects with and serves not only alliances between elites in the West and in India, but colonial discourses of tradition and women and neocolonial discourses of assimilationism.

Vinay Lal suggests that ethnic strife within the category "South Asian" is tied into discursive tensions between East and West, premodern and modern, masculine and feminine.[28] The nation-state, in many ways a masculine construction, has been a show of prowess and bravado, a contest among nations to prove their ability to deal with the ruthlessness of the modern world. Lal argues that the ethnic strife between Hindus and Sikhs, for example, relates to transforming a national identity that has, in the past, been seen to capitulate to the feminine by not asserting its rigid boundaries. Sikh nationalism is seen to threaten the Indian nation-state. This discourse of peril draws on notions of emasculation — the idea that the Indian nation-state is not able to control terrorist and separatist activities within its borders. In turn, Lal maintains, Sikh separatists have drawn on masculine notions of identity by attempting to construct Hindus as the feminine other to Sikh militarism. Anand Patwardhan in his controversial film, *Father, Son and the Holy War* (1994), makes a similar connection between masculinity and discourses of Hindu fundamentalism. He shows how factions of the Hindu right wing, in an attempt to inflate their own superiority, have constructed Muslim men as the feminine other by opposing Muslim circumcision to Hindu virility.[29] Some scholars have argued that fundamentalist discourses have become even more rigid and conservative in the West. Lal connects this kind of nationalism to race and modernity. He argues that living in the lap of the West, where assimilationism is a reality, heightens anxieties around the solidity and cohesiveness of ethnic boundaries.[30]

Lal's arguments around masculinity and nationalism translate well to the context of youth subculture in Toronto. The scene of fusion music continues to be male dominated and mobilizes masculine posturing and bravado in an effort to assert a cultural/racial presence. The existence of gangs, violence, and sexual harassment at dances is testimony to this posturing. Bhangra music and dance, while providing a brown signifier, reproduce a notion of common South Asian identity that is dominated by Punjabi/Sikh and Hindi/Hindu. This cultural space is also one that emulates dominant discourses of femininity and ultimately constructs women as passive.

In a celebration of culture, South Asian youth have asserted a singular and narrowly defined aesthetic that is not inclusive of all points of South Asian identity. In this sense, the community of second-generation youth in the West continues to reproduce colonial notions of community and nation. The narrative of identity for diasporic youth is multiple. It is both subversive and status quo. While it breaks with static notions of traditional authenticity, it represents a form of cultural resistance that is fashioned around a narrative of nationalism and masculinity.

CHAPTER 7

# Endings:
## From Barbie to Bindis

*I* *remember a day in Mrs. Mathews' grade five*
*class. The bell rang and I dragged myself inside.*
*We all sat cross-legged on the floor in rows in front of a big screen. "Now*
*we are going to watch student presentations. There will be questions after,*
*so pay attention."*

*Cindy began. The show began, "This is a presentation about India.*
*In India people wear long cloths like curtains and wrap themselves in it.*
*They don't know how to use forks and knives so they eat with their hands.*
*In India, they don't know how to read. Everybody lives in shanty towns.*
*India is located very close to the equator so the climate is very hot."*

*The heat went right into me. I felt dizzy now and my stomach hurt. I*
*could no longer concentrate. I felt people looking at me. "That's where she's*
*from," someone said and giggled. Someone else looked on sympathetically;*
*they seemed to feel so sorry. I closed my eyes and then the strangest thing*
*happened. I heard Mrs. Mathews' voice come straight toward me. Only her*
*tone seemed so different. It seemed softer and inquisitive. She had never paid*
*me this kind of attention before. Our eyes met for a moment and the class*
*hushed at the sound of her question. She pointed to me, wrinkled her nose,*
*touched her forehead and asked, "Why do women wear those red stickers?"*

*This was too much for this bunch of fifth graders. People were now telling scratch and sniff jokes. My jaw dropped down and all I could do was imagine Mrs. Mathews with a bindi on. Even I began to laugh. The whole class was in a frenzy and as I began to answer we were all interrupted by the loud ringing of the lunch bell.*

*My mouth hung open, orally suspended. And as I made the sounds that form words, for a moment time separated me from the others. Nobody listened. Even Mrs. Mathews had forgotten as she busied herself in dispensing new directives about classroom order for those who rushed into the hall to grab at coats, hats, and mitts.*

Since the time that I was in school, fed steadily on a diet of Dick and Jane stories, blonde Barbie, and Nancy Drew, the popular icons, culture, and educational curricula in North America have definitely changed. In fall 2001, blonde Mary-Kate and Ashley Olsen paraded on the cover of their magazine in saris and bindis. Their cover lineup included: "Gear Guide, Stuff That Puts the Cool in School, " "So Sari Now: It's a Fashion Wrap with Mary-Kate and Ashley." Sari is described as a "chunk" of fabric the twins are trying to understand. Though they date it back to 3000 BC and ask, "Why do women still wear them?" they respond, "Why not? Perhaps it's a measure of India's pride as a nation — why should India adapt to the Western world? India's not known to be a place of great change. It is, in fact, one of the few countries with virtually unchanged social and religious structures for more than 4,000 years."[1] Their back-to-school fashion spread includes Indian silks and prints.

In this snapshot, it looks like we made it. Bindis and mehndi (henna) have ornamented famous bodies like Madonna and Prince and sell in such stores as Claire's Boutique and Le Chateau as "body jewels" and "body art." The product menu at Iguana, an online gift shop, lists items like Kama Sutra oils and Indian lunch boxes featuring Krishna, Ganesh, and dancing Shiva.[2] The banner ad on the home page reads,

"Tell Osama Yo' Mama." With racial profiling now accepted as a necessary means of protecting national security interests in the world post–September 11, 2001, the melting pot has truly reasserted itself. While before South Asians looked the same, Arabs looked the same, and blacks looked the same, now we all look suspiciously like each other.

Seeing the Ganesh lunch boxes and saris as part of "back-to-school" makes me experience many things. On the one hand, there is a feeling of acceptance that comes from knowing that my culture is part of the public domain, that in today's consumer society, it too is considered marketable. But I still wonder whether Mary-Kate and Ashley's cool is the same as ours. It is doubtful that South Asians would be able to set a market trend on a cover of a magazine in the same way as the Olsen twins. Brown girls in saris are immigrant and ethnic, not mainstream and fashionable.

Much of the struggle of the young women I interviewed is about negotiating between a white making of the nation and a diasporic one. In both instances their own voices are displaced. This book began with an examination of some of the theories that attempt to make sense of the process of migration. One such theory, stressing assimilation and acculturation, assumes that in order to maintain a sense of national identity immigrants should conform to the values, aesthetics, consumer trends, and institutional structures of the dominant group. This perspective often portrays second-generation immigrant youth as being caught at a crossroads between their parents' culture and the culture of the dominant society in which they live. Any resulting conflict between youth and parents is explained with reference to the parents' retention of the values of "back home" and their resistance to adopting the cultural values of the host community, and to youths' desire to adopt those values. In this framework racism and prejudice are seen as an outcome of ethnic minorities' refusal to integrate with mainstream Canadian society.

I have suggested that young South Asian women are positioned in different ways as in need of protection, either by their own communities or by white Canadian mainstream society. While the concern over conflict between immigrant parents and their daughters, and the question of excessive restriction versus liberty, seemingly result from a clash between Canadian and South Asian community values over the issue of parenting, they also stem from a clash between the boundaries of Canadian and South Asian cultural values, aesthetics, and identities, and from a question of jurisdiction. Who has the authority over immigrant children, their parents or the mainstream Canadian society? Both communities have different stakes in these young South Asian women. As women we are responsible to our community as reproducers and transmitters of cultural values.[3] As young South Asians we are future adult citizens of Canada and are responsible for the aesthetics and values of Canadian society. If we do not acculturate appropriately, we could tamper with the very social and moral fabric of a Canadian identity based on white sensibilities and values.

What I set out to understand was how and why the issue of generational clash has come to be seen as an ethnic phenomenon. While there is, admittedly, conflict between the generations in all cultural, ethnic, and racial communities, the conflict between immigrant parents and youth is more visible than, for example, generational conflict within white Canadian families. For the South Asian community, the conflict is more conspicuous due to the overlapping discourses of race, cultural difference, and inequality it has been historically intermeshed with. I understand the strictness of South Asian parents as a culmination of several modern perspectives and practices around community, culture, nation, tradition, and womanhood. The chain of signifiers — youth, woman, and racial "other" — and the crossroads at which young South Asian women find themselves, are enmeshed in a series of protective discourses. There are similarities in the ways in which these three categories are conceptualized in the modern era. Youth, women, and racial "others" are constructed as subjects in need of guidance, protection, supervision, or development. The issue of generational conflict between youth and parents, far from being an ethnic phenomenon, is a contradiction inherent in modernity. The conflict is actually between the culture and values of premodern and modern ways of thinking and understanding the world.[4]

The generational clash has much to do with registering social ambivalence and anxiety toward modern social change. Anxiety about how development and the consequent need for imported labour were affecting the moral, social, and cultural fibre of the West became most obvious in debates about racial purity at the turn of the last century. Although imported labour was important to the expansion of the British Empire and the building of its colonies, exclusion and segregation of South Asian and other immigrant populations from mainstream society was accomplished through arguments about adjustability and cultural compatibility. Here there were contradictions between the needs of colonial capitalism and the desire to maintain white cultural authority. Indeed, a historical review of South Asians in Canada reveals a trend of ambivalence on the part of British Canadians. Implicit in the acceptance of new Canadians was the condition that they not be too different in values, aesthetics, and sensibilities from their white British counterparts. The result in early-twentieth-century Canada, as Buchignani et al. conclude, was "a compromising immigration policy that tempered common ethnic and racial biases with practical economic considerations."[5]

White identity has been constructed in reference to an outside community. Circulating notions of "barbarity," "uncivilized," "backward," and "rapist" in relation to visible minorities has served as a means to secure a relative identity that could, at the very least, appear more cultivated in relation to its "native" counterpart.[6] Pajaczkowska and Young explore such practices of representation as a strategy of maintaining white centrality. They argue that white identity is rooted in a history of representation that has favoured denial and disavowal of its own subjectivity as ruthless and aggressive. This is accomplished in part through the invention of representations of the colonial "other" as dirty, violent, or licentious. White identity, Pajaczkowska and Young argue, is an illusion based in the fear of loss of individuality which is projected onto the "other" in order to leave intact "white, middle class male identity as one of safety, power, control, independence and contentment. ... The illusory identity needs narratives constantly to reaffirm its fictitious centrality."7

Keeping in mind that the centrality of whiteness and the West relies on the construction of the "other," it is possible to see that discourses about immigrant culture conflict in Canada help to position and protect the fiction of white/Western superiority. I have argued that the moral panics around juvenile delinquency for white middle-class youth in the 1950s were part of a process in which normative notions of Canadian-ness came to be racialized. I have also argued that the arrival of non-white immigrants to Canada, and more specifically to parts of greater Metropolitan Toronto, have mobilized consistent representations of the non-white ethnic as dangerous, culturally incompatible, or "taking over."

## Birthing Nations and Identities

As a young child I would watch voyeuristically, from the point of view of smallness, my father buried behind the shadows of books and papers. And on some days I peered up from his lap into a spill of words, debates, and philosophizing with colleagues. Not quite understanding his talk about the past, about marches and civil disobedience, I watched his eyes illuminate, eyebrows arching, during discussions about Indian independence from British rule — whose significance I cannot even begin to understand, a generation removed and having grown up in the West. My father spoke nostalgically about his days on the campus of Delhi University in the then-famous coffee house, where heated exchanges between students occurred about the model on which this new India should base itself: modern secularism, traditional religious, or indigenous? It is here that I first began to learn about oppression and resistance and the trail of independence movements from the African continent that inspired people like him. It is here that I also learned about national self-determination and identity.

Historian Duara Prasenjit sees history as a constant negotiation between universality and particularity. He argues that history has often involved differentiating the self from an other.[8] Building on this notion, I have shown that diasporic South Asian identity relies on historically constituted notions of womanhood. Women have often been used as the marker for distinguishing "self" from "other." In an effort to seek legitimation in relation to British colonial rule, Indian nationalists, for example, mobilized notions of female chastity, modesty, and sacrifice, in order to differentiate East from West. While being allowed to enjoy some of the freedoms of the modern world, such as education and paid employment, women's innocence was to be maintained by keeping the values of the old in the private sphere of home and family. Women, in the context of colonial India, became enmeshed in discourses about (racialized) cultural difference.

Not only was keeping women innocent a means to resolve some of the fears associated with modernity, but during the nationalist struggle for independence women became an important signifier in East-West battle over political and moral power. They came to signify the Indian-ness of the nation. Consolidating power for Indian nationalists relied on justifying self-rule to the British by following modern notions of progress and prosperity, while simultaneously maintaining the integrity of what needed to be seen as a distinct identity in the eyes of the Indian populace. Thus was forged a distinction between westernization and modernization. The woman question was used as leverage in regaining political self-determination by appealing to notions of cultural authenticity.

Vinay Lal argues that the South Asian diaspora, although fragmented and dispersed, is attempting to hold itself together through constructing a narrative that pulls on discourses of tradition and culture that are very similar to those promoted by the Indian nation-state. He claims that even in diaspora, modernism circumscribes much of the discussion around Indian identity.[9] Both Lal and Ali Rattansi have argued that the diasporic representation of woman as chaste and pure has helped to construct moral superiority in the context of a hostile Western world that is caught up in anxieties over its own disintegrating familial, moral social fabric.[10] Similarly, Inderpal Grewal argues that discourses representing South Asian girls as repressed or victims of a backward culture are essential to maintaining notions of freedom and democracy in the West.[11]

In the case of second-generation South Asians, the category "woman" can be read as a narrative of displacement. This displacement produces a fragmentary reality. Accordingly, young women's subjectivities are always partial and shifting, depending upon the social context. Because of women's (colonial) historical relationship to tradition and national/cultural identity, their negotiation of culture in the present not only threatens the stability of the category "South Asian" but also destabilizes notions of appropriate femininity. Their femininity is interconnected with their sexual behaviour, and their sexual behaviour is symbolic of the reputation of the collective. South Asian women's identities are also displaced by the external mainstream community and conflicting understandings of what it means to be Canadian within a multicultural (bicultural English/French) framework. They negotiate all these contradictions by articulating a third position of subjectivity, one that is neither traditionally Canadian or South Asian but speaks to the fluidity of categories.

There are extreme emotional costs, however, in negotiating fluidity. The effects of this fragmentation — the constant hiding of selves, the feelings of shame that this can elicit, and how this affects all aspects of self-esteem — still remain untheorized. As Jasbir Puar asks, what are the emotional costs of immigration? What is the impact on "racialized gender spaces of self-esteem, social esteem, mental health ... Do we really have any idea of the toll of immigration?"[12]

## 𝒴  Black and Brown and the Domino of Difference

With the same light that was in my father's eyes when he witnessed history, I watched his sense of urgency and conviction in the struggle against racism and the series of "Paki" bashings that occurred in Toronto in the mid-1970s. One evening when I came home, my father introduced me to a tall, quiet man: "He has a black belt in karate." I learned the meaning of "vigilante" as my father explained in hushed tones that government and police inaction could lead to desperate measures. We had to create our own safety. There were a number of people who had been physically assaulted on the public transport system, some even pushed onto the railway tracks. My mother, who always wore her sari proudly to the school where she taught, now did so with some hesitation. Organizing together, members of the community strategized the necessary systems of protection. For marginal communities living in the West, there is a need for self-protection and a coming together to articulate a cultural space in relation to the dominant mainstream context. Internal differences and power dynamics, however, cannot be forgotten. Notwithstanding his celebration of defiance against the British, my father always included as part of this historical narrative that the moment of birth of the Indian nation state was also a moment of death — a testimony to the brutality of difference, inequality, division, and communal violence. These divisions continue to play out within the subcontinent as well as within the diaspora along religious, class, linguistic, regional, and political lines.

Diasporic celebrations of brownness or South Asian-ness are both defiant of and accomplices in perpetuating racial and cultural inequalities. In a context where blackness is at the bottom of the racial hierarchy, nationalist celebrations of brownness can engender suspicions of complicity. A celebration of South Asian identity that does not recognize and locate itself within a larger system of inequality can be about maintaining a distance from blackness. And maintaining a distinction from a black African-Canadian identity can become a strategy of being closer to whiteness. As I illustrated in Chapter 4, the complicity with whiteness is also found within the category "brown," in the distinction between "refs," "FOBs," and the second-generation, whose dress, style, and accents are more closely aligned with white norms.

Given the historical association of blackness, in the West, to histories of colonization, slavery, and disfranchisement, are young South Asian narratives oppositional or complicit? Are they forging alliances or reproducing forms of racial segregation and inequality in the name of celebration and diversity? Fusion music has brought some of these tensions to the forefront. Canadian diasporic identity in this sense is contradictory. The music scene in Toronto hardly demonstrates a transparent desire to maintain a distinction from black African signifiers. The increasing use of reggae, hip-hop, and R&B denies a simplistic reading of bhangra as an expression of a purist or nationalistic identity. On the other hand, references to black musical styles do not necessarily mean an alliance with, or even a recognition of, the struggles of black youth in an anti-black society. Much referencing of black musical subculture is due, in part, to the alliance between consumerism and youth styles. Hip-hop has now become marketable, and young cultural producers are able to cash in on this popularity by "mixing in." While a political voice of opposition to racism can be found both within South Asian popular culture and in its referencing of black musical and fashion styles (especially the political voice of hip-hop and conscious reggae), this referencing seems to be muted. There is little overt discussion of opposition, even though the music itself stands in opposition to white sensibilities. There is no explicit alliance to a spoken politics of resistance, one that is not just about form but about substance. Despite the intermixing or emulating of black musical groups and the use of seemingly radical names, such as *The Empire Strikes Back* or *Asian Empire,* there seems to be little acknowledgment of historical or contemporary subversive implications.

Perhaps this is testimony to the fact that consumer and class alliances have diluted a radical political voice for both black and South Asian cultural producers.

The space of blackness, however, does provide a home for South Asians who do not align themselves with the status quo and do see the links between South Asian and black as a political and shared cultural space. As Raoul Juneja, a community radio host, explains,

> There have been individuals from both African and Indian cultures who would rather segregate their fellow minorities from each other, rather than see them unite. Despite my current hip-hop work and past South Asian charity work, I've been told I'm "too Indian" for the former and "not Indian enough" for the latter. If anything is to be learned from the history of Gandhi and MLK, or recently from Nelson Mandela's leadership in South Africa, it's that the struggle to end racism has been the common bond between minorities across the globe. And as long as a form of music still exists that attempts to do the same, I can guarantee I'll be a part of it.[13]

Perhaps part of what continues to complicate the relationship between an African diasporic identity and a South Asian one is the lack of knowledge, the historical disconnection, the lack of discursive tools to note the parallel struggles, the political plight, and some of the similarities and differences between us as communities. The 2001 R&B hit "Get Ur Freak On" by Missy Elliott indicates that there is a new reciprocal trend between South Asian and black, in terms of borrowing and fusing cultural elements. In this song, Missy interweaves Ustad Zakir's tabla beats throughout the track and creates a South Asian version of modern rhythm and blues. This track has continued to be popular among both black and brown audiences. More recently (2002), Truth Hurts, the first female artist to be released by Dr. Dre's hip-hop empire, pushes fusion even further. Her track "Addictive" uses Lata

Mangeshkar–style female vocals, bringing the hip-hop audience a taste of Bollywood's Hindi film music, attempting to make black audiences consumers of South Asian sound. From a marketing point of view this fusion package is a seller. Not only does it appeal to and strengthen a South Asian youth market who are already consumers of R&B/hip-hop, but coming from a black artist, it also makes the infusion of Eastern sounds more palatable for a black audience. The risk it takes in blending the two audiences suggests we are ready for a change and speaks to the reality of mixed musical audiences.

A subsequent legal battle between Lata Mangeshkar's Saregama India Limited and Dr. Dre's Aftermath Entertainment sends a message from the East to the West that Bollywood music is established and serious, and cannot be sampled without following standard copyright procedures. Consequently, the hitherto unknown Mangeshkar — a Bollywood singer who has recorded over 50,000 songs — is introduced to pop connoisseurs in the west.

The connection between black and brown in popular culture is a bridge between otherwise separated and divided histories. I wonder what a South Asian diasporic voice, a political one, would look like, had most of us been connected to these voices of struggle and resistance.

## J'ouvert Morning

It was 1994, my first Carnival J'ouvert morning in Trinidad. A kaleidoscope of colours painted my body from the various merrymakers and mud mas enthusiasts with whom I had collided during the course of the long night. My body ached from the steady pace of dance and "chipping down the road" that took place during six straight hours of road march. I had now slowed down, feeling a sense of exhale as I approached the Grandstand, a significant meeting and ending point for some. My face was slightly burnt from the sun that had managed to seep through the cracks of paint and mud dried in various shapes across my cheeks. At this moment of giddiness and fatigue I was hailed by a fellow participant.

"Where are you from?" he panted.

"I was born in England, my parents are from India, I was brought up in Canada, and I am now visiting Trinidad."

"Oh," he exclaimed, "so you are a real Indian! I am Indian too, but not a real Indian. I rarely meet a true Indian."

"But I am no more Indian than you," I explained. "I didn't really grow up there."

It didn't matter. I was still a real Indian and that was enough to elicit a handshake in what was deemed an honorable meeting. I was reminded of being four and spotting other South Asians from my mother's car. This was a moment of cultural recognition, though many lands and borders had been traversed to bring us to together. It seemed my pilgrimage home had gone off the beaten track. While most Indo-Trinidadians spoke about the trip they would take one day to the original homeland, I found myself consistently, over the course of seven years, connecting to a homeland in Trinidad. And what would an Indian from India living in Canada, a "real" Indian, be doing in the Caribbean — wasn't my home India? As a second-generation child of the diaspora, I have no true sense of belonging, because whether I am in Canada, India, or Trinidad, the question "Where are you from?" always remains the same.

Our excited sense of commonality waned a little when I tried out my rusty Hindi and he his patois version. We could not understand each other. Nonetheless, seeing as we had the love of fete in common and had endured a long night, we decided to converge around a big roti and the warmth of the fire it was being cooked on. We spoke of Indian villages from India to Trinidad to Toronto, and about nana nani grandparents and Hindi film stars. While he spoke about doubles, pholourie, and aloo pie, I told of cholay bhatura, pakora, and samosa. Sometimes we talked in cultures, histories, and divisions we could not translate to one another. Other times, we shared a nostalgia as people who had never known each other but understood something about travelling cultures, the splendour of Bollywood cinema therapy, chili peppers, coconut milk, and sari princesses. With my belly full and the sun sleeping in my eyes I knew it was time for siesta. I bid farewell to the meeting of delight and disappointment, recognition and estrangement. As I walked away, I realized that this was part of the human condition as seen through my diasporic lens. While there is no ready-made point of home where all the selves can simultaneously merge, these addresses are in the making in every part of the global village, in all the places where we reside, in the mixtures and confusions, in the accidental crossings and unions, and in the intentional collaborations and making of communities.

# Endnotes

 CHAPTER ONE: The Telling of Secrets

1   *Dahl* is the Hindi/Punjabi/Urdu word for "lentil." *Atta* means
    "whole wheat flour" in the same family of languages.

2   David Hayes, "The Dances, the Firebomb and the Clash of
    Cultures," *Toronto Life,* October 1992, p. 41.

3   I am defining *South Asian* in the diasporic sense. It therefore refers to people who
    have a historical and cultural connection to the South Asian subcontinent (India,
    Pakistan, Republic of Myanmar [formerly Burma], Nepal, Sri Lanka, Bangladesh)
    and those who migrated from the South Asian subcontinent to East Africa,
    Malaysia, Singapore, the Caribbean, Fiji, and other parts of the world.

4   Norman Buchignani et al., *Continuous Journey: A Social History of South Asians in
    Canada* (Toronto: McClelland and Stewart, 1985), p. 110.

5   While I use the term *South Asian* here, I do so realizing that its construction as an
    identity (as opposed to geographical description) is in some ways relevant only in
    the Canadian context. One is not South Asian in Trinidad (one is Indian), Britain
    (Black or Asian), or the United States (Asian), for example. For more on how the
    construction of South Asian as an identity is relevant in the Western context, see
    Chandra Mohanty, "Defining Genealogies: Feminist Reflections on Being South
    Asian in North America," in *Our Feet Walk the Sky: Women of the South Asian
    Diaspora,* ed. The Women of South Asian Descent Collective (San Francisco: Aunt
    Lute Books, 1994), pp. 351–58; Avtar Brah, "Difference, Diversity and
    Differentiation," in *"Race", Culture and Difference,* ed. James Donald and Ali
    Rattansi (London: Sage Publications, 1992).

6   Arjun Appadurai, "Global Ethnoscapes: Notes and Queries for a Transnational
    Anthropology," in *Recapturing Anthropology: Working in the Present,* ed. R.G. Fox
    (Santa Fe, New Mexico: School of American Research Press, 1991), p. 192.

7     Many of the terms used to describe group cultural or racial identities are problematic, and I discuss the issues arising from the concepts of race, ethnicity, and culture later on in this chapter. I use the terms *white* and *South Asian* here with caution, recognizing that I am homogenizing the experiences of a vast range of people. Far from being an essentialist descriptor, I use *white* rather than *European Canadian* in order to point to the hierarchy of colour that continues to operate in Canada. Canadian values in many instances, I argue, are still associated with (white) European values. I use *South Asian* (as opposed to *brown*) for two reasons: to point to the diversity and diasporic nature of the South Asian community in Canada, and to point to the ongoing struggle on the part of minority groups in Canada to be fully acknowledged and included in the citizenship, definition, and entitlements associated with being Canadian.

    The term *Indian* is also problematic and internally contested. I argue in later chapters that the Indian nation-state was constructed through a hegemonic discourse universalizing *Indian* as Hindu, middle-class, and mostly from northern India. This leaves out a number of "others" who comprise the population of India, such as Muslims, tribal groups, and those from other regional, linguistic, and class groups. I also argue that in the diaspora, *Indian* continues to stand in for *South Asian,* leaving out South Asians who are from other parts of the subcontinent and diasporic communities. The young women I interviewed, regardless of whether they were from Pakistan or East Africa, most commonly referred to themselves as "Indian." This points to the continuing dominance of "Indian" as an identity within the South Asian diaspora.

8     Stuart Hall, "New Ethnicities," in *"Race", Culture and Difference,* ed. James Donald and Ali Rattansi (London: Sage Publications, 1992).

9     I had some difficulty in defining first- and second-generation South Asian. I, for example, am among the first in my family to grow up here in Canada. However, I realize that after thirty years of residence in Canada, my parents are not unaffected by Canadian society. It is for this reason I refer to those who have migrated to Canada as the first generation, and their offspring as the second. First-generation South Asians undergo more directly the experience of immigration itself, and the process of integration. Possible language barriers and the issue of Canadian work experience as a systemic barrier preventing them from joining the workforce at par with their qualifications are issues confronted more often by the first generation. Second-generation South Asians face more directly the issue of identity. My parents, for example, never question their identity as Indian, even though one of them holds Canadian citizenship. Most of their peers also prefer a South Asian identification, though some may have opted for a Canadian identity. In general, the Indo-Canadian dilemma remains more powerful for second-generation South Asians. Both generations, of course, experience racism in the Canadian context, although in somewhat different forms.

10     Maria Mies defines purdah as the "most radical form of sex segregation and seclusion of women. The seclusion can be achieved through walls, railings, curtains, veils, separate compartments in trains for men and women, separate seats in buses, through gestures like turning away of the head or looking down, and also through silence. Purdah means above all that a woman should never appear in public, and if that cannot be avoided, must protect herself from being looked at by men." Maria Mies, *Indian Women and Patriarchy* (New Delhi: Concept Publishing, 1980), p. 65.

11  I am referring here to the initial victory of the Hindu-nationalist party BJP (Bharatiya Janata Party) in the Indian national elections of spring 1996. Their national vision is a "Hindu India."

12  Later in this chapter I delineate my reasons for adopting, for the most part, the commonsensical notion of the term *culture* in this book. I situate this within a larger discussion of the terminology of race and ethnicity.

13  G. Collalillo, "Value Structures within Italian Immigrant Families: Continuity or Conflict?" (Ph.D. dissertation, University of Toronto, 1981); N.T. Feather, "Assimilation of Values in Migrants," in *Understanding Human Values,* ed. M. Rokeach (New York: The Free Press, 1979); A. Wolfgang and N. Josefowitz, "Chinese Immigrant Value Changes and Value Differences Compared to Canadian Students," *Canadian Ethnic Studies* 10 (1978): 130–35.

14  P.A.S. Ghuman, *Coping with Two Cultures: British Asian and Indo-Canadian Adolescents* (Clevedon: Multilingual Matters, 1994). N. Issar, *A Comparison of Values of East-Indian, East-Indian Canadian, and European Canadian Adolescents* (Toronto: OISE, 1988). W. Valiente, "Domestic Violence in the South Asian Family: Treatment and Research Issues" in *South Asian Symposium 1992,* ed. C. Sarath (Toronto: Centre for South Asian Studies Graduate Students Union, University of Toronto, 1993): 111–21.

15  B.S. Bolaria and P.S. Li, *Racial Oppression in Canada* (Toronto: Garamond Press, 1985).

16  L. Driedger, *The Ethnic Factor: Identity in Diversity* (Toronto: McGraw-Hill Ryerson, 1989); J.W. Berry, R. Kalin, and D.M. Taylor, *Multiculturalism and Ethnic Attitudes in Canada* (Ottawa: Minister of Supply and Services, 1977).

17  Bhangra, which is traditional Punjabi folk music, in the last decade has been mixed in with such other styles of music as reggae, house, disco, hip-hop, and R&B to create a whole new fusion music. This fusion is particularly celebrated among second-generation South Asian youth. While bhangra is a form of Punjabi folk music and dance, most Western media have used the word to describe any kind of Asian fusion.

18  Hayes, "Dances," pp. 40, 41.

19  How violence, date rape, and harassment affect and constrain the lives of young white Canadian women in both the public and private spheres are questions rendered invisible by this kind of analysis.

20  Berry, Kalin, and Taylor, *Multiculturalism and Ethnic Attitudes,* pp. 36–8.

21  Driedger, *Ethnic Factor,* p. 42.

22  Canadian Press, "Poll Showed Hostility to Immigrants," *Globe and Mail,* September 14, 1992, A4.

23  Canadian Press, "Close Doors, Speak English, Majority Tells Pollster," *Calgary Herald,* May 18, 1995, A13.

24  Peter Weinreich, "Ethnicity and Adolescent Identity Conflicts," in *Minority Families in Britain: Support and Stress,* ed. Verity Saifullah Khan (London: Macmillan Press, 1979). Although this edited collection was written over two decades ago, this piece describes a trend in the literature that continues to exist. Also see Catherine Ballard's work, "Conflict, Continuity and Change: Second-Generation South Asians" also appears in *Minority Families in Britain,* ed. Verity Saifullah Khan (London: Macmillan Press, 1979).

25  Weinreich, "Ethnicity and Adolescent Identity," p. 107.

26    I am referring to, among others, the works of Parmar, Amos, and Brah in the 1980s, which were significant pieces of the time (A. Brah and R. Minha, "Structural Racism or Cultural Difference: Schooling for Asian Girls," in *Just a Bunch of Girls*, ed. G. Weiner. [Philadelphia: Open University Press, 1985]; V. Amos and P. Parmar, "Resistances and Responses: The Experiences of Black Girls in Britain," in *Feminism for Girls: An Adventure Story*, ed. A. McRobbie and T. McCabe [London: Routledge, 1981]; V. Amos and P. Parmar, "Challenging Imperial Feminism," in *Feminist Review* 17 [July 1984]: pp. 3–19). I am not, however, treating their text as a fixed representation of their reflections on young South Asian women and culture conflict. For example, in a 1994 article, Brah points to the complexities and contradictions that Muslim women must negotiate ("'Race' and 'Culture' in the Gendering of Labour Markets" in *The Dynamics of Race and Gender*, ed. H. Afshar and M. Maynard [London: Taylor & Francis, Ltd., 1994]). She offers a useful framework for discussing young women's lives without falling into some of the reductionist traps I am outlining here. I mention the early works of Parmar, Amos, and Brah here because they were among the first to point out, from a feminist perspective, some of the inadequacies of the culture conflict approach. These critiques have greatly informed my own thinking on the subject.

27    Rey Chow calls attention to some of the theoretical flaws underlying what she calls "the representation of the native." She argues that in an attempt to put race into an analysis of women's subjectivities, women of colour have often remained within a reactive framework. This means that race ends up being the defining paradigm and other important variables, such as gender, class, and culture, therefore may end up cast aside. What emerges is a skewed picture, a partial truth. Chow's analysis can serve as a cautionary note to the discussion on women's agency. By portraying women of colour as empowered subjects *only* does not do justice to the totality of their experience. Rey Chow, *Writing Diaspora: Tactics of Intervention in Contemporary Cultural Studies* (Bloomington: Indiana University Press, 1993).

28    Jasbir K. Puar, "Writing My Way 'Home': Traveling South Asian Bodies and Diasporic Journeys," *Socialist Review* (Special Issue: *The Traveling Nation: India and its Diaspora*) 24, no. 4 (1994).

29    Tony Bennett, *Culture, Ideology and Social Process: A Reader* (London: Batsford Academic and Educational in association with the Open University, 1981), p. 77.

30    Edward Said, *Culture and Imperialism* (New York: Alfred A. Knopf, 1993), p. xii.

31    Bennett, *Culture, Ideology and Social Process*.

32    Said, *Culture and Imperialism*, p. xiii.

33    Part of the contention centres on whether these terms are descriptive of an objective, naturally occurring reality or of a socially constructed one. In other words, does racial difference and division exist as a natural biological blueprint, or is its significance merely social and epistemological? In defense of the latter view, Kwame Anthony Appiah has argued that a common culture based on race for black Americans, for example, derives largely from the shared experience of oppression (K.A. Appiah, *In My Father's House: Africa in the Philosophy of Culture* [New York: Oxford University Press, 1992]; see also P. Gilroy, *"There Ain't No Black in the Union Jack"* [London: Hutchinson, 1987]). Others have argued that historical and geographical relationships and conditions have led black Americans to generate a common culture. At the root of this debate is not only the social significance of

the term *race*, but in what an identity based on race is grounded. This raises questions about whether specific theorizations of race/racism/racialization work equally well for different groups and contexts.

While it is beyond the scope of this research, one may explore some of the effects of South Asians in the U.K. being named and naming themselves as "black," in the United States as "Asian," in Canada as "South Asian," and so on throughout the diaspora. Canadian scholar Peter Li emphasizes that it is the social significance bestowed on racial differences that gives race its meaning. Racial difference in itself need not entail a system of racial inequality: "Biological and genetic features that are believed to have produced racial and ethnic groups are also held to determine people's mental, social, and cultural capacities. Accordingly, racial and ethnic groups are seen as forming a hierarchy, based on alleged abilities and potentials, in which some groups are supposedly superior to others. This ranking of racial and ethnic groups along a scale of superiority and inferiority is the essence of racism" (Peter Li, ed. *Races and Ethnic Relations in Canada* [Toronto: Oxford University Press, 1990], p. 3).

Pointing to the state's regulation of immigration and the legal system, Li argues that the definition and relative status of racial and ethnic groups are constantly shifting. This constant flux is indicative of the constructedness of race and ethnicity. For example, he argues that black South Africans have been assigned a legal status based on their colour as opposed to their own subjective affiliation and association to the term *black*. Similarly, in the case of the First Nation peoples of Canada, he contends that the Canadian Indian Act has placed both entitlements and restrictions on those defined as status Indians and that the difference between status and non-status Indians has less to do with their ethnic/racial/cultural attributes than with legal and bureaucratic considerations (p. 6). These are examples of identity being differently constructed, regulated, or legislated by the state in different contexts.

Because *ethnicity* is seen to be tied to liberal notions of multicultural celebrations of difference in multiethnic and -racial societies, some have argued that the term obscures the power relations of race (M. Coombs, "Review Essay: Interrogating Identity," *Berkeley Women's Law Journal* 11 [1996]: 222–49). Pointing out that in a racist society *ethnicity* has come to refer to non-white people *only*, thereby concealing the salience and variations of white ethnicity, some scholars advocate against the usage of *ethnicity* in place of *race* (Rinaldo Walcott, *Critiquing Canadian Multiculturalism: Toward an Anti-Racist Agenda* [Master's thesis: Ontario Institute for Studies in Education, 1993]). According to Floya Anthias, however, any ethnicity can be used as a basis of marginalization and subordination. Anthias argues that "the markers and signifiers that racism uses need not be those of biology or physiognomy but can be those of language, territorial rights or culture" (Floya Anthias, "Race and Class Revisited — Conceptualizing Race and Racisms," *The Sociological Review* 38, no. 1 [1990]: 24). She does, however, distinguish between *race*, defined as reliant on biological markers of difference, and *ethnicity*, defined as "the identification of particular cultures as ways of life or identity which are based on a historical notion of origin or fate, whether mythical or 'real'" (p. 20). Others prefer the use of *ethnicity*, arguing that *race* reifies socially constructed inequality as an immutable fact, thereby increasing its social significance (Hall, "New Ethnicities").

34   Sherene Razack, "What Is to Be Gained by Looking White People in the Eye? Culture, Race, Gender in Cases of Sexual Violence," *Signs* 19 (Summer 1994):

894–923; also see Sherene Razack, *Looking White People in the Eye: Gender, Race and Culture in Courtrooms and Classrooms* (Toronto: University of Toronto Press, 1998); Philomena Essed, *Everyday Racism: Reports from Women of Two Cultures* (Alameda, California: Hunter House, 1990); P. Essed, "Understanding Everyday Racism," in *Sage Series on Race and Ethnic Relations* 2, by P. Essed (London: Sage Publications, 1991); L. Abu-Lughod, "Writing Against Culture," in *Recapturing Anthropology: Working in the Present*, ed. R. Fox (Santa Fe, New Mexico: School of American Press, 1991).

35 Essed, "Understanding Everyday Racism," p. 17.

36 Sherene Razack, "Schooling Research on South and East Asian Students: The Perils of Talking Culture," in *Race, Class and Gender* 2, no.3 (1995): 1.

37 Razack, "What Is to Be Gained."

38 Ibid., p. 4.

39 Calmore, as cited ibid., pp. 4–5.

40 For difference/equality debates within feminism, see Ann Snitow, "A Gender Diary," in *Conflicts in Feminism,* ed. M. Hirsch and E. Fox (New York: Routledge, 1990); M. Barrett, "The Concept of Difference," *Feminist Review* 26 (July 1987): 29–41; Himani Bannerji, ed., *Thinking Through: Essays on Feminism, Marxism and Anti-Racism* (Toronto: Women's Press, 1995); Barbara Smith and Beverly Smith, "Across the Kitchen Table: A Sister-to-Sister Dialogue," in *This Bridge Called My Back: Writings by Radical Women of Colour,* ed. Cherrie Moraga and Gloria Anzaldua (New York: Kitchen Table, Women of Colour Press, 1981); Cherrie Moraga and Gloria Anzaldua, eds., *This Bridge Called My Back: Writings by Radical Women of Colour* (New York: Kitchen Table, Women of Colour Press, 1981).

For critiques of Western feminism, see Chandra Mohanty, "Under Western Eyes: Feminist Scholarship and Colonial Discourses," *Feminist Review* 30 (Autumn 1988): 61–88; Marnia Lazreg, "Feminism and Difference: The Perils of Writing as a Woman on Women in Algeria," *Feminist Studies* 14 (Spring 1988): 81–107; Aihwa Ong, "Colonialism and Modernity: Feminist Re-Presentations of Women in Non-Western Societies," *Inscriptions* (Special Issue on Colonial Discourse) (1988); Valerie Amos and P. Parmar, "Challenging Imperial Feminism," *Feminist Review* 17 (July 1984); Heidi Hartman, "The Unhappy Marriage of Marxism and Feminism: Towards a More Progressive Union," in *Women and Revolution: A Discussion of the Unhappy Marriage of Marxism and Feminism,* ed. Lydia Sargent (Boston: South End Press, 1981); Lydia Sargent, ed., *Women and Revolution: A Discussion of the Unhappy Marriage of Marxism and Feminism* (Boston: South End Press, 1981).

41 Linda Alcoff, "Philosophy and Racial Identity," in *Radical Philosophy* (January/February 1996): 5.

42 Puar, "Writing My Way 'Home': Traveling South Asian Bodies and Diasporic Journeys," pp. 25, 23.

43 While I can be said to be a knowledgeable informant, given my own experience of growing up second-generation South Asian in Canada, I have also observed some profound differences from my experience in the last fifteen years. As I have mentioned, a growing population and concentration of South Asians in certain parts of Toronto have profoundly influenced the experiences of South Asian youth, who now have a number of cultural symbols to draw on in their search for and articulation of identities. It is for this reason that I sought to explore substantively

the experiences of young South Asian women within both the family and the public sphere.

44 I chose this period of study because the early to mid-1990s saw the growth of a second-generation articulation of identity in the form of bhangra dances and South Asian youth fashion.

45 For the survey of newspapers I looked at *Canadian News Index* (1992), *Canadian Periodical Index* (1994, 1995, 1996), and *Canadian Index,* Vol. 3 (Jan.–June 1995) under the heading "immigrants" for a cross-section of early to recent 1990s publications.

46 Finally, I interviewed five social and community workers, all prominent members of the South Asian community, as a means of corroborating some of my research findings. All five were working with youth in some capacity, either as counsellors or service providers. Jasminder Singh, Rupinder Roshan, and Baldev Mutta were all working in the region of Peel, the first two as community health nurses and the last as a community development worker at the Peel Department of Health. At the time of the interviews, Gurpreet Malhotra was the coordinator of the Dixie-Bloor Neighbourhood Centre, and Harjeet Badwall was employed at the South Asian Women's Centre (located in downtown Toronto) as the coordinator of its youth project. For their extensive experience with issues confronting South Asian youth, their commitment to addressing these concerns, and their long-time work within the communities of which they are a part, I value their knowledge and insights. Interviews with them helped me to corroborate trends in the South Asian community as well as the issues confronting the young women in my study. I have also interviewed DJs, such as Jithen and Raoul S. Juneja, who have been involved in the music scene quite extensively.

47 While the experiences of young South Asian women vary in terms of conflict with their parents, for this study I was specifically interested in interviewing women who felt they were experiencing a significant degree of conflict.

48 Lata Mani, "Contentious Traditions: The Debate on *Sati* in Colonial India," in *Recasting Women: Essays in Indian Colonial History,* ed. Kumkum Sangari and Sudesh Vaid (New Brunswick, New Jersey: Rutgers University Press, 1990), pp. 88–126. Also see Lata Mani, *Contentious Traditions: the Debate on Sati in Colonial India* (Berkeley: University of California Press, 1998).

49 Jenny Sharpe, *Allegories of Empire: The Figure of Woman in the Colonial Text* (London: University of Minnesota Press, 1993), p. 7.

CHAPTER TWO: Important Pieces of History

1 Ali Rattansi, "'Western' Racisms, Ethnicities and Identities in a 'Postmodern' Frame," in *Racism, Modernity and Identity on the Western Front,* ed. Ali Rattansi and Sallie Westwood (Cambridge: Polity Press, 1994), p. 24.

2 Australian historian Lesley Johnson argues that the process of modernization led to the fear that individual consciousness would be unable to develop in a stable and coherent way because of the "limitless opportunities to be something else, and to be a multiplicity of things" (Johnson, *The Modern Girl: Girlhood and Growing Up* [Philadelphia: Open University Press, 1993], p. 38). Moreover, authoritarian enforcement based on divine rule was no longer the order of the day (Franco Moretti, *The Way of the World: The Bildungsroman in European Culture* [London:

Verso, 1987]). The emergence of consumer capitalism and "its promises of the endless opportunities for individuals to transform their lives simply through the purchasing of goods" was instrumental in the process of modernization that Johnson talks about (*Modern Girl*, p. 37). These "limitless opportunities" for transformation through consumer capitalism of course are not accessible to everyone, but apply to the bourgeois notion of middle-class individuality. The fantasy of transformation through consumption, Johnson argues, threatens to undermine the (white) individual's ability to develop itself into a coherent unity. The promise of endless choice and opportunity has been seen as a threat to individual cohesiveness, threatening to make it impossible for an individual to know her- or himself and to develop harmoniously.

Here the model of human growth and development is conceptualized linearly: after passing through a series of biological and social developmental stages, a human being reaches adulthood. Adulthood is seen as the state of being a self-determining, autonomous (modern) individual. This model assumes that harmonious development of the individual is possible. The issue confronting eighteenth-century Europe was the modern notion of the self-determining individual and the traditional notion of social responsibility (Moretti, *Way of the World*). The modern idea of freedom was also seen, in some sense, as an individual's burden. One was now burdened by the responsibility of having to forge one's own identity, albeit in a way that also paralleled the new social order. The modern conditions surrounding individual growth "required that they [young people] remain youth for a definite and extended period of time to ensure their successful negotiation of the tasks of growing up, the tasks of becoming a modern individual" (Johnson, *Modern Girl*, p. 44). It demanded young people's responsible participation in the economic sphere, their commitment as reproducers in the private sphere, and their contribution to the political process, while simultaneously promising complete freedom to forge their own identity and destiny.

3   Moretti, *Way of the World*.

4   Johnson, *Modern Girl*, p. 39. The postwar period was a time of reconstruction, economic boom, and consumer capitalism. The re-emergence of youth as a symbol and victim of modernity has been understood as an indication of the cultural impact of Western modernity (ibid.; Mary Louise Adams, "The Trouble with Normal: Postwar Youth and the Construction of Heterosexuality" [Ph.D. dissertation, University of Toronto, 1994]; also see Mary Louise Adams, *The Trouble with Normal: Postwar Youth and the Making of Heterosexuality* [Toronto: University of Toronto Press, 1997]; Stuart Hall, "The Emergence of Cultural Studies and the Crisis of the Humanities" *October* 53 [Summer 1990]: 11–23). Johnson also identifies the introduction of mass secondary education as one of the changes in the postwar era.

5   Adams, "The Trouble with Normal"; Adams, *The Trouble with Normal*.

6   Richard Hoggart, *The Uses of Literacy* (London: Chatto and Windus, 1957). Although I am discussing the 1950s, G. Stanley Hall's ideas about adolescence as determined by biological/hormonal changes, which were developed at the turn of the century, persisted as a dominant discourse around youth in the postwar climate. Hall is one of the most prominent researchers to contribute to the idea of adolescence as a special stage of human development. He viewed puberty — the onset of sexual development — as a delicate period marking the passage into adulthood. Hall is noteworthy for popularizing the notion of this phase as a stressful period, and what has now

come to be popularly understood as the generation gap between adults and youth. See Hall, *Adolescence: Its Psychology and Its Relations to Physiology, Anthropology, Sociology, Sex, Crime, Religion and Education.* (New York: Appleton, 1907).

7    Mary Louise Adams names "attempted rape, destruction of property, robbery, street violence, disobedience in the classroom, and a pronounced unwillingness to respect authority" as the range of behaviours encompassed by the notion of delinquency — all of which were seen as possibly leading to social unrest ("The Trouble with Normal," p. 115).

8    Ibid., p. 94.

9    It has been argued that the idea of youth as a period of allowed instability is a way to resolve some of the contradictions associated with modern development. Some experts saw the "acting out" of the teenager as a normal part of development so long as the rebellious teenager became a mature responsible adult ready to assume her/his role in the production and reproduction process (Hall, *Adolescence*). Others saw this behaviour as an expression of what had gone wrong with the modern era, namely that the freedoms of modernity had undermined the concept of authority itself (F. Tumpane, "The Cruel World vs. Teenagers," *Chatelaine*, May 1950, pp. 4–5).

10   Adams, "The Trouble with Normal," p. 135.

11   Peter Jackson and Jan Penrose, "Placing 'Race' and Nation," in *Constructions of Race, Place and Nation,* ed. Peter Jackson and Jan Penrose (London: University College, 1993).

12   David Theo Goldberg, *Racist Culture and the Politics of Meaning* (Blackwell: University of Minnesota Press, 1993), p. 85.

13   Buchignani et al., *Continuous Journey*, pp. 14, 90.

14   D.M. Indra, "South Asian Stereotypes in the Vancouver Press," *Ethnic and Racial Studies* 2, no. 2 (1979): 166–189.

15   Bolaria and Li use a political economy approach to examine the migration of South Asians, arguing that the systematic recruitment of Indian labour within the British Empire began with the abolition of slavery in 1833–34. Many historians argue that during this time British colonialists were looking for a supply of labour that was cheap and manageable (N. Gangulee, *Indians in the Empire Overseas* [London: The New India Publishing House, 1947]; H.A. Tinker, *A New System of Slavery* [Oxford: Oxford University Press, 1974]; P. Saha, *Emigration of Indian Labour 1834–1900* [Delhi: People's Publishing House, 1970]; K.P. Sandhu, *Indians in Malaya* [London: Cambridge University Press, 1969]). Having exhausted other possible avenues, either because importing labour was too expensive and fraught with legal problems (as in the case of Chinese workers), or because the supply of labour was considered unmanageable (as in the case of recently freed black slaves whose protest against slavery was expressed in the refusal to do plantation work), the British government looked to India as a source of labour for its other colonies (Bolaria and Li, "Colonialism and Labour: East Indians in Canada," in Bolaria and Li, *Racial Oppression*).

16   South Asians first left India in large numbers as indentured labourers. This type of labour was used especially by the British for the development of West Indian colonies. Under the indentured system, the migrant would exchange his/her labour for passage from India to the West Indies. The migrant was not free to work in any other capacity until this debt of passage was paid off, which could take decades. Indentured labour was officially abolished in 1920 (Bolaria and Li, "Colonialism and Labour").

17    Bolaria and Li, "Colonialism and Labour."

18    Buchignani et al., *Continuous Journey.*

19    Buchignani et al., *Continuous Journey;* Bolaria and Li, "Colonialism and Labour."

20    Buchignani et al., *Continuous Journey,* p. 4.

21    House of Commons, Sessional Paper No. 360, 1908, pp. 7–8, as quoted in Bolaria and Li, "Colonialism and Labour," p. 146.

22    See Buchignani et al., *Continuous Journey,* and Bolaria and Li, "Colonialism and Labour," p. 170.

23    R. Holland, "Indian Immigration into Canada: The Question of a Franchise," *Asian Review* 39 (1943): 167–72.

24    First, none of the 5,000 (mainly Sikh) men who first settled in British Columbia were permitted to have their wives or children join them (R. P. Srivastava, "Family Organization and Change Among the Overseas Indian Immigrant Families of British Columbia, Canada," in *The Family in India — A Regional View,* ed. G. Kurian [The Hague, Netherlands: Mouton, 1974]). This restriction remained until 1919 (Holland, "Indian Immigration into Canada," p. 168), and functioned as a kind of imposed birth control method. Second, South Asians living in Canada were denied legal and political rights until 1947. This "alien" status meant that many lived under the fear of deportation, were occupationally and geographically confined, and were residentially segregated (Gangule, *Indians in the Empire Overseas;* Tinker, *New System of Slavery*).

25    See Buchignani et al., *Continuous Journey,* pp. 53–58; and Bolaria and Li, "Colonialism and Labour."

26    Linda Gordon, *Women's Body, Women's Right: A Social History of Birth Control in America* (New York: Viking, 1976).

27    F.A. Walker, "Immigration and Degradation," *Forum* 11, no. 6 (189): 634–44.

28    Robert Hunter, *Poverty* (New York: Harper Torchbooks, 1904).

29    Angus McLaren and Arlene Tigar McLaren, *The Bedroom and the State* (Toronto: McClelland and Stewart, 1986), p. 16. Note the connection here between discourses of youth and the development of the nation.

30    Quoted in Tinker, *New System of Slavery,* pp. 23–24.

31    Wallace, 1907–08, as cited in McLaren and McLaren, *The Bedroom and the State,* p. 360.

32    American feminist scholar Linda Gordon shows that seemingly dissimilar early-twentieth-century movements that supported the use of birth control, such as feminists and eugenicists, shared a connection to the social anxiety around race purity. It is not surprising that the issues of immigration and women's right to control their sexualities were interconnected and manifested themselves in the controversy over birth control. For race purity theorists, the issue of birth control had double implications. Its use by white, middle-class women was condemned as a means by which the reproduction of the white population was being limited; yet it was upheld as a noble gesture when used by non-white and poor populations to restrict their numbers. Those who claimed that the white race was under threat of extinction were concerned about the following issues: that white women in the nineteenth century began to reproduce at a decreasing rate; that this decline in the birth rate was conscious and intentional; and that the fertility rate of "moral" and

"respectable WASP" people was considerably lower than that of immigrants, blacks, and poorer classes (L. Gordon, *Women's Body, Women's Right*, pp. 153–55). A review of the arguments by proponents of the race suicide theory reveals an overall strategy to manage and justify noticeable inequities within the developing modern social order. Much of the controversy around the outnumbering of the white population and the use of eugenics to limit or raise the birth rate of specific groups reflects underlying class, race, and gender disparities and struggles. Gordon concludes that "the societal changes that make large families no longer advantageous — [such as] the high cost of education, food and rent and the end of productive child labour" contributed to the decline in fertility rates among white, middle-class families in the Western world (p. 155).

CHAPTER THREE: Modest and Modern: Women As Markers of the Indian Nation State

1   For example, some women had older siblings whom they could go out with or who would "cover" for them, and some had friends or relatives they could rely on as a network of support or as a means of access to public spaces, such as a dance or club.

2   Mani, "Contentious Traditions"; Mani, *Contentious Traditions*; P. Chatterjee, *The Nation and Its Fragments: Colonial and Post-Colonial Histories* (New Jersey: Princeton University Press, 1993); P. Chatterjee, *Wages of Freedom: Fifty Years of the Indian Nation State* (Delhi: Oxford University Press, 1998); Jasodhara Bagchi, "Colonialism and Socialization: The Girl Child in Colonial Bengal," *Resources for Feminist Research* 22, no. 3/4 (Fall/Winter 1993): 23–30.

3   Nalini Natarajan argues, in the context of India, that women have become the terrain of a nationalist message of "containment of the threat to national culture from diasporic Indian populations" living outside the Indian subcontinent (Natarajan, "Woman, Nation and Narration in *Midnight's Children*," in *Scattered Hegemonies: Postmodernity and Transitional Feminist Practice*, ed. Inderpal Grewal and Caren Kaplan [Minneapolis: University of Minnesota Press, 1994], p. 87). In later chapters, I adopt her notion of modernity as sexual threat in the Canadian context, arguing that similar notions of modernity operate within the South Asian community in Canada.

4   Mani, "Contentious Traditions," p. 90.

5   The contradiction for women within modernity is that the notion of womanhood has to incorporate the freedoms supposedly opened up by modern progress while simultaneously attending to the responsibility attributed to women, of preserving the morality of the individual and the social order, especially through the family. See Joan Landes, "Women and the Public Sphere: A Modern Perspective," *Social Analysis* 15 (1984): 20–31. To refer back to Franco Moretti's argument from the previous chapter, the notion of modern self-government includes both the individual's capacity to govern the self through the ability to reason, and the social capacity to self-govern through democratic participation. Within this construction, the only way that traditional notions of responsibility can be maintained is if the individual perceives the norms of social order as her/his own. As Moretti argues: "The ideal of the self-determining or self-legislating individual meant that social order could no longer be maintained by the force of tradition, and consent to that order could no longer be gained through the exercise of the authority of a sovereign form

of power ... The problem was posed in terms of how the 'free individual' could be required to be, at the same time, the 'convinced citizen' — not as a fearful subject, but as one who perceives 'the social norms as one's own'" (as paraphrased in Leslie Johnson, *The Modern Girl*, p. 37).

6    *Khan dhan* means "kinship/extended family."

7    Joseph Levenson, *Confucian China and Its Modern Fate: A Trilogy* (Berkeley: University of California Press, 1965).

8    Duara Prasenjit, "Bifurcating Linear Histories in China and India," in *Rescuing History from the Nation: Questioning Narratives of Modern China*, by Duara Prasenjit (Chicago: University of Chicago Press, 1995), p. 56.

9    Ibid., p. 66. Prasenjit invents the term *discent* to indicate both "dissent" and "descent."

10    See Benedict Anderson, *Imagined Communities: Reflections on the Origin and Spread of Nationalism*, rev. ed. (London: Verso Press, 1991) for more on nations as imagined communities.

11    Floya Anthias and Nira Yuval-Davis, introduction to *Woman-Nation-State,* ed. Floya Anthias and Nira Yuval-Davis (London: Macmillan, 1989), pp. 113–14.

12    Vinita Srivastava, currently a freelance journalist in New York, is the co-founder of "Masala Mixx" and founder of the on-line magazine (e-zine) *\*BrownSugar* (www.brownsugaronline.com) — a culture and arts magazine for South Asian women.

13    See Mani, "Contentious Traditions"; Mani, *Contentious Traditions;* and Lata Mani, "Multiple Mediations: Feminist Scholarship in the Age of Multinational Reception" in *Feminist Review* 35 (Summer 1990): 24–41.

14    See Gita Sahgal and Nira Yuval-Davis, "Introduction: Fundamentalism, Multiculturalism and Women in Britain," in *Refusing Holy Orders: Women and Fundamentalism in Britain,* ed. Gita Sahgal and Nira Yuval-Davis (London: Virago Press, 1992), pp. 1–25.

15    Brahmanic scriptures form the basis (textually, not necessarily in practice) of Hindu philosophical and religious principles.

16    See Mani, "Contentious Traditions," p. 116, for a more thorough examination of colonialist assumptions of Indian tradition and cultural practices as well as the process by which they became encoded in the legal system. Also see Mani, *Contentious Traditions;* Mani, "Multiple Mediations."

17    Ibid., p. 118.

18    Sumit Sarkar, "Rammohun Roy and the Break with the Past," in *Roy and the Process of Modernization,* ed. V.C. Joshi (Delhi: Vikas, 1975), pp. 52–53, as cited ibid., p. 114.

19    Gita Sahgal, "Secular Spaces: The Experience of Asian Women Organizing," in *Refusing Holy Orders: Women and Fundamentalism in Britain,* ed. Gita Sahgal and Nira Yuval-Davis (London: Virago Press, 1992), pp. 163–97.

20    See Natarajan, "Woman, Nation and Narration"; J. Bagchi, "Colonialism and Socialization," pp. 23–30; Kumkum Sangari and Sudesh Vaid, eds., *Recasting Women: Essays in Indian Colonial History* (New Brunswick, New Jersey: Rutgers University Press, 1990); Mani, "Multiple Mediations," pp. 24–41; Mani, "Contentious Traditions"; Mani, *Contentious Traditions.*

21    Chatterjee, *Nation and Its Fragments,* p. 121; also see pp. 116–34.

22    Ibid., p. 131.

23    Ibid., p. 121.

24    As quoted in Kumari Jayawardena, *Feminism and Nationalism in the Third World* (New Delhi: Kali for Women, 1986), p. 95.

25    Ketu Ketrak, "Indian Nationalism, Gandhian Satyagraha and Representations of Female Sexuality," in *Nationalism and Sexualities,* ed. Andre Parker et al. (New York: Routledge, 1992), p. 396.

      Ketrak argues that Gandhi deliberately chose certain mythological heroines over others because they best embodied these virtues. For example, Gandhi praised the virtues of figures like Sita and Draupadi who, according to Hindu mythology, embodied notions of strength that lay in self-sacrifice and passivity. He chose these symbols over such heroines as the Rani of Jhansi who cloaked herself in male attire and in 1857 led troops into battle against the British Raj (p. 398).

26    Ibid., p. 391.

27    Chatterjee, *Nation and Its Fragments,* p. 131. The West was aligned with the kind of modernity nationalists wanted to distinguish themselves from; they saw Western modernism as contradictory to the Indian identity that needed preserving. According to nationalist discourses, the inner core of this identity was contained within the private sphere, and could be preserved by women. A multitude of claims were made by Indian nationalists about the superior moral character of women that justified their suitability for this role. Women and the true essence of Indian identity became synonymous, and both were seen as in need of protection from the threat of Western modernity.

28    Ibid., p. 129.

29    For more on Hindu womanhood and Indian national identity, see Bagchi, "Colonialism and Socialization."

30    Laura Ann Stoler, "Carnal Knowledge and Imperial Power: Gender, Race and Morality in Colonial Asia," in *Gender at the Crossroads of Knowledge: Feminist Anthropology in the Post-Modern Era,* ed. Micaela di Leonardo (Berkley: University of California Press, 1991), p. 52.

31    Ibid., p. 53.

32    This was justified in relation to particular assumptions about European women. The Dutch argued that women might obstruct permanent settlement. Also, children would not be able to assimilate to the conditions of the colonies and sickness might force families to return back home (ibid.).

33    For example, both Laura Ann Stoler (ibid.) and Jenny Sharpe (*Allegories of Empire*) argue that the panic over the rape of white women by "native men," which circulated in the colonies in the late nineteenth and early twentieth centuries, was due to a crisis in colonial authority. Sharpe contends that rebellions such as the Indian Mutiny of 1857 mobilized a discourse of sexual assault on white women that was really about race. The idea of the native man as incapable of sexual restraint and as a threat to European women and white honour emerged as a means of maintaining the notion of white racial superiority. Stoler maintains that this panic also helped to put in place certain legal measures that increased the regulation of natives, such as the segregation of social spaces, harsher penalties for crossing racial lines, and restrictions on interracial mixing.

34    Stoler, "Carnal Knowledge," p. 70.

CHAPTER FOUR: Fusion or Confusion?

1    Communities of diaspora were originally associated with the Jews, and the term has also come to mean the similar exile or plight of a people. In the past few decades, the idea of diaspora has been applied to a black and pan-African identity and more recently to a South Asian one.

2    For more on how diaspora both defies and reproduces the norms of the nation-state, see J. Clifford, "Diasporas," *Cultural Anthropology* (August 1994): 302–38; Inderpal Grewal and Caren Kaplan, eds., *Scattered Hegemonies: Postmodernity and Transitional Feminist Practices* (Minneapolis: University of Minnesota Press, 1994).

3    Floya Anthias and Nira Yuval-Davis, *Racialized Boundaries: Race, Nation, Gender, Colour and Class and the Anti-Racist Struggle* (London: Routledge, 1993), pp. 21–22.

4    See ibid.; and Gita Sahgal, "Secular Spaces," pp. 163–97.

5    Norman Cafik, "Multiculturalism," in *Multiculturalism*, Canada, Minister of State (Ottawa: Government of Canada, 1978), p. 6

6    I do not believe that a land that is already inhabited can be discovered or founded. I would also like to question the notion of the English and French as "races."

7    The Royal Commission on Bilingualism and Biculturalism as quoted in Cafik, "Multiculturalism," p. 10.

8    Essed, "Understanding Everyday Racism," p. 17.

9    Nineteenth-century arguments about racial inferiority (based on biological and genetic differences) are no longer credible and have been replaced with notions of cultural inferiority (see L. Abu-Lughod, "Writing Against Culture"); also see ibid.

10   By "cultural esteem" I mean the level of pride in one's own cultural, ethnic, or racial identity.

11   While I will be elaborating further on the construction and preservation of internal boundaries around Indian-ness in Chapter 6, I would like to draw attention to the fact that Pinki does not allow for the possibility of West Indians, nor for their inclusion in her definitions of "Indian."

12   Errol Lawrence, "Just Plain Common Sense: The 'Roots' of Racism," in *The Empire Strikes Back: Race and Racism in 70s Britain*, Centre for Contemporary Cultural Studies, University of Birmingham (London: Hutchinson University Library and the Centre for Contemporary Cultural Studies, 1982).

13   G. Tsolidis, "Ethnic Minority Girls and Self-Esteem," in *Hearts and Minds: Self-Esteem and the Schooling of Girls*, ed. J. Kenway and S. Willis (London: Falmer Press, 1990), p. 60.

14   Mary Louise Adams, taking up Michel Foucault's work on discourse and power, argues that the construction of norms and the process of normalization involves "discourses and practices that produce subjects who are 'normal,' who live in 'normality' and, most importantly, find it hard to imagine anything differently" (Adams, "The Trouble with Normal," p. 23). Adams provides an historical overview of the different uses of *norm* as description and *norm* as a standard of measure. In the first instance, *normal* can refer to that which is common or typical, while in the second instance, *normal* is an evaluative category. The normal/pathological dichotomy emerged in the field of medicine in the 1800s when *normal* became associated with health. The norm in this sense came to be seen as more than a description of what was common in that it became a standard of measure, a desir-

able condition, how things should be. The notions of norm and normal, Adams concludes, although different, have contributed to the idea of "normal" as a significant social marker and as a vehicle of measuring difference. She argues that "it is when this measure of difference goes to work through moral discourses that it becomes a norm, a regulatory standard of behaviour, an expression of disciplinary power" (p. 26).

15  I elaborate further on the idea of insider norms in the next chapter, which explores how certain notions of community, ethnicity, and gender work together in regulating the lives of young South Asian women in Canada.

16  Anne Campbell, "Self Definition by Rejection: The Case of Gang Girls," *Social Problems* 34 (December 1987): 452.

17  Ibid.

18  Ibid., p. 456.

19  Campbell (ibid.) does not problematize the hierarchical ordering of "American" and "Puerto Rican."

20  Cafik, "Multiculturalism."

21  Adams, "The Trouble with Normal"; Adams, *The Trouble with Normal.*

22  Teun van Dijk, *Elite Discourse and Racism* (Newbury Park: Sage Publications, 1993), pp. 248.

23  Ibid., 249.

24  Ibid., p. 250.

25  Christopher Husbands, "Crises of National Identity as the 'New Moral Panics': Political Agenda Setting about Definitions of Nationhood," *New Community* 20 (January 2, 1994). This panic has reached notably more critical levels in the aftermath of September 11, 2001, in the United States, Canada, and other NATO countries. Because immigrants, of Muslim denomination in particular, have been associated with the attacks, there has been a heightened focus on people of colour and immigrants in general in relation to crime and terrorism. Three months after the destruction of the World Trade Center, Canada proposed tightened immigration laws, announcing that only those with a job offer and extremely close relatives here will have a chance of getting in. Interestingly enough, Torstar News Service reports the decrease in performance of new skilled worker immigrants in the 1990s — which has "fallen below that of the average Canadian" — as among the reasons for stricter immigration policies (*Metro Today,* December 18, 2001, and December 19, 2001, p. 2).

26  Husbands, "Crises of National Identity," p. 193; also see Stanley Cohen, *Folk Devils and Moral Panics* (London: MacGibbon and Kee, 1972).

27  Canadian Press, "Poll Showed Hostility to Immigrants."

28  "Immigrants' Origins Increasingly Diverse: Demographers Fear Racist Backlash," *Globe and Mail,* December 9, 1992, A9. The 1991 census showed that 4.3 million immigrants are residing in Canada, which is 16.1 percent of the Canadian population, consistent with the 1940s.

29  Associated Press, "Population Crisis Feared As Billions Enter Fertile Years," *Globe and Mail,* March 4, 1995, A1.

30  Harvey Schachter, "Toronto Is a Changed Metropolis," *Montreal Gazette,* December 21, 1994, B3.

31   Lila Sarick, "Ethnic Melting Pot, or Cauldron?" *Globe and Mail,* December 29, 1994, A4.

32   Lila Sarick, "Region Deals with Influx of Immigrants," *Globe and Mail,* December 28, 1994, A1; Lila Sarick, "A Region Grown Like a Gawky Adolescent," *Globe and Mail,* December 30, 1994, A4.

33   Ibid.; Sarick, "Ethnic Melting Pot, or Cauldron?"

34   Sarick, "A Region Grown Like a Gawky Adolescent."

35   Ibid.

36   *Montreal Gazette,* May 18, 1995, A9; *Calgary Herald,* May 18, 1995, A13. Notice the discrepancy in parallels here: not English-speaking and multilingual.

37   In the aftermath of the September 11, 2001, destruction of the World Trade Center in New York, we can add to the list of anxieties the association of South Asian immigrants to acts of terrorist violence.

38   Alanna Mitchell, "Immigrants' Origins Increasingly Diverse: Demographer Fears Racist Backlash," *Globe and Mail,* December 9, 1992, A9.

39   Ibid.

40   My objective here is not to single out David Hayes ("The Dances, the Firebomb and the Clash of Cultures") or Trish Woods (CBC Television, *The Fifth Estate,* November 1993) for partiality. According to a rationalist framework, their representations of the South Asian community would fall under the category of balanced, fair, and objective reporting. My purpose is to look at some of the ways in which discourses around race, ethnicity, gender, modernity, and culture are hidden under commonsense representations and readings of demographic change.

CHAPTER FIVE: The Hall of Shame

1   Leslie Roman, "Intimacy, Labour, and Class: Ideologies of Feminine Sexuality in the Punk Slam Dance," in *Becoming Feminine: The Politics of Popular Culture,* ed. Leslie G. Roman and Linda K. Christian-Smith with Elizabeth Ellsworth (London: The Falmer Press, 1988).

2   M. Douglas, *Purity and Danger* (London: Routledge, 1984).

3   Roman, "Intimacy, Labour, and Class," pp. 134, 136.

4   Quoted in David Hayes, "The Dances, the Firebomb, and the Clash of Cultures," pp. 120, 123. While Mr. Pandoori is one voice within the South Asian community, his perspective is representative of its conservative element. He is also an influential leader within the Punjabi community, especially among Peel residents.

5   Angela McRobbie, *Feminism and Youth Culture: From "Jackie" to "Just Seventeen"* (London: Macmillan, 1991), p. 193.

6   Floya Anthias and Nira Yuval-Davis, introduction to *Woman-Nation-State,* p. 102.

7   The regulation of women's bodies through social sanctions and controls, such as the bodily controls that Leslie Roman speaks about (in "Intimacy, Labour, and Class"), has been documented in both sociological as well as anthropological research. See S. Ardener, "Introduction: The Nature of Women in Society," in *Defining Females,* ed. S. Ardener (New York: Wiley, 1978); S. Ortner and H. Whitehead, "Introduction: Accounting for Sexual Meanings," in *Sexual Meanings,* ed. S. Ortner and H. Whitehead (Cambridge: Cambridge University Press, 1981),

pp. 1–28; E.M. Schur, *Labelling Women Deviant* (Philadelphia: Temple University Press, 1984); C. Smart and B. Smart, *Women, Sexuality and Social Control* (London: Routledge, 1978). Feminist scholars have also illustrated that women who challenge the norms of appropriate feminine behaviour are often open to social disapproval through the "sexualization" of their behaviour. For example, L.S. Smith has argued that girls who transcend the norms of femininity through delinquent behaviour are portrayed by adults in the legal system as sexually promiscuous (L.S. Smith, "Sexist Assumptions and Female Delinquency: An Empirical Investigation," in *Women, Sexuality and Social Control*, ed. B. Smart and C. Smart (London: Routledge, 1978), pp. 74–86.

8    Susan Lees, *Losing Out: Sexuality and Adolescent Girls* (London: Hutchinson, 1986).

9    Christine Griffin, *Representations of Youth: The Study of Youth and Adolescence in Britain and America* (Cambridge: Polity Press, 1993), p. 160.

10    I will be exploring further the complexity of narratives of South Asian-ness in relation to the context of racism in the concluding chapter of this book.

11    Chatterjee, *The Nation and Its Fragments*.

## CHAPTER SIX: A Patch of "Indian"

1    Although *bhangra* in its original sense refers to traditional Punjabi folk music, now most South Asian music, whether it has traces of bhangra or not, is commonly referred to in the mainstream media as bhangra.

2    *Desi* is a South Asian word for "homemade" and "authentic," also commonly used as self-reference.

3    Several scholars have attempted to demythologize the sameness associated with South Asian diaspora. In order to resist hegemonic notions of diasporic identity, says Jasbir Puar, we must pay attention to "class positionings, immigration histories, nation-state formations, nationalisms, and racisms [all of which] enable and disable different configurations of home, of belonging, of being" (Puar, "Writing My Way 'Home'," p. 57). Amarpal K. Dhaliwal argues that while diaspora works to subvert hegemonic notions of nation it does not "automatically" or always do so. He argues that the "South Asian diaspora constitute[s] diaspora in nationalist terms by privileging India as nation and a Hindu notion of India, at that" (Dhaliwal, "Reading Diaspora: Self-Representational Practices and the Politics of Reception," *Socialist Review* [Special Issue: *The Traveling Nation: India and Its Diaspora*] 24, no. 4 [1994]: 18).

4    Certain voting rights are reserved for Canadian citizens only (permanent residents or those with landed immigrant status cannot vote in federal and most provincial elections). Landed or permanent status is not as permanent as the term implies. For example, those who are found guilty of certain criminal and civil crimes, those deemed to be a danger to the public, and those who leave the country for more than six months are subject to having their status revoked. Also, some government jobs and grants are reserved for Canadian citizens. (See Community Legal Education Ontario [CLEO], "Immigration and Refugee Fact Sheet" [Toronto: Community Legal Education Ontario, 2000].)

5    Mohanty, "Defining Genealogies," p. 352.

6    Ibid.

7   See Discography for more detail.

8   Paul Willis has suggested symbolic work is not something specific to the official
    world of art alone, but is part of the daily practice of all individuals, who through
    signs and symbols "establish their presence, identity and meaning" (Willis, *Common
    Culture: Symbolic Work at Play in the Everyday Cultures of the Young* [Milton Keynes:
    Open University Press, 1990], p. 1). Willis claims that young people as a group are
    most indicative of the dynamics of symbolic activity because it is at this age "where
    people are formed most self-consciously through their own symbolic and other
    activities ... It is also the stage where people begin to construct themselves through
    nuance and complexity, through difference as well as similarity" (p. 8).

9   Rattansi, "'Western' Racisms," p. 77.

10  Satpal Ram was wrongfully accused of murder and sentenced to ten years in prison
    for a crime he committed in self-defence to ward off a racially motivated attack in
    the U.K. He ultimately spent fifteen years in prison, and was released in June 2002,
    though his conviction still remains to be overturned.

11  As quoted in Sahgal, "Secular Spaces," p. 180.

12  I have been host and producer of the show "Masala Mixx" since co-founding it
    with Vinita Srivastava in 1992 at CKLN 88.1 FM, a community radio station based
    at Ryerson University in Toronto.

13  Interview with DJ Jithen, July 26, 1996.

14  Interview with DJ Jithen, December 17, 2001.

15  Ibid.

16  For more on South Asians' tradition of resistance and solidarity with black resist-
    ance movements, see Prashad Vijay, *The Karma of Brown Folk* (Minneapolis:
    University of Minnesota Press, 2000), pp. 157–83.

17  Amarjit Singh, "African Americans and the New Immigrants," in *Between the Lines:
    South Asians and Postcoloniality*, ed., Deepika Bahri and Mary Vasudeva
    (Philadelphia: Temple University Press, 1996).

18  For more information regarding the demolition of the Babri Masjid, see Ramesh
    Thakur, "Ayodhya and the Politics of India's Secularism: A Double Standards
    Discourse," *Asian Survey* 33, no. 7 (1993: 653–57).

19  While Muslim separate schools do exist in Toronto, they are privately funded.

20  C. Dwyer, "Constructions of Muslim Identity and the Contesting of Power: The
    Debate over Muslim Schools in the United Kingdom," in *Constructions of Race,
    Place and Nation,* ed. P. Jackson and J. Penrose (London: University College, 1993).

21  Ibid.

22  For a comprehensive look at the Sikh community in Ontario, see J. Bali and S.L.
    Manohar, eds., *Sikhs in Ontario* (Toronto: Ontario Council of Sikhs, 1993).

23  While I am suggesting parallel positions of dominance for Hindu and Sikh commu-
    nities in Canada, I do so with caution. Punjabi Sikhs within India do not have the
    same access to structural power as Hindus do, and therefore in some ways comprise
    a minority. I am suggesting that Hindu/Hindi-speaking and Sikh/Punjabi-speak-
    ing South Asians in Canada dominate as cultural groups in relation to South Asians
    from other diasporic communities, such as the Caribbean and other parts of the
    subcontinent, and from other linguistic and religious backgrounds.

24     See, for example, Vinay Lal, "Sikh Kirpans in California Schools: The Social Construction of Symbols, Legal Pluralism, and the Politics of Diversity," *Amerasia* 22(1) (Spring 1996); also see Vinay Lal, "Sikh Kirpans in California Schools: The Social Construction of Symbols, the Cultural Politics of Identity, and the Limits of Multiculturalism in *New Spiritual Homes: Religion and Asian Americans*, ed. David K. Yoo (Honolulu, Hawaii: University of Hawaii Press, 1999).

25     See, for example, *India-West*, June 9, 1995, and June 23, 1995, for the connection between Hindu fundamentalism in the United States and in India.

26     Grewal and Kaplan, *Scattered Hegemonies*, p. 56.

27     I would like to point out that the mid-1970s wave of immigration to Canada differed significantly from the 1960s wave of professional migrants from the South Asian subcontinent. At this time there was an increasing need for semi-skilled labour in Canada. This shift in labour needs, of course, greatly affected the class profile of South Asian immigrants (Bolaria and Li, *Racial Oppression in Canada*). While most of the parents of the young women in my study are 1970s migrants, I am unable to make any substantive conclusions regarding class and notions of tradition in the way that Grewal has suggested for 1960s migrants to the United States. My sample is too small for any speculation regarding transnational class alliances and the implications for the 1970s wave of South Asian immigrants, or any similarities or differences in notions of tradition or ties to the subcontinent.

28     Vinay Lal, "The Nation, Nation-State and the Cultural Politics of Hindu/Indian Womanhood in the Indian Diaspora" (paper presented at "Challenge and Change: The Indian Diaspora in Its Historical and Contemporary Contexts," St. Augustine, Trinidad, University of West Indies, August 11–18, 1995).

29     For the masculine-feminine contestation in relation to British and Indian nationalisms, see Mrinalini Sinha, *Colonial Masculinity: The 'Manly Englishman' and the Effeminate Bengali' in the Late Nineteenth Century* (Manchester: Manchester University Press, 1995). She argues that British superiority was accomplished through discourses that posited British men as masculine in relation to "bengali babu."

30     Lal, "The Nation."

CHAPTER SEVEN: Endings: From Barbie to Bindis

1     *Mary-kateandashley* magazine, August/September 2001.

2     Iguana Cultural Gift Shop Web site, www.artworldiguana.com, July 20, 2002.

3     See Anthias and N. Yuval-Davis, *Racialized Boundaries*; V.M. Moghadam, ed. *Gender and National Identity: Women and Politics in Muslim Societies* (London: Zed Books, 1994).

4     In suggesting that the issue of culture clash is situated between the values of modernity and premodernity, I am not assuming that the significance or meanings attached to the categories "modern" and "traditional" are the same for every ethnic/racial group, or that the conflicts for South Asian youth are no different from those of white youth. The issue of generational clash between the values of a premodern society and a modern one is for South Asian youth embedded in racialized discourses of cultural difference. The East-West contest over cultural difference can be traced back to the colonial period and has continued to manifest itself in various ways in neocolonial North America since the turn of the last century.

5     Buchignani et al., *Continuous Journey,* p. 4.

6     Jenny Sharpe, *Allegories of Empire;* Stoler, "Carnal Knowledge and Imperial Power," pp. 51–101.

7     Claire Pajaczkowska and Lola Young, "Racism, Representation, Psychoanalysis," in *"Race", Culture and Difference,* ed. James Donald and Ali Rattansi (London: Sage Publications, 1992), p. 204.

8     Prasenjit, *Rescuing History from the Nation.*

9     Lal, "The Nation."

10    Rattansi, "'Western' Racisms," pp. 15–86.

11    Grewal, "The Post-Colonial, Ethnic Studies and the Diaspora," *Socialist Review* (Special Issue: *The Traveling Nation: India and the Diaspora*) 24, no. 4 (1994): 45–74.

     In arguing that the South Asian diaspora emulates features of the Indian nation-state, both in its exclusion of identities and in its notions of womanhood and community, I do not want to reproduce the very erasures that I am critiquing by displacing already marginalized communities. I am not suggesting, for example, that Pakistan, Bangladesh, and other parts of the subcontinent do not mobilize their own particular iconographies, symbols, and formulae in the womanhood-nation construction. I am arguing that the discourse of Indian nationalism has tended to dominate much of the diaspora. Evidence of this can be seen, for example, in the constant displacement of "other" South Asians: Indians from India have to be reminded that there are Indians from other places, such as the Caribbean and Fiji. In my own research, testimony to this brand of indocentrism was found in young women's self-identifications as "Indian" over "Pakistani," "East African," or "South Asian" and the omission of "West Indian." Also, while there are parallels between colonial discourses of identity and diasporic ones, there are also differences between diasporic and Indian nationalist and nation-state narratives of Indian-ness.

     I would argue that living in the West, in diaspora, has in many ways threatened the distinction between westernization and modernization that was a central component of nationalist discourses. More than on the subcontinent itself, notions of identity, culture, and tradition seem static and historically dated in diaspora. This is partly due to the fact that the anxiety about westernization and cultural dilution is a contemporary reality and not just a relic of the past. Consequently South Asian communities are charged with being more traditional or conservative than those within the subcontinent. The anxiety over loss of identity is very real in the face of Canadian assimilationism.

12    Puar, "Writing My Way 'Home'," p. 97.

13    Interview with Raoul Juneja, January 10, 2002. Juneja is the founder and current head of Lyrical Knockout Entertainment, and former co-host of CHRW 94.7 FM, the radio station of the University of Western Ontario.

# Bibliography

 Abu-Lughod, L. *Remaking Women: Feminism and Modernity in the Middle East.* Princeton, NJ: Princeton University Press, 1998.

———. "Writing Against Culture." *Recapturing Anthropology: Working in the Present.* Ed. R. Fox. Santa Fe, New Mexico: School of American Press, 1991.

Adams, M.L. "The Trouble with Normal: Postwar Youth and the Construction of Heterosexuality." Ph.D. dissertation: University of Toronto, 1994.

———. *The Trouble with Normal: Postwar Youth and the Making of Heterosexuality.* Toronto: University of Toronto Press, 1997.

Ajello, R. "New Talk of A B.C. Influx." *Maclean's* 109 (Feb. 5, 1996): 28.

Alcoff, L. "Cultural Feminism Versus Post-Structuralism: The Identity Crisis in Feminist Theory." *Signs* 13 (Spring 1988): 405–36.

———. "Philosophy and Racial Identity." *Radical Philosophy* (Jan./ Feb., 1996): 5–14.

Althusser, L. *For Marx.* Trans. B. Brewster. London: Verso Press, 1979.

———. "Ideology and Ideological State Apparatuses (Notes Towards an Investigation)." *Lenin and Philosophy and Other Essays.* Trans. B. Brewster. New York: Monthly Review Press, 1971.

Amos, V. and P. Parmar. "Challenging Imperial Feminism." *Feminist Review* 17 (July 1984): 3–19.

―――. "Resistances and Responses: The Experiences of Black Girls in Britain." *Feminism for Girls: An Adventure Story.* Ed. A. McRobbie and T. McCabe. London: Routledge, 1981.

Anderson, B. *Imagined Communities: Reflections on the Origin and Spread of Nationalism.* Revised Edition. London: Verso Press, 1991.

Antaki, C., ed. *Analyzing Everyday Explanation.* London: Sage Publications, 1988.

Anthias, F. "Race and Class Revisited ― Conceptualizing Race and Racisms." *The Sociological Review* 38, no. 1 (Feb. 1990): 19–42.

Anthias, F. and G. Lazaridis. *Gender and Migration in Southern Europe: Women on the Move.* New York: Oxford Berg, 2000.

Anthias, F. and N. Yuval-Davis. *Racialized Boundaries: Race, Nation, Gender, Colour and Class and the Anti-Racist Struggle.* London: Routledge, 1993.

―――. Introduction to *Woman-Nation-State.* Ed. F. Anthias and N. Yuval-Davis. London: Macmillan, 1989.

Appadurai, A. "Global Ethnoscapes: Notes and Queries for a Transnational Anthropology." *Recapturing Anthropology: Working in the Present.* Ed. R.G. Fox. New Mexico: School of American Research Press, 1991.

Appiah, K. A. *In My Father's House: Africa in the Philosophy of Culture.* New York: Oxford University Press, 1992.

Ardener, S. "Introduction: The Nature of Women in Society." *Defining Females.* Ed. S. Ardener. New York: Wiley, 1978.

Ashworth, M. "Results and Issues from a National Survey of ESL Programs." *Education of Immigrant Students.* Ed. A. Wolfgang. Toronto: OISE Press, 1975.

Back, L. "The Unity Beat." *Guardian Newspaper.* October 13, 1993, 25.

Bagchi, J. "Colonialism and Socialization: The Girl Child in Colonial Bengal," *Resources for Feminist Research* 22, no. 3/4 (Fall/Winter 1993): 23–30.

―――. *Indian Women, Myth and Reality.* Hyderabad: Sangam Books, 1995.

Bali, J. and S.L. Manohar, eds. *Sikhs in Ontario.* Toronto: Ontario Council of Sikhs, 1993.

Ballard, C. "Conflict, Continuity and Change: Second-Generation South Asians." *Minority Families in Britain: Support and Stress.* Ed. V.S. Khan. London: Macmillan Press, 1979.

Ballard, R., ed. *Desh Pardesh: The South Asian Presence in Britain.* London: Hurst and Company, 1994.

Bannerji, H. "But Who Speaks for Us? Experience and Agency in Conventional Feminist Paradigms." *Unsettling Relations: The University as a Site of Feminist Struggles.* Ed. H. Bannerji. Toronto: Women's Press, 1991.

———, ed. *Thinking Through: Essays on Feminism, Marxism and Anti-Racism.* Toronto: Women's Press, 1995.

Barrett, M. "The Concept of Difference." *Feminist Review* 26 (July 1987): 29–41.

Barvth, L.G., and M.L. Manning. *Multicultural Education of Children and Adolescents.* Needham Heights, MA: Allyn and Bacon, 1992.

Bennett, T. *Culture, Ideology and Social Process: A Reader.* London: Batsford Academic and Educational in association with the Open University, 1981.

Berman, M. *All That Is Solid Melts into Air.* London: Verso Press, 1985.

Berry, J.W., R. Kalin, D.M. Taylor. *Multiculturalism and Ethnic Attitudes in Canada.* Ottawa: Minister of Supply and Services, 1977.

Bolaria, B.S., and P.S. Li. "Colonialism and Labour: East Indians in Canada." *Racial Oppression in Canada.* 2nd ed. Ed. B.S. Bolaria and P.S. Li. Toronto: Garamond Press, 1988.

———. *Racial Oppression in Canada.* Toronto: Garamond Press, 1985.

Bonnet, A. and G.L. Watson, eds. *Emerging Perspectives on the Black Diaspora.* New York: University Press of America, 1990.

Borland, K. "That's Not What I Said: Interpretive Conflict in Oral Narrative Research." *Women's Words: the Feminist Practice of Oral History.* Ed. D. Patai and S.B. Gluck. New York: Routledge, 1991.

Brah, A. *Culture and Identity: The Case of South Asians.* E 354, Block 3, Units 8–9: Open University, 1982.

———. "Difference, Diversity and Differentiation." *"Race", Culture and Difference.* Ed. J. Donalds and A. Rattansi. London: Sage Publications, 1992.

———. *Inter-Generational and Inter-Ethnic Perceptions among Asian and White Adolescents and Their Parents.* Ph.D. dissertation: Bristol University, 1994.

———. "'Race' and 'Culture' in the Gendering of Labour Markets." *The Dynamics of Race and Gender.* Ed. H. Afshar and M. Maynard. London: Taylor & Francis, Ltd., 1994.

Brah, A. and R. Minha. "Structural Racism or Cultural Difference: Schooling for Asian Girls." *Just a Bunch of Girls.* Ed. G. Weiner. Philadelphia: Open University Press, 1985.

Breman, J. and P. du Roy. *Imperial Monkey Business: Racial Supremacy in Social Darwinist Theory and Colonial Practice.* Amsterdam: VU University Press, 1990.

Buchanan, J. "Young Women's Complex Lives and the Idea of Youth Transitions." *Youth Subcultures: Theory, History and the Australian Experience.* Ed. R. White. Hobart: National Clearinghouse for Youth Studies, 1993.

Buchignani, N. et al. *Continuous Journey: A Social History of South Asians in Canada.* Toronto: McClelland and Stewart, 1985.

Bullivant, B.M. "Culture: Its Nature and Meaning for Educators." *Multicultural Education: Issues and Perspectives.* 2nd ed. Ed. J. Banks, A. Cherry, and M. Banks. Boston: Allyn and Bacon, 1993.

Butler, J. *Gender Trouble: Feminism and the Subversion of Identity.* New York: Routledge, 1990.

Cafik, N. "Multiculturalism." *Multiculturalism.* Canada, Minister of State. Ottawa: Government of Canada, 1978.

Calmore, J. O. "Critical Race Theory, Archie Shepp, and Fire Music: Securing an Authentic Intellectual Life in a Multicultural World." *Southern Law Review* 65 (July 5, 1992): 2129–30.

Campbell, A. *Bridging Cultures.* Belconnen, Australia: Faculty of Education, University of Canberra, 1995.

———. "Self Definition by Rejection: The Case of Gang Girls." *Social Problems* 34 (December 1987): 451–66.

Carby, H. "Schooling for Babylon." *The Empire Strikes Back: Race and Racism in 70s Britain.* Centre for Contemporary Cultural Studies, University of Birmingham. London: Hutchison University Library and The Centre for Contemporary Cultural Studies, 1982.

Centre for Contemporary Cultural Studies, University of Birmingham. *The Empire Strikes Back: Race and Racism in 70s Britain.* London: Hutchison University Library and The Centre for Contemporary Cultural Studies, 1982.

Chatterjee, P. *The Nation and Its Fragments: Colonial and Post-Colonial Histories.* New Jersey: Princeton University Press, 1993.

———. *Wages of Freedom: Fifty Years of the Indian Nation-State.* Delhi: Oxford University Press, 1998.

Chew, D. "The Case of the 'Unchaste' Widow: Constructing Gender in 19<sup>th</sup>-century Bengal." *Resources for Feminist Research* 22, no. 3/4 (Fall/Winter 1993): 33–41.

Chow, R. *Writing Diaspora: Tactics of Intervention in Contemporary Cultural Studies.* Bloomington: Indiana University Press, 1993.

Chowdhury-Sengupta, I. "The Return of Sati: A Note on Heroism and Domesticity in Colonial Bengal." *Resources for Feminist Research* 22, no. 3/4 (Fall/Winter 1993): 41–44.

Clifford, J. "Diasporas." *Cultural Anthropology* (August 1994): 302–38.

Cohen, S. *Folk Devils and Moral Panics.* London: MacGibbon and Kee, 1972.

Collalillo, G. "Value Structures Within Italian Immigrant Families: Continuity or Conflict?" Ph.D. dissertation: University of Toronto, 1981.

Community Legal Education Ontario (CLEO). "Immigration and Refugee Fact Sheet." Toronto: Community Legal Education Ontario, 2000.

Coombs, M. "Review Essay: Interrogating Identity." *Berkeley Women's Law Journal* 11 (1996): 222–49.

Cotterill, P. "Interviewing Women: Issues of Friendship, Vulnerability and Power." *Women's Studies International Forum* 15, no. 5/6 (1992): 593–606.

Daly, M. *Gyn/Ecology: The Metaethics of Radical Feminism.* Boston: Beacon Press, 1978.

Das Gupta, S., ed. *A Patchwork Shawl: Chronicles of South Asian Women in America.* New Jersey: Rutgers University Press, 1998.

Davies, B. *Shards of Glass: Children Reading and Writing Beyond Gendered Identities.* Sydney: Allen and Unwin, 1993.

Davies, B. and C. Banks. "The Gender Trap: A Feminist Post-Structuralist Analysis of Primary School Children's Talk About Gender." *Journal of Curriculum Studies* 24, no. 1 (1992): 1–25.

Dei, G. *Anti-Racism Education: Theory and Practice.* Halifax: Fernwood Publishing, 1996.

Dhaliwal, A. K. "Reading Diaspora: Self-Representational Practices and the Politics of Reception." *Socialist Review* (Special Issue: *The Traveling Nation: India and Its Diaspora*) 24, no. 4 (1994): 13–43.

Dijk, T. van. *Elite Discourse and Racism.* Newbury Park: Sage Publications, 1993.

Donald, J. and A. Rattansi, eds. *"Race", Culture and Difference.* London: Sage Publications, 1992.

Douglas, M. *Purity and Danger.* London: Routledge, 1984.

Driedger, L. *The Ethnic Factor: Identity in Diversity.* Toronto: McGraw-Hill Ryerson, 1989.

Dua, E. "Racism or Gender: Understanding Oppression of South Asian-Canadian Women." *Canadian Women Studies* 13, no. 1 (1992): 6–10.

Dwyer, C. "Constructions of Muslim Identity and the Contesting of Power: The Debate over Muslim Schools in the United Kingdom." *Constructions of Race, Place and Nation.* Ed. J. Peter and J. Penrose. London: University College, 1993.

*Encyclopaedia Britannica.* Vol. 6. Chicago: William Berton Publisher, 1943–73. Helen Heningway Berton Publisher, 1973–74, 1976.

Essed, P. *Everyday Racism: Reports from Women of Two Cultures.* Alameda, California: Hunter House, 1990.

Essed, P. and D.T. Goldberg. *Race Critical Theories: Text and Context.* Malden, Mass: Blackwell Publishers, 2002.

———. *Understanding Everyday Racism: Sage Series on Race and Ethnic and Relations 2.* London: Sage Publications, 1991.

Everett, J. "The Upsurge of Women's Activism in India." *Frontiers* Vol. 7, no. 2 (1983): 18–26.

*Father, Son and the Holy War.* Directed by Anand Patwardhan. 120 min. Bombay, 1994.

Feather, N.T. "Assimilation of Values in Migrants." *Understanding Human Values.* Ed. M. Rokeach. New York: The Free Press (1979): 97–128.

Finch, J. "It's Great to Have Someone to Talk To: Ethics and Politics of Interviewing Women." *Social Research: Philosophy, Politics and Practice.* Ed. M. Hammersley. London: Sage Publications, 1993, pp. 166–80.

Fine, M. *Framing Drop-Outs: Notes on the Politics of Urban Public High School.* New York: State University of New York Press, 1991.

Firestone, S. *The Dialectic of Sex: The Case for Feminist Revolution.* New York: Morrow, 1970.

Fleras, A., and L.J. Elliot. *The Challenge of Diversity: Multiculturalism in Canada.* Scarborough: Nelson Canada, 1992.

Forbes, G. "Caged Tigers: First Wave Feminist in India." *Women's Studies International Forum* 4, no. 6 (1982): 525–36.

Foucault, M. *History of Sexuality.* First American Edition. New York: Pantheon Books, 1978.

———. "What Is an Author?" *Language, Counter-Memory, Practice.* Ed. D. Bourchard. New York: Cornell University Press, 1977.

Friedan, B. *The Feminine Mystique.* New York: Norton, 1963.

Furnham, A. "Commonsense Theories of Personality," *Everyday Understanding.* Ed. G. R. Semin and K. J. Gergen. London: Sage Publications, 1990.

Fyfe, A., and P. Figueroa, P., eds. *Education for Cultural Diversity: The Challenge for a New Era.* London: Routledge, 1993.

Gandhi, N. *When the Rolling-Pins Hit the Streets: The Anti-Price Rise Movement — 1972.* Unpublished paper manuscript: Bombay, 1985.

Gangule, N. *Indians in the Empire Overseas.* London: The New India Publishing House, 1947.

Ghuman, P.A.S. *Coping with Two Cultures: British Asian and Indo-Canadian Adolescents.* Clevedon: Multilingual Matters, 1994.

Giddens, A. *The Consequences of Modernity.* Cambridge: Polity Press, 1990.

———. "Living in the Post Traditional Society." *Reflexivity and Its Doubles: Structures, Aesthetics and Community.* Ed. U. Beck, A. Giddens, and S. Lash. Cambridge: Polity Press, 1994.

Gillis, J. *Youth and History.* New York: Academic Press, 1974.

Gilroy, P. *Against Race: Imagining Political Culture Beyond the Colour Line.* Cambridge, Mass: Belknap Press of Harvard University Press, 2000.

———. *Between Camps: Race, Identity and Nationalism at the End of the Colourline.* London: Allen Lane, 2000.

———. *The Black Atlantic.* Cambridge, MA: Harvard University Press, 1993.

———. *"There Ain't No Black in the Union Jack."* London: Hutchinson, 1987.

Goldberg, D.T. *Racist Culture and the Politics of Meaning.* Blackwell: University of Minnesota Press, 1993.

Gordon, L. *Bad Faith and Anti-Black Racism.* New Jersey: Humanities Press, 1995.

———. *Women's Body, Women's Right: A Social History of Birth Control in America.* New York: Viking, 1976.

Gramsci, A. *Selections from the Prison Notebooks of Antonio Gramsci.* New York: International Publishers, 1971.

Grewal, I. *Home and Harem: Nation, Gender, Empire, and the Cultures of Travel.* Durham, NC: Duke of University Press, 1996.

————. "The Post-Colonial, Ethnic Studies and the Diaspora." *Socialist Review* (Special Issue: *The Traveling Nation: India and its Diaspora*) 94, no. 4 (1994): 45–74.

Grewal, I. and C. Kaplan, eds. *Scattered Hegemonies: Postmodernity and Transitional Feminist Practices.* Minneapolis: University of Minnesota Press, 1994.

Griffin, C. *Representations of Youth: The Study of Youth and Adolescence in Britain and America.* Cambridge: Polity Press, 1993.

————. *Typical Girls? Young Women From School to the Job Market.* London: Routledge, 1985.

Hacking, I. "Normal." A discussion paper prepared for the "Modes of Thought" workshop: Toronto, September 1993.

Haggis, J. "Gendering Colonialism or Colonising Gender? Recent Women's Studies Approaches to White Women and the History of British Colonialism." *Women's Studies International Forum* 13, no. 1/2 1990: 105–15.

Hall, G. S. *Adolescence: Its Psychology and Its Relations to Physiology, Anthropology, Sociology, Sex, Crime, Religion and Education.* New York: Appleton, 1907.

Hall, S. "The Emergence of Cultural Studies and the Crisis of the Humanities." *October* 53 (Summer 1990): 11–23.

————. "New Ethnicities." *"Race", Culture, Difference.* Ed. J. Donalds and A. Rattansi. London: Sage Publications, 1992.

————. *Questions of Cultural Identity.* London: Sage Publications, 1996.

Handa, M.L. *Manifesto for a Peaceful World Order: A Gandhian Perspective.* Delhi: Gandhi Bhavan, University of Delhi, 1983.

Hartman, H. "The Unhappy Marriage of Marxism and Feminism: Towards a More Progressive Union." *Women and Revolution: A Discussion of the Unhappy Marriage of Marxism and Feminism.* Ed. L. Sargent. Boston: South End Press, 1981.

Hartsock, N. "Post-Modernism and Political Change: Issues for Feminist Theory." *Cultural Critique* (Winter) (1989–90): 15–25.

Hayes, D. "The Dances, the Firebomb and the Clash of Cultures," *Toronto Life* (October 1992): 39.

Herberg, W. *Protestant, Catholic, Jew.* New York: Doubleday, 1955.

Hoggart, R. *The Uses of Literacy.* London: Chatto and Windus, 1957.

Holland, R. "Indian Immigration into Canada: The Question of Franchise." *Asian Review* 39 (1943): 167–72.

Hunter, R. *Poverty*. New York: Harper Torchbooks, 1904.

Husbands, C. T. "Crises of National Identity as the 'New Moral Panics': Political Agenda Setting about Definitions of Nationhood." *New Community* 20 (January 2, 1994): 101–206.

Indra, D.M. (1979). "South Asian Stereotypes in the Vancouver Press," *Ethnic and Racial Studies* 2, no. 2 (1979): 166–89.

Issar, N. *A Comparison of Values of East-Indian, East-Indian Canadian, and European Canadian Adolescents*. Toronto: OISE, 1988.

Jackson, P. and J. Penrose. "Placing 'Race' and Nation." *Constructions of Race, Place and Nation*. Ed. P. Jackson and J. Penrose. London: University College, 1993.

Jamal, S. "Home — Waffling with Cunning in the Border Country: A Conversation with Ramabai Espinet, Sherazad Jamal and Yasmin Ladha." *Rungh* 1, no. 1/2 (1992): 30.

Jayawardena, K. *The White Women's Other Burden: Western Women and South Asia During British Rule*. New York: Routledge, 1995.

———. *Feminism and Nationalism in the Third World*. New Delhi: Kali for Women, 1986.

Johnson, L. *The Modern Girl: Girlhood and Growing Up*. Philadelphia: Open University Press, 1993.

Jolly, M. "Colonizing Women: The Maternal Body and Empire." *Feminism and the Politics of Difference*. Ed. S. Gunew and A. Yeatman. San Francisco: Westview Press, 1993.

Jones, A. "Becoming a 'Girl': Post-Structuralist Suggestions for Educational Research." *Gender and Education* 5, no. 2 (1993): 157–66.

Kallen, H. M. *Culture and Democracy in the United States*. New York: Liverright, 1924.

Kenway, J. and S. Willis. *Hearts and Minds: Self-Esteem and the Schooling of Girls*. London: Falmer Press, 1990.

Ketrak, K. H. "Indian Nationalism, Gandhian Satyagraha and Representations of Female Sexuality." *Nationalism and Sexualities*. Ed. A. Parker et al. New York: Routledge, 1992.

Lal, V. "The Nation, Nation-State and the Cultural Politics of Hindu/Indian Womanhood in the Indian Diaspora." Unpublished paper. Prepared for the conference "Challenge and Change: The Indian Diaspora in its Historical and Contemporary Contexts." St. Augustine, Trinidad: University of West Indies, August 11–18, 1995.

———. "Sikh Kirpans in California Schools: The Social Construction of Symbols, the Cultural Politics of Identity, and the Limits of Multiculturalism." *New Spiritual Homes: Religion and Asian Americans.* Ed. David K. Yoo. Honolulu, Hawaii: University of Hawaii Press, 1999.

———. "Sikh Kirpans in California Schools: The Social Construction of Symbols, Legal Pluralism, and the Politics of Diversity." *Amerasia* 22, no. 1. (Spring 1996): 57–89.

Landes, J. *Feminism, the Public and the Private.* Oxford, U.K.: Oxford University Press, 1998.

———. "Women and the Public Sphere: A Modern Perspective." *Social Analysis* 15 (1984): 20–31.

Lash, S. and J. Urry. *Economies of Sign and Space.* London: Sage Publications, 1994.

———. *The End of Organized Capitalism.* Cambridge: Polity Press, 1987.

Law Union of Ontario. *The Immigrants Handbook.* Montreal: Black Rose Books, 1981.

Lawrence, E. "Just Plain Common Sense: The 'Roots' of Racism," *The Empire Strikes Back: Race and Racism in 70s Britain.* Centre for Contemporary Cultural Studies, University of Birmingham. London: Hutchison University Library and The Centre for Contemporary Cultural Studies, 1982.

Lazreg, M. "Feminism and Difference: The Perils of Writing as a Woman on Women in Algeria." *Feminist Studies* 14 (Spring 1988): 81–107.

Lees, S. *Losing Out: Sexuality and Adolescent Girls.* London: Hutchinson, 1986.

Lemelle, S. and R. Kelly. *Imagining Home: Class Culture and Nationalism in the African Diaspora.* London: Verso, 1994.

Lesko, N. "The Curriculum of the Body: Lessons from a Catholic High School." *Becoming Feminine: The Politics of Popular Culture.* Ed. Leslie G. Roman, L.K. Christian-Smith, with E. Ellsworth. London: The Falmer Press, 1988.

Levenson, J.R. *Confucian China and Its Modern Fate: A Trilogy.* Berkley: University of California Press, 1965.

Li, P., ed. *Race and Ethnic Relations in Canada.* Toronto: Oxford University Press, 1990.

Liu, L. "The Female Body and Nationalist Discourse: The Field of Life and Death Revisited." *Scattered Hegemonies.* Ed. I. Grewal and C. Kaplan. Minneapolis: The University of Minnesota Press, 1994, pp. 37–62.

Lugones, M. "Hablando Cara a Cara / Speaking Face to Face: An Exploration of Ethnocentric Racism." *Making Face, Making Soul, Haciendo: Creative and Critical Perspectives by Women of Colour.* Ed. G. Anzaldua. San Francisco: Aunt Lute, 1990.

Lynch, J., C. Modgil, and S. Modgil, eds. *Cultural Diversity and the School: Equity or Excellence? Education and Cultural Reproduction.* Vol. 3. London: The Falmer Press, 1992.

MadhavaRau, L. "Perfecting the Juggling Act: Young Gujurati Women Speak." Unpublished paper. London: University of Western Ontario, 1992.

Mani, L. *Contentious Traditions: The Debate on Sati in Colonial India.* Berkeley: University of California Press, 1998.

———. "Contentious Traditions: The Debate on *Sati* in Colonial India." *Recasting Women: Essays in Indian Colonial History.* Ed. K. Sangari and S. Vaid. New Brunswick, New Jersey: Rutgers University Press, 1990, pp. 88–126.

———. "Multiple Mediations: Feminist Scholarship in the Age of Multinational Reception." *Feminist Review* 35 (Summer 1990): 24–41.

Marshall, B.L. *Engendering Modernity: Feminism, Social Theory and Social Change.* Boston: Northeastern University Press, 1994.

McClintock, A. *Imperial Leather: Race, Gender and Sexuality in the Colonial Contest.* New York: Routledge, 1995.

McLaren, P. *Schooling as Ritual Performance: Towards a Political Economy of Educational Symbols and Gestures.* London: Routledge, 1993.

McLaren, A. and A.T. McClaren. *The Bedroom and the State.* Toronto: McClelland and Stewart, 1986.

McRobbie, A. *Feminism for Girls: An Adventure Story.* London: Routledge, 1981.

———. *Feminism and Youth Culture: From "Jackie" to "Just Seventeen."* London: Macmillan, 1991.

———. *Postmodernism and Popular Culture.* London: Routledge, 1994.

McRobbie, A. and M. Nave, eds. *Gender and Generation*. London: Macmillan, 1984.

Mies, M. *Indian Women and Patriarchy*. New Delhi: Concept Publishing, 1980.

Mock, K.R. and V.L. Masemann. *Implementing Race and Ethnocultural Equity Policy in Ontario School Boards*. Toronto: Ontario Ministry of Education, 1990.

Moghadam, V.M., ed. *Gender and National Identity: Women and Politics in Muslim Societies*. London: Zed Books, 1994.

Mohanty, C. "Defining Genealogies: Feminist Reflections on Being South Asian in North America." *Our Feet Walk the Sky: Women of the South Asian Diaspora*. Ed. The Women of South Asian Descent Collective. San Francisco: Aunt Lute Books, 1994, pp. 351–58.

———. "Under Western Eyes: Feminist Scholarship and Colonial Discourses." *Feminist Review* 30 (Autumn 1988): 61–88.

Moraga, C. and G. Anzaldua, eds. *This Bridge Called My Back: Writings by Radical Women of Colour*. New York: Kitchen Table, Women of Colour Press, 1981.

Morgan, R. *Sisterhood Is Powerful: An Anthology of Writings from the Women's Liberation Movement*. New York: Vintage Books, 1970.

Moretti, F. *The Way of the World: The Bildungsroman in European Culture*. London: Verso, 1987.

Morris, M. "Things To Do With Shopping Centers." *Grafts: Feminist Cultural Criticism*. Ed. S. Sheridan. London: Verso, 1988.

Mosse, G. *Nationalism and Sexuality: Respectability and Abnormal Sexuality in Modern Europe*. New York: Howard Fertig, 1985.

Nagel, J. "The Ethnic Revolution: Emergence of Ethnic Nationalism." *Sociology and Social Research* 69 (1984): 417–34.

Natarajan, N. "Woman, Nation and Narration in *Midnight's Children*." *Scattered Hegemonies: Postmodernity and Transitional Feminist Practices*. Ed. I. Grewal and C. Kaplan. Minneapolis: University of Minnesota Press, 1994, pp. 76–89.

Newman, W.M. *American Pluralism: A Study of Minority Groups and Social Theory*. New York: Harper and Row, 1973.

Oakley, A. "Interviewing Women: A Contradiction in Terms." *Doing Feminist Research*. Ed. H. Roberts. London: Routledge, 1981, 30–61.

Oliver, W. "Black Males and Social Problems: Prevention Through Afrocentric Socialization." *Journal of Black Studies* 20, no. 1 (1986): 15–39.

Ong, A. "Colonialism and Modernity: Feminist Re-Presentations of Women in Non-Western Societies." *Inscriptions* (Special Issue on Colonial Discourse) (1988).

———. *Flexible Citizenship: The Culture of Logics and Transnationality.* Durham, NC: Duke University Press, 1999.

Ortner, S. and H. Whitehead. "Introduction: Accounting for Sexual Meanings." *Sexual Meanings.* Ed. S. Ortner and H. Whitehead. Cambridge: Cambridge University Press, 1981, pp. 1–28.

Pajaczkowska, C. and L. Young. "Racism, Representation, Psychoanalysis." *"Race", Culture and Difference.* Ed. J. Donald and A. Rattansi. London: Sage Publications, 1992, pp. 198–219.

Park, Robert. "The City: Suggestions for the Investigation of Human Behaviour in the Urban Environment." *The City.* Ed. R. Park and E.W. Burgess. Chicago: University of Chicago Press, 1967.

———. "Human Migration and Modern Man." *American Journal of Sociology* 33 (1928): 881–93.

Parker, A., M. Ruso, D. Sommer, and P. Yaegar., eds. *Nationalism and Sexualities.* New York: Routledge, 1992.

Patai, D. and S.B. Gluck, eds. *Women's Words: The Feminist Practice of Oral History.* New York: Routledge, 1991.

Pierson, R.P. *"They're Still Women After All": The Second World War and Canadian Womanhood.* Toronto: McClelland and Stewart, 1986.

Poovey, M. "Speaking of the Body: Mid-Victorian Constructions of Female Desire." *Body/Politics: Women and the Discourses of Science.* Ed. M. Jacobus, E. Fox Keller and S. Shuttleworth. New York: Routledge, 1990.

Pransenjit, D. *Rescuing History from the Nation: Questioning Narratives of Modern China.* Chicago: University of Chicago Press, 1995.

Prashad, V. *The Karma of Brown Folk.* Minneapolis: University of Minnesota, 2000.

Prentice, S. "Militant Mothers in Domestic Times: Toronto's Postwar Childcare Struggle." Ph.D. dissertation: Toronto, York University, 1993.

Preyra, C. *Experiences of South Asian Women in a Canadian Shelter for Battered Women.* Master of Arts thesis: Toronto, OISE, 1988.

Puar, J.K. "Resituating Discourses of 'Whiteness' and 'Asianness' in Northern England." *Socialist Review* 24, no. 1/2 (1994): 21–53.

———. "Writing My Way 'Home': Traveling South Asian Bodies and Diasporic Journeys." *Socialist Review* (Special Issue: *The Traveling Nation: India and Its Diaspora*) 24, no. 4 (1994): 75–108.

Radhakrishan, R. "Nationalism, Gender and the Narrative of Identity," *Nationalisms and Sexualities*. Ed. A. Parker et al. New York: Routledge, 1992, pp. 77–95.

Rattansi, A. "'Western' Racisms, Ethnicities and Identities in a 'Postmodern' Frame." *Racism, Modernity and Identity on the Western Front*. Ed. A. Rattansi and S. Westwood. Cambridge: Polity Press, 1994, pp. 15–86.

Razack, S. *Looking White People in the Eye: Gender, Race and Culture in Courtrooms and Classrooms*. Toronto: University of Toronto, 1998.

———. "Race, Space and Prostitution: Towards an Historical Methodology." Unpublished paper. Toronto: OISE/University of Toronto, 1996.

———. "Schooling Research on South and East Asian Students: The Perils of Talking Culture." *Race, Class and Gender* 2, no. 3, 1995.

———. "Storytelling for Social Change." Unpublished paper. Toronto: OISE/University of Toronto, 1992.

———. "What Is to Be Gained by Looking White People in the Eye? Culture, Race, Gender in Cases of Sexual Violence." *Signs* 19 (Summer 1994): 894–923.

Resources for Feminist Research. "Colonialism, Imperialism and Gender." *Resources for Feminist Research* 22, no. 3/4 (Fall/Winter 1993).

Rich, A. *Of Woman Born: Motherhood As Experience and Institution*. New York: Bantam, 1977.

Roberts, H., ed. *Doing Feminist Research*. London: Routledge, 1981.

Roman, L.G. "Intimacy, Labour, and Class: Ideologies of Feminine Sexuality in the Punk Slam Dance." *Becoming Feminine: The Politics of Popular Culture*. Ed. L.G. Roman, L.K. Christian-Smith, with E. Ellsworth. London: The Falmer Press, 1988.

Rudolph, L.I. and S.H. Rudolph. *The Modernity of Tradition: Political Development in India*. Chicago: Chicago University Press, 1967.

Saha, P. *Emigration of Indian Labour 1834–1900*. Delhi: People's Publishing House, 1970.

Sahgal, G. "Secular Spaces: The Experience of Asian Women Organizing." *Refusing Holy Orders: Women and Fundamentalism in Britain.* Ed. G. Sahgal and N. Yuval-Davis. London: Virago Press, 1992, pp. 163–97.

Sahgal, G. and N. Yuval-Davis, eds. *Refusing Holy Orders: Women and Fundamentalism in Britain.* London: Virago Press, 1992.

————. "Introduction: Fundamentalism, Multiculturalism and Women in Britain." *Refusing Holy Orders: Women and Fundamentalism in Britain.* Ed. G. Sahgal and N. Yuval-Davis. London: Virago Press, 1992, 1–25.

Said, E. *Culture and Imperialism.* New York: Alfred A Knopf, 1993.

————. *Orientalism.* New York: Vintage Books, 1979.

Sandhu, K.P. *Indians in Malaya.* London: Cambridge University Press, 1969.

Sangari, K. and S. Vaid. *Recasting Women: Essays in Indian Colonial History.* Ed. K. Sangari and S. Vaid. New Jersey: Rutgers University Press, 1990.

Sargent, L., ed. *Women and Revolution: A Discussion of the Unhappy Marriage of Marxism and Feminism.* Boston: South End Press, 1981.

Sarkar, S. "Rammohun Roy and the Break with the Past." *Roy and the Process of Modernization.* Ed. V.C. Joshi. Delhi: Vikas, 1975, pp. 46–68.

Schur, E.M. *Labelling Women Deviant.* Philadelphia: Temples University Press,1984.

Sharpe, J. *Allegories of Empire: The Figure of Woman in the Colonial Text.* London: University of Minnesota Press, 1993.

Singh, A. "African Americans and the New Immigrants." *Between the Lines: South Asians and Postcoloniality.* Ed. D. Bahri and M. Vasudera. Philadelphia: Temple University, 1996.

Sinha, M. *Colonial Masculinity: The 'Manly Englishman' and the 'Effeminate Bengali' in the Late Nineteenth Century.* Manchester: Manchester University Press, 1995.

Smart, B. *Modern Conditions, Postmodern Controversies.* London: Routledge, 1992.

Smart, C. and B. Smart. *Women, Sexuality and Social Control.* London: Routledge, 1978.

Smith, B. and B. Smith. "Across the Kitchen Table: A Sister-to-Sister Dialogue." *This Bridge Called My Back: Writings by Radical Women of Colour.* Ed. C. Moraga and G. Anzaldua. New York: Kitchen Table, Women of Colour Press, 1981.

Smith, D.E. *The Everyday World as Problematic: A Feminist Sociology.* Toronto: University of Toronto Press, 1987.

Smith, L. S. "Sexist Assumptions and Female Delinquency: An Empirical Investigation." *Women, Sexuality and Social Control.* Ed. B. Smart and C. Smart. London: Routledge, 1978, 74–86.

Smith, S. "Immigration and Nation-Building in Canada and the United Kingdom." *Constructions of Race, Place and Nation.* Ed. J. Peter and J. Penrose. London: University College, 1993.

Snitow, A. "A Gender Diary." *Conflicts in Feminism.* Eds. M. Hirsch and E. Fox. New York: Routledge, 1990.

Srivastava, R.P. "Family Organization and Change Among the Overseas Indian Immigrant Families of British Columbia, Canada." *The Family in India – A Regional View.* Ed. G. Kurian. The Hague, Netherlands: Mouton, 1974.

Stanley, L. "How the Social Science Research Process Discriminates Against Women." *Is Higher Education Fair to Women?* Ed. S. Acker and D. Warren-Piper. Guildford, Surrey: SRHE & NFER-Nelson, 1984.

Stoler, L.A. "Carnal Knowledge and Imperial Power: Gender, Race and Morality in Colonial Asia." *Gender at the Crossroads of Knowledge: Feminist Anthropology in the Post-Modern Era.* Ed. M. di Leonardo. Berkley: University of California Press, 1991, pp. 51–101.

———. "Making Empire Respectable: The Politics of Race and Sexual Morality in Colonial Cultures." *Imperial Monkey Business: Racial Supremacy in Social Darwinist Theory and Colonial Practice.* Ed. J. Breman and P. du Roy. Amsterdam: VUP, 1990.

———. *Race and the Education of Desire: Foucault's History of Sexuality and the Colonial Order of Things.* Durham, Duke University Press, 1995.

———. *Tensions of Empire: Colonial Cultures in a Bourgeois World.* Berkeley, California: University of California Press, 1997.

Strathern, M. "An Awkward Relationship: The Case of Feminism and Anthropology." *Signs* 12 (Winter 1987): 276–92.

Taylor, J. *The Social World of Batvia.* Madison: University of Wisconsin Press, 1983.

Thakur, R. "Ayodhya and the Politics of India's Secularism: A Double Standards Discourse." *Asian Survey* 33, no. 7 (1993): 653–57.

Thapar, S. "Women as Activists; Women as Symbols: A Study of the Indian Nationalist Movement." *Feminist Review* 44 (Summer 1993): 81–95.

Tinker, H.A. *Separate and Unequal.* Vancouver: University of British Colombia Press, 1976.

———. *A New System of Slavery.* Oxford: Oxford University Press, 1974.

Torgovinick, M. *Gone Primitive: Savage Intellects, Modern Lives.* Chicago: University of Chicago Press, 1990.

Trivedi, P. "To Deny Our Fullness: Asian Women in the Making of History." *Feminist Review* 17 (July 1984): 39.

Tsolidis, G. "Ethnic Minority Girls and Self-Esteem." *Hearts and Minds: Self-Esteem and the Schooling of Girls.* Ed. J. Kenway and S. Willis. London: Falmer Press, 1990, p. 60.

———. *Schooling, Diaspora and Gender: Being Feminist and Being Different.* Philadelphia: Open University Press, 2001.

Tumpane, F. "The Cruel World vs. Teenagers." *Chatelaine* (May 1950): 4–5.

Valiente, W. "Domestic Violence in the South Asian Family: Treatment and Research Issues." *South Asian Symposium 1992.* Ed. C. Sarath. Toronto: Centre for South Asian Studies Graduate Students Union, University of Toronto, 1993, 111–21.

———. "Social Work Practice with South Asian Women: Issues, Concerns and Problems." *South Asian Symposium 1991.* Ed. C. Sarath. Toronto: Centre for South Asian Studies Graduate Students Union, University of Toronto, 1992, pp. 81–99.

Vijay, P. *The Karma of Brown Folk.* Minneapolis: University of Minnesota Press, 2000, 157–83.

Walcott, R. *Critiquing Canadian Multiculturalism: Toward an Anti-Racist Agenda.* Master's thesis. Toronto: OISE, 1993.

———. *Performing the Post-Modern: Black Atlantic Rap and Identity in North America.* Ph.D. dissertation. Toronto: University of Toronto, 1995.

Walker, F.A. "Immigration and Degradation." *Forum* 11, no. 6 (1981): 634–44.

Weber, M. *Economy and Society,* Volumes I and II. Ed. G. Roth and C. Wittich. Berkeley, California: University of California Press, 1978.

Weiner, G., ed. *Just a Bunch of Girls.* Philadelphia: Open University Press, 1985.

Weinreich, P. "Ethnicity and Adolescent Identity Conflicts." *Minority Families in Britain: Support and Stress.* Ed. V.S. Khan. London: Macmillan Press, 1979.

Williams, R. *The Analysis of Culture.* London: Open University, 1981.

———. *Keywords: A Vocabulary of Culture and Society*. Revised and expanded edition. London: Fontana, 1983.

Willis, P. *Common Culture: Symbolic Work at Play in the Everyday Cultures of the Young*. Milton Keynes: Open University Press, 1990.

Wilson, B. and J. Wyn. *Shaping Futures: Youth Action For Livelihood*. Sydney: Allen and Unwin, 1987.

Wolfgang, A. and N. Josefowitz. "Chinese Immigrant Value Changes and Value Differences Compared to Canadian Students." *Canadian Ethnic Studies* 10 (1978): 130–35.

Wyn, J., "Youth, Transition and Education: The Concept of Youth in Educational Policy and Practice." Unpublished paper. Presented as "What's Youth Got to Do with Curriculum?" for Critical Pedagogy Series. Toronto: OISE, November 30, 1994.

Yuval-Davis, N. *Women, Citizenship and Difference*. New York: St. Martin's Press, 1999.

· · ·

For the survey of newspapers, I looked at *Canadian News Index* (1992); *Canadian Periodical Index* (1994, 1995, 1996); and *Canadian Index*, Vol. 3 (January–June 1995). I searched under the heading "immigrants" for a cross-section of early to recent 1990s publications.

## ꙮ Newspapers

Associated Press. "Population Crisis Feared as Billions Enter Fertile Years." *Globe and Mail*, March 4, 1995, p. A1.

Canadian Press. "Close Doors, Speak English, Majority Tells Pollster." *Calgary Herald*, May 18, 1995, p. A13.

———. "Most Canadians Favour Five-Year Ban on Immigration, Poll Finds." *Montreal Gazette*, May 18, 1995, p. A9.

———. "Poll Showed Hostility to Immigrants." *Globe and Mail*, September 14, 1992, p. A4.

Field, D. "Multiculturalism Undermines Values Held by Canadians." *Toronto Star*, December 23, 1994, p. A27.

*India-West*. June 9, 1995, and June 23, 1995.

Mitchell, A. "Immigrants' Origins Increasingly Diverse: Demographers Fear Racist Backlash." *Globe and Mail,* December 9, 1992, p. A9.

Sarick, L. "Ethnic Melting Pot, or Cauldron?" *Globe and Mail* (National Affairs), December 29, 1994, p. A4.

———. "Region Deals with Influx of Immigrants," *Globe and Mail* (National Affairs), December 28, 1994, p. A1.

———."A Region Grown Like a Gawky Adolescent." *Globe and Mail* (National Affairs), December 30, 1994, p. A4.

Schachter, H. "Toronto Is a Changed Metropolis." *Montreal Gazette,* December 21, 1994, p. B3.

Torstar News Service. Article on new immigration rules. *Metro Today,* December 18 and 19, 2001, p. 2.

## ➴ Discography

Apache Indian. "Aids Warning." *No Reservations.* London, England: Island Records, 1993.

———. "Come Follow Me." Bootleg. London, England, 1991.

———. "Drink Problems." *No Reservations.* London, England: Island Records, 1993.

———. "Make Way for the Indian." *Make Way for the Indian.* London, England: Island Records, 1995.

———. "Movie Over India." Bootleg. London, England, 1990.

Apache Indian and A.R. Rahman. "No Problem." *Lovebirds.* Bombay, India: Venus Records, 1996.

Asian Boyz Club. *Judgment Night.* Toronto, Canada: Asian Boyz Club Productions, 1994.

Asian Empire. *Empire Strikes Back.* Toronto, Canada: Asian Empire Productions, 1994.

DJ Sanjay. *One Nation Equals Justice.* Toronto, Canada: Sunshine Records, 1994.

R.A.S. *Stardust: An Asian Scandal.* Toronto, Canada: Asian Boyz Club Productions, 1991.